DATE DUE

A Democracy of Facts

EARLY AMERICAN STUDIES

Series editors
Daniel K. Richter, Kathleen M. Brown, Max Cavitch,
and David Waldstreicher

Exploring neglected aspects of our colonial, revolutionary,
and early national history and culture, Early American
Studies reinterprets familiar themes and events in fresh ways.
Interdisciplinary in character, and with a special emphasis
on the period from about 1600 to 1850, the series is published in
partnership with the McNeil Center for Early American Studies.

A complete list of books in the series
is available from the publisher.

A DEMOCRACY OF FACTS

Natural History in the Early Republic

ANDREW J. LEWIS

UNIVERSITY OF PENNSYLVANIA PRESS

PHILADELPHIA

Published by
University of Pennsylvania Press
Philadelphia, Pennsylvania 19104-4112
www.upenn.edu/pennpress

Printed in the United States of America
on acid-free paper

10 9 8 7 6 5 4 3 2 1

Library of Congress Cataloging-in-Publication Data
ISBN 978-0-8122-4308-6

For Nancy, Asher, and Phoebe

Contents

Introduction

From an Empire of Reason
to a Democracy of Facts

This is a book about a campaign for respect and legitimacy. The American general populace regarded naturalists and natural history of the 1780s warily, associating both with a genteel, deferential cosmopolitan culture, and esoteric knowledge. Yet naturalists and their practices exited the early republic fifty years later transformed: considered by most Americans of the 1830s and 1840s as individuals whose knowledge and techniques contributed to society. Rather than elitist aesthetes, naturalists at the twilight of the new republic were possessors of important and vital skills. They were doing the people's work. This transformation—unsteady, unstable, sometimes unconscious but always circuitous—is the subject of this book.

In the 1780s naturalists' genteel trappings and their claims to an exclusive expertise met challenges from citizens suspicious of their social betters and convinced of their own observations of nature. The ensuing contests over nature were multivalent. In some cases they were relatively straightforward and concerned the identification of animals or an aspect of their behavior, the conclusive identification of a plant or whether a region might contain more of these specimens. Yet these challenges could also extend to the core of natural history, the aims and goals of the practice. Ordinary Americans and naturalists themselves were asking similar questions: Just what was natural history for? What exactly did it do? Who should be considered a naturalist and why? Early republic Americans agreed that natural history could catalog and describe nature, but, as practiced by an orthodox elite in the United States, it imposed limitations on theorizing about nature's causes and emphasized the assembly of individual facts. Naturalists were not willing or able, it seemed to those outside its closed orthodox circle, to interpret the world around them. To many Americans, naturalists' reluctance to interpret and explain nature made their practices foreign; interesting to be sure, but precious, remote, and not meaningful. It also deprived natural history and its advocates of its most powerful asset: to serve as a tool to make sense of the natural world and Americans' place within it.

Ordinary Americans refused to be silenced regarding nature. They filled the vacuum between their aspirations for the practice and naturalists' limitations on it by borrowing from the experts their observational techniques and rhetoric. To this they added their own interpretive elements to explain the natural world and their place within it. They cobbled together a dynamic, heterodox method that engaged the natural world through observation and employed a fact discourse just as naturalists did. But their method did not stop with the fact collecting and empirical inquiry; they answered the questions they posed about nature. Ordinary Americans asked and answered why phenomena in nature occurred, oftentimes with theological reasoning, adding religious import to nature study and nationalist gloss. This powerful amalgam of science and sentiment made possible for Americans an understanding of nature and an ownership stake in the national landscape's past and present, as well as prognostications of its future potential. Ordinary Americans made natural history a part of the nation building process, an exercise as much involved with the creation of natural character as it was with plants and animals.

Challenged vigorously by a rival method, elite naturalists also found themselves and their practices engaged with the larger public. They and their techniques situated, sometimes uneasily and uncomfortably, in a variety of spaces both public and private, arenas in which their authority and credibility could be as easily questioned and contested as established and confirmed. Such spaces included universities and academies where natural history was practiced within a closed community, largely behind shut doors; in public, academic, and popular lectures in which the authority of natural history was performed and established before a largely polite audience. But the spaces also extended into the swirling and ungovernable print and market economies where specialists were challenged by the rules that determined prices, financial interests, other writers' agendas. Thus, natural history in the early republic found itself participating in a *democracy of facts*: a volatile, exciting, enthusiastic, and exhausting arena in which the authority of natural historical expertise was not yet solid, the observations and convictions of ordinary Americans held particular sway, the motivations of its most august practitioners were constantly questioned, the overriding sense was that conclusions about American nature were uncertain and provisional until proven otherwise (a time that for many never arrived). It is in these spaces, in the back and forth between naturalists and the public, and from the lively exchanges and contentious debates that characterized them that this examination takes flight.

A small episode involving an ancient tooth illustrates, briefly, how the democracy of facts operated. Dr. William Read, proprietor of Rice Hope plantation in South Carolina, wrote a brief note to Thomas Jefferson in 1806. In it he presented Jefferson with a "fossil which you may consider a curiosity & not unworthy of your contemplation." Read related that the object was excavated while digging a canal for field irrigation in the marshlands that bounded the adjacent Cooper River. Read praised Jefferson as "attentive to Natural Philosophy as well as to the other branches of science," so it seems that Read knew Jefferson to be president of the American Philosophical Society in Philadelphia, that city's oldest and most august scientific organization, as well as President of the United States. More facts followed: the specimen "lay with several others of similar form in a stratum of Earth resembling decay'd shells"; Read included a second example, "a broken one," should "your Excellency" choose to "direct a chemical analysis on it." Read ended his note by relating that his own experiments on the object proved it "dentous," and that community deliberation among the neighborhood's "curious & learned" concluded the fossils "to be the teeth of some Monster unknown at this day."[1]

On its surface this letter seems to be a relatively simple matter: one gentleman plantation owner writing another his observations about nature, a note that includes the genteel protocols of flattery and deference, the rhetoric of natural history, the results of experiment, and the inclusion of specimens. In the late eighteenth and early nineteenth centuries, letters possessing these characteristics were the lifeblood of natural history practice and were one of the primary means though which gentlemen and those who wished to correspond with genteel naturalists communicated and disseminated information about American nature in the Anglophone world.[2]

Yet, this letter also hints that natural history was not the province of elites alone and beckons a closer examination. It is unlikely that Read, the owner of a substantial rice plantation supported and sustained by slave labor, dug the canal from which the teeth were excavated. More probably his slaves did. It is possible, if not probable, that it was his slaves who brought the teeth to Read's attention and not without precedent that a slave might have assisted Read with his experiments on them.[3] Read did not write Jefferson of his slaves' participation in the episode but he does record that at least two distinct categories of people—the "curious & learned"—joined in helping him determine that these teeth were not from any known animal but from an unfamiliar one. It stands to reason that such a conversation or series of conversations would have drawn on the collective experience of many individuals and their knowledge, casual and intimate, of the area's animals, their natural history, and their anatomy. Read regarded himself among the "learned," no doubt, and his letter leaves open the possibility that he consulted others whom he considered of this same status. As to whom he classified as the "curious," Read's note is silent, but such a group may have included his neighbors less experienced with natural history, other laborers working on the excavation, perhaps even those in bondage. These were the citizens of the democracy of facts.[4]

This very brief glimpse into the early nineteenth century suggests that natural history practice was a more variegated and far richer enterprise than white gentlemen observing nature and writing letters about it to one another. Read's note is too spare to reconstruct whether the conversations about the teeth dug from the marsh were facile or erudite, calm or disputatious. Moreover, moderns must also take on faith that Read accurately described community deliberation as coming to a consensus; it is quite possible, probable even, that there were more opinions about the teeth than Read suggests. Nevertheless, such discussions were certainly populated by a wide cross section of the population of the early republic: the learned, those such as Read with genteel educations if not some amount of scientific training, as well as the curious, an amorphous class of unidentified individuals possessing differing levels of education, experience, and the capacity for critical inquiry and thought. For certain the majority of them were men, but readers should not assume that women did not contribute too.[5] Finally, slaves were likely involved even if their participation and contributions were attenuated. Natural history in early republic America, this single, small episode suggests, possessed a full cast of characters and involved the work of many hands and the contributions of many minds. The democracy of facts was defined overwhelmingly by a wide range of opinions about the natural world from those who recorded their thoughts for posterity as well as those whose thoughts were ignored, not recorded, and are now lost.

The early republic saw Americans across all segments of society closely scrutinizing plants and animals, artifacts and antiquities, geologic formations and natural phenomena. As readers of this book consider—among other things—pursuits resembling the modern scientific disciplines of botany, ornithology, archaeology, and geology; fact collecting and empiricism; and the role of natural history in state building, they may find themselves as perplexed by what they have picked up as those who excavated the ancient teeth from the Cooper River marsh: "What should I make of this object in my hand?" Why so many seemingly separate subjects in one volume? The answer is that this study approaches natural history as did most early-republic Americans: as an ill-defined and capacious set of practices that resists easy delineation; an unfragmented cluster of activities pursued by ordinary folks as well as those who moderns would regard as putative scientists, many if not most of whom slipped easily and effortlessly from one modern discipline to another. Rather than treat natural history as an aggregated antecedent to the modern biological and earth sciences, as the umbrella term for a collection of demarcated disciplines with codified sets of settled rules and investigative protocols, this study regards early-republic natural history as a constellation of unstable and contested practices that comprise a *method* of interrogating the natural world as well as a *means* of explaining that collected information about nature.

As a method, natural history for Americans in this period was largely, though not exclusively, observational, classificatory, and taxonomic. It sought facts: isolated particulars from nature that once sufficiently accumulated promised to reveal the deep structures of the natural world and explain natural phenomena. To collect facts the practices of natural history relied on individuals' ability to see and to hear, touch, taste, and smell. Clear-headed, commonsense use of one's faculties as well as a sound mind were at once the minimum and, in some respects, the sole requirement to participate in the era's natural history, although depending on the situation these observations might demand some use of instruments: scales, weights and measures, tools for discerning distance, thermometers, and on very rare occasion microscopes or telescopes. It was also a practice that eschewed theorizing about nature as well as the assembling of those facts into a "system" to explain nature's causes; those activities were germane to natural philosophy, a related discipline that many American naturalists and the general public took pains to avoid because it was deemed too scholastic and speculative. (That naturalists and Americans generally avoided theorizing about the causes in nature does not mean that they lacked opinions about the natural world; they had plenty.) Thus, early republic natural history possessed a low threshold for entry and participation and overwhelmingly took advantage of and valorized Americans' predominant experience with nature: that of living in it. It celebrated individuals' time spent with plants and animals, their observations of the nation's forests and fields, lakes, steams, and mountains. As much as naturalists might claim for themselves a unique expertise to catalog and explain the natural world, in short to create natural knowledge, the backbone of early republic natural history as broadly understood was founded on the convictions of Americans' every-day engagements with nature.

As a means to explain the natural world, early republic natural history was descriptive, relying on words put into print as well as on images and maps. These descriptions ran the gamut from an accounting of an individ-ual species—for example, the close-read characteristics of a single tree—to a description of an entire neighborhood, state, or region. The latter would list the area's animals and plants, lakes and rivers, mountains and caves, rocks, and ores, as well as its peoples: an exemplary text is Jefferson's *Notes on the State of Virginia*.[6] That natural history depended on the printed word meant that the descriptive practices were, to some degree, bookish and scholastic; and they were argumentative too, often to a fault. Most early republic Americans considered it axiomatic that very little about American nature was settled and much about American nature was left to be discov-ered. Existing and emerging knowledge about American nature, they thought, was provisional. Consequently they quibbled about the contours of nature incessantly, most of the time calmly, interestedly, bemusedly, occasionally vituperatively. To read early republic scientific journals and the natural history passages and articles in the period's personal letters, literary magazines, and newspapers is to immerse oneself in a practice characterized by a prideful, excited, enthusiastic, swirling, and raucous debate, the indi-vidual writings marked by the effort to persuade the reader that the writer's view of nature was the correct one.

In these writings, authors relied on the rhetoric and discourse of fact to effect persuasion. They might marshal any combination of personal testi-mony and eyewitness accounts, the testimony of those whom they knew and could trust, the experiences of others reported to them through trusted sources, as well as other forms of hearsay evidence.[7] Writers also relied heavily on the authority of existing texts from contemporaneous as well as past naturalists, including those of the ancients on occasion. Natural history was thus a formal, quasi-legalistic literary endeavor as much as it was a simple observational examination of American nature. Natural history was not a practice that made itself comprehensible predominantly through experiment, though experiment could and did play a role in some natural historical matters.

If commonsense observation and the ability to produce clear description were the requirements for admission to participate, then what, the modern reader might ask, was the role of education and training; for that matter, what of experts and expertise in early republic natural history? It is anachronistic to put in place a clear divide between amateur and professional natural history in this period as there were no professional requirements for describing oneself a naturalist, nor was it possible for most naturalists to make a consistent living from natural history, largely obviating it as a profession or career in the modern sense. It was an avocation, though one that could (and did) prove profitable to a few individuals. Early republic natural history was theoretically open to all who could master the informal, if rigorous, requirements to participate: the mastery of key concepts, the command of the contents of important texts, an awareness and implementation of proper observational techniques, and an ability to translate those observations into the recognizable rhetoric and discourse that suggested a transparent rendering of one's observations onto the page. But such skills were not just learned; they were signs of cosmopolitan sociability and were generally acquired and mastered through formal and informal genteel education.

There was little doubt that into the early republic, natural history practice retained its elite associations with metropolitan and cosmopolitan elites: those who trafficked in learned discourse and possessed access to erudite transatlantic correspondents and membership in polite institutions. The scientific societies in the early republic's largest cities—the American Philosophical Society in Philadelphia, the Lyceum of Natural History in New York, the American Academy of Arts and Sciences in Boston—served as the repositories of these sentiments and protocols, and these organizations as well a few others worked to make themselves into centers of calculation, the arenas in which accumulated natural historical information from throughout the new nation would be sifted, examined, and vetted: in short, facts made into natural knowledge.[8]

It was in institutions such as these, among their membership, and through publication that naturalists worked to establish their credibility and challenge the democracy of fact. In its stead, elite naturalists worked to create what one called "an empire of reason," a methodological counterbalance they imagined would pursue a codified discipline and be directed by those who believed they had to authority to determine and police the proper methods of nature study. The empire of reason was, in practice, defensive rather than offensive. As a ballast of erudition in a democracy of facts, it proved persuasive only to those who already believed themselves deserving of the respect they did not possess. Against popular charges that naturalists had a financial stake and personal interest in their identifications of plants and animals, they stressed to the public that their method was disinterested. Against claims that their knowledge was esoteric, naturalists argued for its utility. To those critics who suggested that natural history was self-indulgent, naturalists pleaded that their knowledge and techniques would contribute to the betterment of the nation.

Over time naturalists wearied of engaging the public directly and looked to state and federal governments for support. The second and third generations of early republic naturalists—those who came of age between 1810 and 1840—realized the limitations of a democratic natural history practice as they endlessly fought and refought disputes about evidence and evidentiary rules and evaluated reports of hard-to-believe natural wonders and marvels. Not only were arguments with untrained Americans tiresome and distracting but natural history itself was an expensive endeavor that the public failed to support in the ways the first-generation naturalists had hoped for and advocated. Collecting and preserving specimens was costly, dangerous, and slow; natural history publications had limited popular appeal; and the financing of expeditions was beyond the means of individuals or most scientific societies. Only government, state and federal, had the resources to fund natural history, and by the 1830s and 1840s the symbiosis of interests between trained naturalists and state had coalesced around independent but shared goals.

Naturalists needed the state and federal governments to support their research, their collecting expeditions, and their publications. The state, in turn, profited by having naturalists assist in the rationalization of already owned and newly acquired lands—boundary surveying, geological descriptions, and natural resource and wildlife assessments. As federal, state, and local governments pursued economic development and provided incentives for immigration and settlement, funding infrastructure projects with land grants and low land prices, they wanted to know more about what they were selling. Naturalists provided that service and became crucial members in the creation of a science/state nexus that increasingly resembled the science-friendly governments of Europe. Just as an empire cannot function without a bureaucracy to support its ambitions, so natural history and science, specialists realized, needed government to support their aims and bolster their authority.

State-supported science neither replaced nor eradicated democratic science, and by the fourth and fifth decades of the nineteenth century the two sets of coherent if chaotic practices had diverged substantially. In the decade before Darwin, a thriving democratic natural history that was as much about sentiment and spirituality as it was about empiricism was moving away rapidly from a state-supported science that was aligning itself with the long-term project of land rationalization and domestic expansion.

So many subjects are considered in the following pages that it is necessary, briefly, to define its parameters. As the foregoing indicates, natural historical epistemology, fact discourse, and empiricism are important components in this study; thus, it draws upon and brings to bear on the early republic the methodology and work of scholars who have fleshed out the social and intellectual history of early modern, Enlightenment, and early nineteenth-century science in Europe and the United States.[9] This book contributes to this literature, first, by finding that American naturalists of this period were not the scientific provincials they imagined themselves to be but were part of and on par with the international community of scientific inquiry, attuned to and participants in its debates and aware of its ongoing controversies. Early republic natural history and science was maturing rapidly and demonstrating a confidence that had been missing during the years of British rule, when American naturalists, save a select few, served primarily as peripheral collectors and correspondents to European savants. The early national period saw an efflorescence of activity: the founding of numerous medical and scientific journals, the creation of natural history and scientific societies, the establishment of scientific higher education, and from that a growing, if still small, community of experienced naturalists. American naturalists' frequent complaints of their uniquely difficult situation notwithstanding, the struggles and successes of early republic natural history were different from those of European naturalists only in degree, not in kind.

Second, this study shows that American naturalists were part and parcel of the large-scale epistemological changes that scholars associate with the history of science in this period.[10] If European scientific societies and individuals were expanding their correspondent communities of interested individuals the world over, then early republic naturalists were cultivating exchanges with many of these same people as well, though more modestly, and with their fellow citizens in other cities and on the frontiers. The early republic saw the establishment of local and putatively national scientific communities similar to those being formed and reformed in Europe, communities characterized by attempts to settle the debates about the rules for creating natural knowledge, the adoption and use of a unified discourse, and the proper literary and representational forms for the communication of findings of fact. These scientific communities grew in tandem with those of related specialist groups—instrument makers and illustrators, engineers and surveyors, printers and engravers—who helped to foster science and establish it as a vital interest in the modern state.

This book joins in conversation the vibrant literature that extends the European history of science into the early modern and Enlightenment colonial peripheries, where concerns over the circuits and circulation of information, specimen exchange, and the cooptation and transformation of natural knowledge dominate.[11] It reveals the central and vital contributions of non-European male elites to making New World natural knowledge, even as legal regimes and cultural practices worked to marginalize and make invisible their contribution. And it extends this scholarship by highlighting the contributions of historical actors not always associated with natural history—the young nation's farmers and mechanics, ordinary men and women, those who were literate but not learned—as well as contributes to the story of marginalization by showing how the natural knowledge of Indians and slaves continued to be overlooked and ignored.

Though the following pages examine epistemology and empiricism, contested knowledge and attempts to establish scientific authority, this book is not primarily a history of science, or at least not one that focuses on the development of professional institutions or individual biography. Readers searching for that would be better served by other studies.[12] Rather, it is a history of interactions with natural world, experiences determined and shaped by the observational methods of natural history and expressed in its language and terminology; it is a history that describes how Americans made natural knowledge and made sense of themselves and the new nation through that knowledge. Along the way it probes the implicit, inarticulate standards that governed natural historical aspiration and praxis to lay bare natural historical epistemology in the early republic. This study unearths subtle but significant disputes in scholarly and popular natural history alike about what evidence overrode what other evidence, about what constituted evidence, and indeed what counted as a fact in the first place. In doing so, it reveals the premium that naturalists and ordinary Americans in the early republic placed on possibility—a concept with enormous political and cultural authority—and the consequent reluctance to dismiss eyewitness accounts however contrary to common sense, received wisdom, experiment, or theory. As a result, by modern standards, many naturalists of the early republic were scarcely scientists at all. They disdained systematic thinking and theory. Many insisted that no laboratory experiment could ever count for as much as the testimony of untrained but credible observers. Yet these men and women were certainly naturalists, if natural history is historicized adequately to show how foreign it is from contemporary practice.

At its core, this study is concerned with the processes and methods through which the first generation of early republic naturalists attempted to establish disciplinary credibility and cultural authority by, paradoxically, experimenting with a democratic natural history. Rather than emulate what they perceived as the rigidly hierarchical natural history practices of Europe, American naturalists initially advertised for and welcomed the participation of their fellow citizens. Natural history, they urged, was a tool to investigate, to catalog, to explore, and, ultimately, to know the new nation. It was a method and means for a new citizenry to take ownership of a new nation, a very large one at that. Ordinary Americans enthusiastically answered this call. The following pages record the excitement many Americans experienced as they observed and wrote about nature to naturalists and for one another. But these same Americans also took liberties with natural history and empiricism, using its rhetoric and its techniques to further their own agendas, projects not always in accord with aims of a more disciplined practice. So what follows is also an examination of naturalists' efforts to wrest control of the unleashed practice, a process at which they succeeded less modestly than post-Enlightenment moderns might imagine.

The book follows a loosely chronological arc by investigating episodes and spaces of contestation in natural historical matters from approximately 1790 to roughly 1840. In the fifty years covered here, naturalists and early republic Americans demonstrated an enthusiastic interest in nature, one that depended for its comprehension on their willingness to believe that nature mirrored society and society reflected nature. Americans argued about nature, their observations, and its lessons not only in the language of natural history and science but also in the rhetoric of political theory and American politics. In exchanges about plants and animals, geologic features and natural wonders, Americans interlaced ideas about domestic and international economics, entrepreneurial risk, and how to make a dollar. Investigations of American antiquities and pre-Columbian ruins, practices not entirely divorced from natural history and naturalists, inspired speculation about the continent's ancient past and anxious wonder about the new nation's future. As Americans gazed up at the stars and looked down at the earth they pondered God's designs in nature and providential designs for the United States. Americans talked about those designs when they discussed the contours of American character and the course of national destiny. In short, the practices of natural history as well as conversations and debates about the natural world were woven into the fabric of early national everyday life: into discussions of local and national politics, into descriptions of the economy, into understandings of the past and visions of the future, and into individuals' and the nation's relationship with God.

The Revolution in Natural History Practice: Democratic Science and the Case of Submerging Swallows

The first issue of Boston's *Memoirs of the American Academy of Arts and Sciences* (1785) contains a letter from Samuel Dexter, a judge from Dedham, Massachusetts, to James Bowdoin, president of the academy. Dexter wrote that his friend, Judge Foster of Brookfield, Massachusetts, had witnessed "a multitude of swallows, endeavoring to disengage themselves from the mud" of a drained pond in the spring. Aware that bird migration "has been a problem among naturalists," Dexter wished to add his observations to the debate of "whether certain species of birds migrate in autumn to distant countries, or remain with us during the winter, in a torpid state." Dexter agreed with the latter opinion, at least with regard to the "house-swallow," and offered "other facts" which he believed "render it probable" that swallows "sink into ponds and rivers, in the fall of the year, and lie there, benumbed and motionless, until the return of spring."[1]

Dexter marshaled evidence to support this opinion. A former neighbor told him when warm weather returned that " 'it is almost time for the swallows to come out of the mud where they have lain all winter.' " Dexter related how he called his unnamed neighbor's "philosophy" into question, but the man recounted that every fall swallows would congregate on the reeds near the edge of the river. It seemed to the neighbor that their "torpitude had already begun" since the swallows were nearly motionless. The weight of the birds bent the grass to the water and although the neighbor had never seen them sink, he "doubted not of their immersion any more than if he had been a witness to it." The swallows' complete disappearance and their spring struggle from the mud further convinced the neighbor. He instructed Dexter to "look out for their resurrection."[2]

"Although I paid little attention to it for some years," Dexter wrote Bowdoin, "yet I followed his advice at length, and watched for their appearance several seasons, as carefully as I could." He confessed that he never saw firsthand the swallows rising out of the muck. Yet, "in more years than one" and "at the proper time in the spring," Dexter witnessed large flocks at river's edge unable to use their wings and covered with viscous ooze. Noting that they could fly but a few yards and "seeming to want to rest themselves, as if feeble, or fatigued," Dexter believed them recently emerged from the mud and not recovered from their winter posthibernation stupor. Circumstantial evidence was enough to persuade. Dexter admitted that while he "may possibly overrate these discoveries," he agreed with previous informants, concluding that swallows spent the winters submerged in the subaqueous mud of ponds, lakes, and rivers.[3]

Admittedly strange on first reading, swallow submersion was considered a legitimate subject for a scientific journal in the early republic because it met the threshold to be considered as such. Late eighteenth- and early nineteenth-century natural history practice in America was bounded by two important parameters and one essential working assumption. First, practitioners avoided and rejected absolute conclusions about the natural world in favor of probabilistic claims. Those with an interest in nature study based their conclusions on relative degrees of plausibility, quite often relying on analogy. Thus, swallow submersion probably did or, at least, could occur, since more than one person witnessed the phenomenon (Dexter and his neighbor), and because there were already documented analogues for hibernation. Second, naturalists in the earliest decades of the republic employed a "philosophical modesty" that admitted and celebrated human limitations in understanding the natural world. They exhibited an openness to experience that emphasized sociable and unsystematic sensory philosophizing over the solipsism often found in rational systems. Therefore, even if one doubted swallow submersion, it was poor science to dismiss it completely, since nature was exceedingly complex and human understanding quite limited. Finally, Americans interested in the natural world labored under the working assumption that nature and natural laws were universal throughout the world in most cases, but that particular deviations from these universals within nature distinguished the New World. They inherited this belief from three centuries of European writings that suggested the fecundity of American nature and reports of its deviance from known forms in the Old World. Americans harbored a suspicion that wonderful natural phenomena and untold new creatures awaited discovery and readied themselves to find them.[4]

These men and a few women compared nature and science in America to that in Europe. Anxious about European judgments regarding the status of intellectual life in the United States, those with interests in nature took pains to distinguish and denote the country's bounty. Yet the very attention devoted to these efforts belied their articulated confidence. For example late eighteenth- and early nineteenth-century Americans took umbrage with the infamous European claims about the New World's degenerative potential and the implication that New World nature was limited and inferior. They accused European closet philosophers of system building, or drawing definitive conclusions prematurely from insufficient facts. American naturalists admired European natural history for its accomplishments and its attention to the collection of information and facts. Yet they lambasted its conclusions. "System builder" became a politically charged epithet for a European naturalist who was overreaching and it furnished a unifying call to action among American naturalists to set the record straight. American naturalists believed themselves to be redefining, reforming, and reorienting the field even as they replicated the methods of European natural history through observation, fact collection, and a reluctance to theorize.

Some American naturalists sought to remedy the mistakes of their European counterparts by opening their practice to all Americans, seeking out and inviting natural historical data from their countrymen regardless of the reporter's educational background or social standing. Facts would be collected and then pitted against one another in public forums such as newspapers and magazines. This competition between facts—what one naturalist called the "democracy of facts"—would result in probable truth overwhelming and canceling out falsehood. [5] Consequently, an informed public, according to this permissive method, would be able to discern and decide about that which appeared most true, or at least most probable in the natural world. In a period extremely sensitive to the operations of secret agendas and the discovery of hidden interests in politics and economics, a transparent, fact-based method had the benefit of exposing and eliminating the problems of individual subjectivity and political prejudices. Most American naturalists could have confidence that they and their method would discover knowledge or collect information about the natural world through observation. They did not think of themselves as creating or making knowledge about nature. Their methodology was designed to take natural knowledge away from the theorist and the philosopher and return it to the natural world and its observers, where American naturalists believed it belonged.

Still, some naturalists, even some who advocated a permissive natural historical method and the democracy of facts, were decidedly less inclusive when it came time to draw conclusions about the natural world. Many of these naturalists demurred when stories about fantastic nature found their way into print. Swallow submersion stories highlighted tensions between a view of fact collecting as the work of many hands and one of reserving knowledge making for the learned. For some naturalists, swallow stories proved too incredible, marking those who reported them as either mistaken or, more damning, lacking the observational skills and sound thinking necessary for the natural historical project. Permissive rhetoric notwithstanding, many eighteenth- and nineteenth-century naturalists living and working in the United States strove to recreate the hierarchical protocols and practices they inherited from Europeans, with one important twist. Instead of serving as peripheral actors collecting specimens and facts for European metropolitans to interpret and arrange as part of the natural order, American naturalists now played the role of arbiter of nature to their countrymen who collected samples and facts for them to interpret. For these naturalists the study of natural history in America was not and should not be a democracy. The early United States was to be an "empire of reason," with an educated elite determining the boundaries of nature and the natural world for their countrymen. Despite their rhetoric some American naturalists were unwilling to discard all the imperial overtones of natural history practice that predated the American Revolution. Yet writers placed so much emphasis on gathering data from the field and were so wary of theorizing and prematurely generalizing that would-be American savants found themselves deferring to the (epistemologically) sovereign people.[6]

Dexter's report on swallow submersion is an example of the correspondence that naturalists sought and only one of numerous print and countless eyewitness testimonials about swallow submersion that circulated in the forty years following the American Revolution. Swallow stories generally supplied eyewitness accounts or secondhand testimonies detailing the discovery of swallows in mudflats or hollow trees during winter or early spring. The birds were removed from the cold and reanimated by the warmth of fires or in the pockets of the individuals who found them.

Related accounts offered circumstantial or eyewitness descriptions of individual swallows, sometimes entire flocks, plunging into rivers or lakes, not to be seen again until spring. Skeptics sought less dramatic destinations for wintering swallows and offered contrasting accounts. They testified to having seen swallows in migratory flight or having identified species peculiar to northern regions appearing in southern climates. Some went further and performed dissections and experiments, the results suggesting the anatomical impossibility of swallow submersion.

Swallow submersion stories adhered to cognitive patterns formulated by Francis Bacon and refined in the scientific societies of Europe, a methodology of fact seeking that would allow experts to determine the veracity of various natural phenomena. During the sixteenth and seventeenth centuries, natural philosophers and natural historians adopted an approach to knowledge creation, a fact discourse, which favored testimonies of individual experience and observation as the primary means of collecting information about the natural world. Members of scientific societies and consumers of natural history literature scrutinized testimonies through rhetorical analysis and a consideration of the social situation of the witness. These analyses tended to reject hearsay evidence; in turn, they elevated individual ocular testimony and multiple witnessing as the highest standards of discovery. Facts were matters to be pleaded and proved by one side against the contrary pleadings and proofs by the other and not, as in the modern sense, already considered true or worthy of belief.[7]

These discursive and epistemological practices of fact were part of a transatlantic culture of natural history in which a few colonials living in America participated before the Revolution.[8] Most often North American colonists played the role of collectors for European, usually English, patrons or savants. Through contact with organizations like the Royal Society, colonists adopted the research methodologies and goals of these institutions, going so far as to model America's first scientific organization, Philadelphia's American Philosophical Society, after London's Royal Society. Through these exchange networks, Americans were exposed to and participated in the major natural history endeavors and debates of the late eighteenth century. But for natural historians of the late eighteenth and early nineteenth centuries the American Revolution offered an opportunity to reverse their roles in the collector/interpreter equation. The American Revolution signaled for naturalists not only political change but also an opportunity for an authoritative new role as interpreters of nature in the new nation and an opportunity to reform natural history practice to accommodate the new nation's needs.

The hopeful prospects for the new nation were intertwined with those of science. David Ramsay, historian of the Revolution, argued that arts and sciences that languished under British rule "will now raise their drooping heads; and spread far and wide, till they have reached the remotest parts of this untutored continent."[9] Joel Barlow, poet and natural history advocate, believed that the present was an "age of philosophy" and imagined that America would soon take its place as the world's "empire of reason."[10] Freedom, liberty, and independence provided science with the climate it needed to flourish; America, these men believed, offered the "fresh soil."[11] The attention of its citizens now freed from the exigencies of war, natural history enthusiasts looked forward to "instructing the world in useful arts—and extending the empire of science." Natural history and science would lead to an improved and efficient agriculture; they would generate new technologies of manufacture; they would assist the expansion of commerce; and they would propel an "attentive perusal" of America's little read "Book of Nature."[12] Charles Willson Peale, in a lecture at the University of Pennsylvania, called natural history "the science comprehending all nature"; sketching the history of humankind, he argued that observation of the natural world was the key to "the progress of society from a rude to a civilized state." Peale considered the study of natural history of individual interest; however, with reference to the United States, he argued that "it ought to become a NATIONAL CONCERN, since it is a NATIONAL GOOD."[13] Nationalizing the practice and methods of natural history, Peale promised that agriculturists, theologians, merchants, and mechanics would benefit from the pursuit, each profession learning something new about the material world.

This heady enthusiasm for nature study was tempered by the recognition that natural history had an equally powerful ability to obscure and to injure. In the right hands, natural history could explain natural phenomena and offer practical solutions to vexing problems of life and nation; in its purest form it created and extended "useful knowledge." When practiced by the biased, however, natural history could be as devastating as an invading army, perhaps more so. Not only could it teach false lessons about the natural world, its biased conclusions could irreversibly damage the reputation of peoples and nations. In his *History of New-Hampshire*, Jeremy Belknap wrote that European natural historians stated "facts in a delusive light" and represented America "as a grave to Europeans" to "throw discouragement on emigration to this country" and harm its chances for success.[14] For natural history to be a successful enterprise, it needed to be practiced by individuals untainted by narrow interests. Interest occluded the senses, produced false observations, and eventually led to testimonies of natural phenomena that were not only inaccurate but simply not true.[15] Of these dangers consumers of European natural history were well aware.

American thinkers considered the European treatment of American nature the direct result of this corruption. The writings of the French naturalist Georges Louis Leclerc, Comte de Buffon, and others, notorious for their gross assertions about the American climate, landscape, and its degenerative potential, attracted the ire and condemnation of American natural history writers.[16] Buffon was artfully countered by Thomas Jefferson in Query VI of *Notes on the State of Virginia*; Jefferson's famous refutation was but one of many that attacked the sources, logic, and conclusions drawn by European natural historians.[17] This logic of climatic determinism and degeneration caused American naturalists to begin a major effort not only to refute European conclusions but to launch an attack on the sources and reasoning of these accounts.

Many late eighteenth- and early nineteenth-century American natural history texts begin with a thoroughgoing challenge leveled against the European treatment of American nature. Critics were consistently irritated that European natural history writers recycled biased travel accounts as evidence to support their opinions. Jeremy Belknap argued that accounts by European "closet philosophers" had been written by those "who have not seen [America] at all" and relied heavily on the writings of "those who have passed through it with rapidity of a traveler." Samuel Williams, a former professor of mathematics at Harvard and author of *The Natural and Civil History of Vermont*, likewise argued that because Buffon had depended on "transient or partial accounts" he had "fallen into many mistakes respecting the natural productions of America, which, more accurate observations would have corrected."[18] Travel accounts were suspect because natural historical accuracy was not the aim of the writers. In critiquing Buffon's assertions Jefferson asked of the naturalists' sources, "Who were these travelers? . . . Was natural history the object of their travels? Did they measure or weigh the animals they speak of? or did they not judge of them by sight, or perhaps even from report only?"[19] James Mease, a student of the

American climate, thought that if European naturalists "profess to write as philosophers" they should seek information from the "purest sources" and not "content themselves with theorising on subjects, which can be determined only by fact and observation." Mease believed that travelers "can be very inadequate judges" and their accounts "have gained more credit than they deserve."[20]

If faulty sources leading to false conclusions irritated American natural history writers, the logic found within the European accounts generated their greatest consternation. Instead of relying on careful observation and reporting "fact," European authors were repeatedly accused of theorizing and speculating, of forcing their findings into a "system" to create artistic rather than accurate descriptions of America. It is "amusing to observe the inconsistent conclusions of these theorizing philosophers" Belknap wrote, "for whilst one condemns the air of woodlands as destructive to life and health, another celebrates it as containing nutritive particles." Benjamin Smith Barton, a professor of natural history at the University of Pennsylvania, told listeners in a lecture that "it must appear obvious" to readers of Buffon and Cornelius De Pauw "that upon almost every subject connected with the Natural History of America, these writers have erred, because they have had a system to gratify." Barton thought that De Pauw's writings "show him to be a Stranger to Truth." More disturbing was the recognition that Buffon's conclusions were erroneous, lamentable "because the errors of this great French Naturalist are most intimately blended with some of the chastest and most beautiful truths in Nature." It was "system" that led him astray. Jefferson thought that "there has been more eloquence than sound reasoning displayed in support of [Buffon's] theory; that it is one of those cases where judgment has been seduced by a glowing pen." Jefferson added that "while I render every tribute of honor and esteem to the celebrated Zoologist . . . I must doubt whether in this instance he has not cherished error also, by lending her for a moment his vivid imagination and bewitching language." Since it was clear to many that European natural historians were incapable of producing valid or accurate observations, critics agreed with Belknap that "America can best be described by those who have for a long time resided in it."[21]

While many natural history works begin with a scathing denunciation of European naturalists, these critiques are more than formulaic complaints to generate attention. The passages suggest the degree to which American naturalists considered their practice of natural history distinct and ultimately superior to that of their European counterparts. Unlike Europeans who relied on untrustworthy sources and forced their findings into systems, American naturalists called for a study of particulars. American naturalists imagined themselves stripping away "philosophy" from nature study and basing their practice on collected facts. More than anything, they wanted to avoid the rush to generalization that diluted the efficacy of European natural history writings. Like Francis Bacon two hundred years earlier, American naturalists imagined themselves righting the practice of natural history. At the beginning of the seventeenth century, Bacon attempted to purge natural history of its medieval scholastic tendencies. He insisted that before generalizations about nature could be made, a thorough foundation of fact needed to be established.[22] American naturalists employed a similar reformist sensibility and applied it to natural history practice. By insisting on "fact," they saw themselves eradicating the theorizing tendencies that dominated European natural history while returning the practice to its foundations.

American naturalists hoped to discover and to discern the underlying structures and processes of nature but were hesitant to make definitive claims. To do so, at a moment when so little about American nature was known, would replicate the generalizing tendencies of European science. Rather, they argued that naturalists should collect facts regardless of the seeming improbability. When a critical mass of facts was assembled, then naturalists could proceed to generalize about the large-scale processes and structures that determined the operation of the natural world and could reject false claims. In late eighteenth- and early nineteenth-century America, to err on the side of caution was not considered poor science; if anything, it was better to withhold judgment until more evidence could be collected than to rush to a decided opinion. If testimonies and observations seemed to establish the plausibility of a claim but left considerable room for reasonable doubt, it was considered better to avoid making definitive assertions. To suggest outright that something like swallow submersion was impossible would be to rule too authoritatively and would limit the possibilities in American nature.

The practice American natural historians imagined and described would overcome the limitations of European science by basing itself on "reason" manifested through the works of nature. Their method would be antitheoretical, antisystematic, and, since it was would be founded upon experience and direct observation, available to all. Francis Hopkinson, in an address before the American Philosophical Society in 1784, gave this method its fullest expression. His message was a forecast, an invitation, and a prospectus. In America, he wrote, "The door to knowledge seems to be wider open than it ever was." The authority of the schools, he believed, is daily giving way "to the authority of nature." Hopkinson wished to eliminate the exclusionary impediments to natural knowledge. He wrote "that it is not absolutely *necessary* that a man should be what is called *learned* in order to be a philosopher"; instead, a "judicious and careful examination of the phenomena of nature, and experiments, made simple and easy, may, and often do, lead the attentive enquirer to most important discoveries." Many of the great advances in philosophical knowledge, he argued, had been made by men "not eminent in their learning" (Benjamin Franklin the most notable) and many of the most useful improvements in "mechanics" had been produced by "men of the most scanty education." Imploring his audience to open their eyes to nature, he reminded them that "the language of nature is not written in Hebrew or Greek." The understanding of the natural world "is not involved in the contemptible quirks of logic, nor wrapt in the visionary clouds of metaphysical hypothesis." Rather, "the great book of nature is open to all—all may read therein."[23]

As optimistic as Hopkinson was about the "advantageous possibilities" for American natural history, he felt that it was necessary to ask the "mortifying question—what are we doing?" to promote its advancement. The American prospects for the extension of the science appeared great. The deficiency, he believed, "is not owing to a want of men of strong abilities, or a sufficiency of acquired learning among us." America has been noted for the "sagacity of her citizens"; this climate was "favourable to the production of genius" and the "uncultivated abilities of the lowest class of natives of this country, seem to be as keen and discerning as those of any country whatever." The deficiency, he concluded, "must be owing merely to a want of attention, which, in our situation, is unpardonable."[24] To rectify this problem, Hopkinson reasoned, natural history must be promoted throughout the nation in the form of learned societies—the American Philosophical Society and the American Academy of Arts and Sciences most notably—and by educating citizens through books, public lectures, and newspapers. Promoting inquiry into the natural world was vital to the success of the American experiment. But this inquiry would be less hierarchical, less institutional, and more fluid than its European counterpart, whose methodology was directed more by philosophical hypotheses. American natural history, in its earliest years, followed a pattern that "depends not always upon the intrinsic degree of probability, but upon facts founded on the testimony of people of noted veracity."[25] The investment made by American natural history enthusiasts in the observations of "people of noted veracity" created the environment in which swallows submersion stories could flourish and the belief in possibility in American nature could thrive.

Dexter was not alone in his opinion of the winter destination of swallows. In the late eighteenth and early nineteenth centuries, swallow submersion—the belief that come autumn swallows hibernated in the mud of lakes and rivers rather than migrate—was one of the most actively discussed and frequently recurring natural history subjects in American print. Its advocates and detractors filled the pages of the leading scientific journals, natural history books, literary magazines, and newspapers with accounts of phenomena, experiment, and their theories about both. Swallow submersion was the subject of both public and academic lectures on natural history, the subject occupying the meetings of America's scientific societies and becoming a currency of exchange among a growing collection of natural history enthusiasts, a self-identified group of men and women interested in the natural world who believed themselves capable of unbiased, commonsense observation and immune to prejudice.

New to America, the controversy over the wintering destination of swallows had ancient roots, a history of which American nature observers were well aware. Aristotle believed that most birds migrate while others, notably the swallow, hibernate in the holes of cliffs and banks; hibernation remained one of the most popular explanations for the wintering habits of swallows through the early modern period. Olaus Magnus, Archbishop of Upsala, wrote of fishermen pulling their nets from the sea and finding balls of fish and swallows clinging together. The clusters were brought from the water and warmed by fires, reanimating the torpid birds.[26] Other naturalists argued for migration. Pierre Belon, a French naturalist, advocated for hibernation in his 1555 *History of the Nature of Birds*, as did Francis Willoughby, the English natural historian, in his 1676 *Ornithologia*, the first book devoted entirely to the study of birds.

The controversy occupied naturalists into the eighteenth century as well. Mark Catesby, a traveler-naturalist to eighteenth-century Florida and Carolina, thought the "want of food" causes birds "by Instinct, to resort to

Figure 1. Olaus Magnus, *Histoire des pays spetentrionaus* (Paris, 1561).
Magnus's *Histoire* contains an engraving illustrating fishermen pulling
swallows and fish from beneath frozen bodies of water. Courtesy Beinecke
Rare Book and Manuscript Library, Yale University.

some other Parts of the Globe, where they may find a fresh Supply."[27] A
series of letters and reports about swallow migration published in the Royal
Society's *Philosophical Transactions* gave the controversy its highest profile
in the Anglophone world in the years immediately preceding its appearance
in the United States. Peter Collinson—the English botanist and patron of
the colonial American naturalists John Bartram, Benjamin Franklin, and
Cadwallader Colden—argued vehemently for migration, primarily on the
basis of information he gathered from his extensive network of correspondents around the world. His counterpart, Daines Barrington, vice-president
of the Royal Society, sided with the hibernationists. While Collinson and
Barrington disagreed about the wintering habits and whereabouts of swallows, they did agree on how to settle natural history disputes. Both men
sought natural history information and testimony from individuals around
the world. In short, they sought "facts" that would allow them to determine
the legitimacy of various natural phenomena.[28] Thomas Pennant, a Scottish
natural historian, agreed with Collinson, writing that submersion is "too

amazing and unnatural to merit attention, if it was not that some of the learned have been credulous enough to deliver, for fact, what has the strongest appearance of impossibility; we mean the relation of swallows passing the winter immersed under ice, at the bottom of lakes, or lodged beneath the water of the sea at the foot of rocks." Though earnestly delivered, Pennant wrote, these stories "must provoke a smile."[29] When Americans engaged this debate, many did so with a historical awareness, wondering if New World swallows would prove or disprove the ancient texts and informants from around the world as accurate reporters of natural phenomena or deluded observers of nature.[30]

The debate over swallow submersion, migration, and hibernation, however, is more than a quaint or quirky episode in the history of American science.[31] While singular in its many details, it shares common characteristics with other public natural historical and scientific disputes over whether mastodons were alive and well in the American west or the efficacy of electrical treatments for chronic ailments.[32] Still, this vibrant controversy offers an opportunity to examine the inner workings and dominant rules of natural history, its culture, and practice in the late eighteenth- and early nineteenth-century United States.[33] As Americans witnessed, wrote, and argued about whether swallows migrated, hibernated, or submerged under water, they exposed the boundaries within which they created and contested natural knowledge, even as those who participated in this debate fused three distinct, interrelated, and dense discourses about natural historical method, purpose, and nationalist cant.

The first, evidenced in Dexter's letter, concerned natural history as a practice and the rules that governed, or were supposed to govern, that practice: namely, how to observe nature; the correct procedures for gathering and communicating eyewitness and secondhand testimony; the proper literary forms, genres, and rhetoric for writing about natural phenomena; and the protocols for experiments and experimentation (discussed below concerning the swallow experiments conducted by Dr. Charles Caldwell). These discussions introduced one of the central tensions within the period's natural history and the swallow submersion debate: an oppositional relationship between eyewitness experience from the field and experiments removed from nature.

The second discourse concerned the contributions natural history could make to the encyclopedia of human knowledge and the long-term project of furthering human progress. Francis Hopkinson and Charles Willson

Peale, as well as many others, vigorously promoted natural history in America during the early years of the republic and urged the citizenry to contribute in the transnational republic of letters. Advocates described natural history's purposes and methods in cataloging and describing nature; they explained its central role in propelling the advancement of human societies from more primitive to more advanced stages of development; and they traced the discipline's own history from its beginnings among the ancients through its modern manifestations in chorography and travel writing, the Linnaean classificatory system, and, later, the establishment of the geographic and biogeographic traditions commonly attributed to Alexander von Humboldt.[34]

The third discourse was nationalistic in character and celebrated the distinctive and unique qualities of the new American nation, among them its nature. Promoters attempted to distinguish natural history as practiced in the early United States as a different and improved method of natural inquiry from that being practiced by Europeans, highlighting the debate over American nature as evidence of European naturalists' faulty methods and erroneous conclusions. Individuals such as Benjamin Smith Barton, David Ramsey, and Joel Barlow linked natural history practice and natural historical epistemology to a soaring nationalistic optimism. These "prophets of glory" saw natural history and themselves as playing a pivotal role in securing the economic foundation of the new nation through the identification of natural resources, revealing the moral lessons embedded in nature. They also saw naturalists as among the class of people who could establish the United States on solid economic footing and serve as examples for other citizens to emulate.[35]

A careful examination of swallow submersion exposes a vigorous discussion about natural history methodology, evidentiary rules, codes of conduct, and the place of human reason in gathering information about the natural world. The theory of swallow submersion incurred conversation and dispute about the possessors of and definition of fact, as well as the relative value of fact and theory. And as they argued about swallow submersion, these Americans determined and debated the place and role of natural history in the new republic, who could participate in it, and how they would do so. In short the controversy surrounding swallow submersion reveals Americans in the late eighteenth and early nineteenth centuries working from an epistemology of scientific inquiry attuned to the particulars and unknown contours of American nature, an approach to the natural world shaped by the era's political culture and its particular interests and anxieties. Stories of swallow submersion are not the folklore of a prescientific era but the by-product of the cultural and political context of the era's natural history, when Americans were self-consciously creating a nation and, they believed, an improved scientific practice grounded in observed fact, not abstract theory.

While the antihierarchical and antitheoretical overtones to nature observation can partly explain the persistence and expansion of swallow stories, equally important is the expanding access to printed material.[36] Swallow stories tended to spread, it appears, through the frequent reprinting of an account written for one newspaper or journal to another, intriguing people who were unaware of the theory and reinforcing the beliefs of those who already considered the theory true. Drawing from the scientific discourse of fact and the earlier rhetorical conventions to report wonders and marvels, published swallow stories show little variation from one to the next, following a similar literary pattern.[37] Swallow stories emphasize the writer's presentation of himself as a reasonable and trustworthy reporter of fact; they include other testimonies to corroborate his sightings; often they present eyewitness testimony, not just secondhand or hearsay evidence; and they describe the narrator's own conversion experience from initial incredulity to a position of surprised but firm belief.[38]

Josiah Blakeley's 1789 swallow testimony exhibits most of these characteristics. Following the lead of Dexter, Blakeley wrote in New York's *American Magazine* that "the history of our common Swallow has long been a problem in ornithology." While people in general "supposed them birds of passage, a few who appear to have been better informed, supported the contrary." Blakeley reasoned that the "opinion of many was founded on what they thought probable—that of the few, on fact." When he was a boy, his nurse told him that swallows wintered on the moon, and as he grew older, others tried to convince him that they migrated. Though exposed to the "doctrine of their descending to pass the winter in the gloomy descent of water, I was a real sceptic." However, having pieced together enough credible testimonies to swallow submersion, "I now as much doubt the theory of those naturalists who contend they are birds of passage, as I disbelieve the philosophy of my nurse." His letter not only provided more evidence for the phenomena; it also offered an account of his conversion to the "truth."[39]

Blakeley's conversion was a combination of suggestion and witnessing.

A conversation in 1780 with a "zoologer" started his change of mind. While talking with his unnamed companion about the "phenomena of the sudden exit, but gradual and irregular return of swallows," Blakeley noted that geese "were observed both in their flight from and return to the sea" and "black birds, in the fall of the year, were seen in flocks of vast numbers directing their course to the south-west." But having never seen swallows in migration, "I thought it probable when they began their passage, they flew only in the night, or, that they ascended beyond the reach of the human eye." His companion told him that swallows were not birds of passage; that the cause of their sudden disappearance but irregular return was that "they had a fixed day for immersing into the water, but none for emerging from it." When Blakeley called this idea into question, the zoologer told a story of a neighbor who, on draining a pond, was attracted to what appeared to be "moving mud." The neighbor took some of the mud to his house, warmed it slowly by a fire "till from it there rose a number of swallows, hovering over the head of himself and family, who had been spectators of their resurrection."[40]

Still a doubter, Blakeley made more observations and gathered more testimonies. In 1782 he lived near the millpond in Boston. That August the pond "was covered with swallows, some flying just above the surface of the water—others lighting upon the rushes and water lilies that raised their heads above it." Speaking with a neighbor about the collection of swallows, Blakely was informed that " 'for some days before they take their annual flight . . . they rendezvous at this pond.' " The neighbor "mentioned the day of the month (August) which I do not remember, on which he said they would all disappear." Blakeley missed the event, but his neighbor assured him that it "took place accordingly." The testimony of these men began to work on Blakeley.

"Before I was convinced that swallows passed the winter under the water," he wrote, "I was in the month of August at Bethlehem [Pennsylvania]." Blakeley wrote that "a little before sun-set" each evening he would walk along Monocras Creek and the Lehigh River. During his walk he was "astonished at the collection of swallows that were alighting upon, and hovering over the willows which grow on the bank of the creek." Asking about "the cause of their leaving their nests in old buildings and collecting to pass the night in those green willows," he was informed by the Rev. Mr. Vanvleek, a resident of the area, that it happened every year at that season. Blakeley noted that by August 20 the birds had disappeared. He offered a possible explanation: "Perhaps it is from the branches of those willows, that hang over the creek that they altogether immerse into the water."[41] Blakeley's conversion was slow; he became convinced of the truth of swallow submersion through a preponderance of credible evidence.

The conversion process operated as a device that invited a reader to identify with the reporter. As the reporter described his reluctance to accept the swallow submersion theory, the questions he asked as he investigated the idea led the reader toward the moment of belief. The conversion narrative also reinforced the agenda of American natural history: theoretical expectations of American nature could not compete with the reality of lived experience. Conversion underscored distinctly the foolishness of theoretical natural history and emphasized the importance of fact. And as swallow stories circulated, they engendered bolder, first-person eyewitness testimony.

Peter Cole, an individual from New York City, contributed a letter to the *Medical Repository*, one of America's leading scientific and medical journals, in 1798. Cole witnessed large flocks of swallows flying over the water toward the east corner of a New York City pond, where "in the twinkling of an eye, [they] disappeared under the water and rose no more." Watching the swallows with his "spy-glass," Cole was approached by his neighbor, Mr. Brooks, who agreed with what Mr. Cole saw. Cole mused about the importance of what he had seen in his letter. These few observations, "however imperfect, may possibly afford a field for speculation to the philosophic mind, and lead to useful discoveries." Cole admitted that after witnessing this event he had become a "proselyte" to the submersion doctrine; however, he had done so not from "speculative researches, but *ocular demonstrations*."[42]

Multiple eyewitness testimonies were vital to establishing submersion as a possible explanation for wintering swallows. Another New Yorker corroborated Cole's observations the next year. H. Pollack's testimony, related in a letter by W. Johnson to the *Monthly Magazine and American Review*, described how large flocks of swallows "plunged into the water and disappeared." Pollack, "aware of the importance of affording any additional information on this long disputed question in the natural history of the swallow," obtained a telescope to observe the swallows' behavior. He would not need it. One flock of approximately two hundred birds plunged into the water within thirty yards of him and "instantly disappeared, without the least appearance of opposition that might be expected to arise from their natural buoyancy." He was confident that his eyes were not deceiving him. The evening was serene and his friend, Mr. Seebor, said he saw the same thing.[43]

Accounts of swallow submersion did not go unchallenged. Skeptics attempted to shift the terms of debate away from individual observation to the use of reason and experiment. An anonymous correspondent to the *Medical Repository* penned a lengthy critique. The author wrote after having read Peter Cole's piece about submersion, a theory, "which I thought had been exploded." While limited space prevented him from detailing all the arguments against submersion, the author offered a summary of them for those "who have not yet examined the merits of both sides of the question." He reasoned that it was impossible for any "land animal" to exist without respiration; the internal structure of the swallow lacks the organs necessary for water respiration; and the "specific levity" of the swallow would make months under water a "physical impossibility." He believed that all people should doubt testimonies about submersions. "It is not my intention to doubt the word of your correspondent [Mr. Cole]. I believe he relates what he thinks he distinctly saw." But, the author continued, "is it not possible that he might have been mistaken?" The correspondent thought Cole too far from the events to have seen the particulars of what happened to the birds. He wished that Cole "*would have the goodness to inform us, whether he actually saw them plunge into the water, and saw the waves which must have ensued their submersion.*" Should he do so, then the anonymous author "will give up the controversy"; but, if not, the "mere 'disappearance' of the swallows cannot be admitted as a certain proof of their submersion."[44]

The anonymous author cited an experiment related in the *Gentleman's Magazine*, an English publication, in which the submersion was tested on swallows.[45] The experimenter "immersed" two swallows. He related that the experimenter "immediately had cause to conclude they were drowning" for when they came into contact with the water "the air escaped from them copiously, causing large bubbles on the surface of the water." He left them in the water overnight, returned to recover the birds and placed them in his house next to the fire. He warmed their bodies to "natural blood-heat" but not the least signs of "re-animation" appeared. Not wont to judge too quickly, the experimenter waited two more days until a time when "their bodies were hastily becoming corrupt" before abandoning the experiment. The anonymous critic believed that experimental evidence confirmed that the birds lacked the organs necessary for water respiration, making submersion impossible.[46]

This critique was joined the next year by an extended essay that also refuted swallow submersion with reasoned arguments and experimental results. Its author, Dr. Charles Caldwell, a Philadelphia physician and likely the author of the earlier anonymous letter, informed his readers that he would "controvert" the hypothesis of the winter submersion of swallows "rather by endeavouring to expose its improbability, than by advancing facts in direct opposition." In place of submersion, Caldwell argued for swallow migration. Caldwell questioned the accuracy of the statements attesting to swallow submersion, even condemning Cole's article as the "loose story of a man relating a common event" rather than the "accurate statement of a philosopher, drawn up after a faithful examination of his subject."[47]

Caldwell performed an experiment to suggest the impossibility of swallow submersion and, in doing so, attacked the methodology of fact collecting through observation. "In the close of the summer of [seventeen] ninety six," he wrote, "I was so fortunate as to become possessed of two swallows, (the hirundo rustica) just before the annual disappearance of these birds. I kept them uninjured, till such disappearance actually took place." Learning that local people noted the disappearance of the neighborhood swallows, Caldwell and a colleague, Dr. Cooper, "lost no time in repairing to the Schuylkill, where we immersed our two little prisoners in the river, with weights appended sufficiently heavy to sink them to the bottom." In an attempt to replicate the conditions described in submersion testimonies "the weights were fixed in such a manner, as to draw one of the swallows down headforemost, and the other in the contrary direction." Caldwell and Cooper chose a place in the river of sufficient depth where they could observe the actions of the birds and submerge the birds completely.

"These little animals no sooner came in contact with the water, than they manifested signs of great alarm, and struggled with their wings, as if desirous to escape from the embraces of an element that was unnatural to them." When submerged to the bottom "air began to escape from them" partly from their lungs and partly from air trapped in the feathers. "They exhibited," Caldwell thought, "the anxiety and convulsions of animals in a drowning state, but, in less than three minutes, became perfectly motionless." Having allowed the swallows to remain submerged three hours, Caldwell and Cooper took them out carefully "and made use of every means we could devise, to restore them to life." All efforts proved fruitless. "Our birds were reduced, not to a state of torpidity, or suspended animation, but, of absolute death." He noted that similar experiments conducted at different seasons by different gentlemen produced the same results. Caldwell wondered, "Have we not ample reason, then to conclude" that all swallows would share precisely the same fate "whether immersed in water, by their own act, or by the hand of the experimenter?"[48]

He concluded his essay arguing that the submersion theory belied a rational, intelligent design. Faulty observations, poor human reasoning, and distortions in common sense observing produced testimonies for swallow submersion. Caldwell wondered why nature, "as if in sport and wantonness of the swallow alone," would force a swallow to become torpid and deprive it of the advantages resulting from migration. "Such tantalizing inconsistency," he concluded, "is incompatible with the wisdom of arrangement, and benignity of design, so conspicuously displayed in the economy of the universe." Caldwell challenged the discourse and protocols of fact collecting, asserting that "no splendour of talents, nor authority of names, will ever be able to give permanency to a belief in the submersion of swallows"; rather, his belief would be based on the witnessed results of experiments and reasoned conclusions that followed such procedures.[49]

Caldwell, much to his disappointment, did not end the controversy over swallows; nor is there evidence that he persuaded many believers to doubt submersion. Even with experimental evidence to the contrary, fact creation in early decades of the new nation relied predominately on individual observation, witness testimony, and an overriding belief that, in American nature, possibility should be the default position until proven incorrect. Results of contrived experiments and human reason did not unseat prevailing opinion and the authority of testimony. Reviews of Caldwell's memoir show this to be the case. The reviewer in the *American Review* went right to the heart of the matter, the determination of fact. He wrote that "four reputable witnesses" had given their testimony. These testimonies "are the facts, and these, connected with many others on record, tend confirm an opinion, held by some naturalists, of the hybernation of these birds in the bottom of ponds and rivers." Doctor Caldwell, however, "is a strenuous opposer of this notion" and endeavored to show that there might be deception of sight in making these observations. "But as we know the persons, and have heard their statements," the reviewer continued, "we find no reason to distrust their accuracy either in seeing or in relating what they saw."

Trusting the discourse of fact, the reviewer had no doubt "that swallows, in great number sometimes go under water."[50] Swallow submersion "is an odd phenomenon," the reviewer admitted. But Caldwell had erred by attempting to prove "from pathological considerations, and *a priori* estimates," in short through human reason, the impossibility of swallow submersion and resuscitation. "We do not view the matter as either absurd in itself, or impossible in nature." The reviewer wrote that "life is sometimes held from its grantor under very singular conditions"; while its characteristics and dimensions may be different in swallows than in humans, "man ought to see and admire them, and not deny the existence of such peculiarities, or contradict those who have witnessed their reality."[51]

The reviewer believed that experimental procedures could not replicate the natural conditions and attacked Caldwell's methods; deductive conclusions should not be employed to settle these matters, the reviewer thought. "Speculations are of little avail, and of no value, in these cases," he wrote. Caldwell's reasoning would conclude that an animal deprived of air for a year or more would die; "and yet experience teaches that toads have been found alive, after enclosure in blocks of marble for centuries unknown."[52] Caldwell's logic "assures us" that animals once frozen could not reanimate; "yet fishermen know that perch and eels, and several other animals, can sometimes revive after having been frozen as stiff as an icicle." Trout brought to market "in a state of congelation . . . have revived in the kitchen of the purchaser when put into a pail of cold water to thaw." The reviewer offered examples of insects revived after drowned in wine and humans kept alive without sustenance for months. Should Dr. Caldwell "undertake to enclose toads in rocks, to render fishes rigid by frost, to keep a man six months without aliment, or to preserve the lives of insects in vinous liquors, he would, probably, fail to resuscitate them in every instance." Such experiments would militate against the related facts but, the reviewer continued, "this is a subject not to be established by reasoning; but the fact being established, we are to reconcile it to our own reason as well as we can." Dr. Caldwell, the reviewer concluded, has not "in any degree increased our knowledge of this part of natural history." That swallows may migrate was not in dispute; that they hibernate "is as little to be doubted." The genus *hirundo* consists of several species, the particulars of each little known. Before an ultimate decision is made, the reviewer continued, more information on their respective habits and ways of life should be collected. After that "we shall be enabled to form a better judgment which of them fly away to warmer latitudes, which shelter themselves in holes and caves, and which commit themselves to the protection of the waters."[53]

A review in the *Medical Repository* similarly criticized the memoir, citing Caldwell's folly in attempting to replicate nature through experimentation as its basis for critique. This reviewer could not agree with Caldwell that his experiment or his physiological arguments "have any decisive effect on the determination of the submersion question." If the submersion of swallows was true, the reviewer thought, "it must be performed at certain times and places, in modes and under circumstances which we cannot arrange nor imitate." The reviewer did note that Caldwell's treatise served as a reminder that readers should scrutinize the authenticity and the details of every narrative on the subject. That noted, the reviewer thought that there exists "an assignable weight of testimony (much greater, perhaps than has been hitherto obtained)" which should "compel belief" and "render the explanation of the principle altogether to the admission of the fact."[54] Reviews such as these demonstrate the inclination among American naturalists to value multiple testimony over human reasoning. They regarded experiments as useful, perhaps illuminating, but not conclusive. Experiments required human thought, planning, and execution: that is, they required some degree of theory, which was to be avoided in natural historical matters. Facts, by contrast, seemed to require no reasoning, no mediation, no thought. To these reviewers facts were visceral, uncorrupted evidence and required only the confidence that the senses had not been compromised to compel belief.[55]

This epistemic pattern dominated late eighteenth- and early nineteenth-century natural history and was embraced and defended at the American centers of natural knowledge creation. A letter from Robert Dunbar, resident of Virginia, to Benjamin Smith Barton, professor of natural history at the University of Pennsylvania, shows that swallow submersion came to the attention of the American Philosophical Society in Philadelphia. Dunbar wrote Barton after hearing his public lecture on natural history that included a description of swallow submersion and assured the professor that "you may depend upon the statement, as I was myself a witness to the facts." He continued: "It is more than two years since I chanced to be in company with a gentleman of information, and an accurate observer of the works of nature" when the subject of swallow submersion was mentioned. The gentleman informed Dunbar that he had seen the birds dive underwater for winter so many times that "the circumstance had ceased to create the smallest curiosity." Dunbar was encouraged to follow him to the site of submersion, where he would "then have it in my power to satisfy myself, surely, as to the fact."[56]

Dunbar's letter is notable for its specifics. On the second of September 1800, the swallows collected at the edge of a marsh where Dunbar witnessed large flocks "very much agitated, and distressed." Soon they plunged into the water and totally disappeared. Some of the swallows attempted to immerse themselves near the margin of the marsh "where the water and mud were more intimately incorporated; so much so, as completely to prevent those swallows from sinking." After the birds' initial attempt to submerge, "they again renewed the effort, until they finally succeeded." One swallow "having attempted to sink itself, where there was but little water, failed in the attempt, and lay, apparently without life, it being near the margin on side of the pond." Dunbar's companion picked it up and laying it in his hand, revived it. The swallow then "ascended to a considerable height in the air; again, descended into the water, and finally disappeared." Recounting the experience, Dunbar wrote that while the majority of the birds had submerged before his arrival at the pond, he had "no doubt of the truth" of what the gentleman told him. The man lived near the pond and was, Dunbar wrote, "a person of veracity."[57]

Dunbar's letter was referred to the American Philosophical Society's committee on natural history where it was scrutinized and vetted. On 4 February 1803 the committee read their report to the entire organization. Jonathan Williams, vice-president of the society and author of the report, laid the logic of natural history uncommonly bare. "Natural history," he wrote, "is generally speaking a Collection of Facts," and the "great object" in natural history researches is "to obtain the highest degree of authenticity that such Facts are susceptible of." When determining authenticity, he continued, it is not "necessary to insist on those strict Rules of Evidence, which are indispensable in cases where Interest or Ambition may operate as strong motives to pervert the truth." Instead it is merely "the deception of the senses, and the illusions of the imagination" that need to be guarded against, at least, "when we can depend on the intelligence of observers." Williams continued that "we ought not therefore to reject hearsay testimony altogether, and a chain of perspicuous communications, through several respectable hands, may be considered as almost tantamount to a statement made to the Society of each individual." In the case before the organization, he wrote, the writer "is introduced to the Society by one of

Figure 2. Alexander Wilson, *American Ornithology* (Philadelphia, 1812), 5, plate 2. Wilson produced the first illustrated comprehensive American ornithological text. This plate shows barn (*Hirundo rustica*), white-bellied (renamed the tree swallow, *Tachycineta bicolor*), and bank swallows (*Riparia riparia*). These species were cited frequently by witnesses as those that submerged. Courtesy Beinecke Rare Book and Manuscript Library, Yale University.

its Vice Presidents [Barton] in a manner sufficient to establish full confidence in what he himself has seen, and, (on the principles mentioned,) what he has heard from other seems to deserve credibility."[58]

Williams wrote of the letter's merits and anticipated the critiques of skeptics. "These Facts will, it is conceived, form a valuable addition to those already obtained on this subject, especially as they tend to obviate two objections which have been opposed to the belief of them." First, Williams wrote, "It has been said that the want of specific gravity in the bird would render its submersion impossible." But in the letter "we here see that the swallows acquire a great degree of velocity before plunging, as if on purpose to overcome their buoyancy." So too, it has been argued "that the proof of the submersion did not prove the resurrection;" yet the letter stated that swallows had been observed in the spring covered in mud, "which corroborates other testimony too forcibly to be resisted." Williams concluded and summarized the methodology of natural history: "It is vain to oppose reasoning to Such Facts;—they are either true, or false." Since Williams thought it difficult to conceive that anyone would propagate such "gross falsehoods . . . merely for the pleasure of deceiving"; and since Dunbar followed the proper channels to induce belief and his testimony was verified by multiple witnesses, Williams concluded "all reasoning is at an End."[59] Dunbar's letter and swallow submersion were accepted by the American Philosophical Society. A letter on swallow submersion similar to Dunbar's, written by Colonel Frederick Antes, was published in the society's next volume of *Transactions* in 1806.[60]

Williams's call for a halt to reasoning was reflective of the milieu through which possibility became the dominant outlook on nature. While many naturalists suspected swallow submersion to be a trick of the eye or a folk tale retold, most naturalists preferred to withhold judgment until more data could be collected. This epistemological caution, while supporting natural history, had the ironic result of engendering confidence in those beliefs that naturalists ultimately hoped to disprove. And once these stories found their way into print, naturalists found them increasingly difficult to displace. Eyewitness testimonies of moving boulders, living frogs found in rocks, and snakes with the capacity to charm their prey not only made appearances in the magazine and journals in the first decades of the nineteenth century; these testimonies acquired adherents. Hoping to avoid putting eyewitness testimony into direct conflict, naturalists attempting to disprove these kinds of accounts had to rely on arguments from experiments. Yet these claims were met with skepticism as their methodology and their critics thought experimental procedures and theories too close to deductive conclusions made by naturalists. The resulting situation was a view of America as a place where it seemed anything was probable, or at least possible, until proven otherwise by facts.

Naturalists who valued truth came to realize that this reliance on facts derived from individual observation had a Janus face. In 1796, Benjamin Smith Barton published a memoir investigating and challenging the existence of the "fascinating faculty" attributed to the rattlesnake, the ability to "charm" and lure its prey. Barton considered it one of "the earliest prejudices imprinted on [children's] tender minds," a prejudice "which often increases with their years." Barton desired to release the "bondage of the mind" by proving that such a faculty did not exist and aimed to give "a general, though correct, view of the question, uninfluenced by the bold assertions of ignorance, or by the plausible conjectures of science." His investigation "sought for facts: these have been my guides."[61] By constructing an argument on personal observation, he followed the dominant rules of natural history and presented a rebuttal that relied on observation rather than theory and experiment as Caldwell had done in refuting swallow submersion.

Barton considered a snake's ability to charm its prey "destitute of a solid foundation." Although he had read and heard many stories "by men whose veracity I could not suspect . . . the mere force of argument never compelled me to believe." He suspected that there was a "deficiency in the extent of observation" and it was on the retold tales that he focused attention. According to testimony, the snake "lying at the bottom of the tree or bush upon which the bird or squirrel sits, fixes its eyes upon the animal which it designs to fascinate or enchant." Then the "unhappy animal" utters "a most piteous cry," runs or flies wildly about until it "runs into the snake's jaws, and is swallowed at once, if it be not too big." But Barton offered observations suggesting that snakes did not possess this capacity. He noted that the birds most often "charmed" were ground birds or made their nests near the ground and that spring or early summer, when young are most vulnerable, were the seasons in which these stories were most often set. Coupled with information from Timothy Matlack, the onetime secretary of the American Philosophical Society and an "ingenious friend of mine," whose snake dissections produced only one bird and one squirrel from the specimens' stomachs, Barton suggested that other explanations might be necessary. Barton offered the testimony of Philadelphia clock and instrument maker David Rittenhouse, the "cautious and enlightened philosopher," who observed a female bird protecting her nest from a snake. Sometimes she flew right at the snake, intending to scare off the snake; she was not being charmed. Rittenhouse observed from the "enlarged belly" that snake had already eaten two or three of her young and was in the process of consuming another. Rittenhouse told Barton that the cry and actions of the bird were "precisely similar" to those said to be under the influence of a snake and that the species, a red-winged blackbird, builds its nest close to the ground. From this testimony and from his own observations, Barton believed "the strong democracy of facts should exert its wholesome sway." A snake employs "no machinery of enchantment" to obtain prey; rather it relies on its cunning and its strength.[62]

Barton failed to convince, even with observational facts driving his memoir. There were many who still believed in the existence of a true fascinating faculty, Barton admitted, and "what change time and further attention to the subject may accomplish, I know not."[63] It is difficult to discern a marked shift in understanding of snakes. Stories of the fascinating faculty continued throughout the nineteenth century and into the twentieth.[64] In a supplement to his memoir, Barton paused to ponder an answer as to why his observations failed to convert. "Prejudices," he wrote, "or, to name them by a milder phrase, the earlier biases of our minds, frequently detain us, in the investigation of science. Our first love is said to be the strongest." Likewise, the "first principles in science," as in politics and in religion, "are often adhered to with the extreme of pertinacity." Belief reinforced by experience was more powerful than even the illuminating rays of science, Barton admitted, and "he who turned of fifty years of age, relinquishes a favourite error, has infinitely more merit, than the world may be willing to allow him." Against entrenched experience and overwhelming opinions to the contrary, Barton knew that his task of overturning belief in charming snakes, like Caldwell's efforts to disprove swallow submersion, was a difficult and arduous one.[65] Aware that his efforts to convert would be in vain, he resorted to the language of those who doubted Caldwell's experiments. Barton asked, "Why should we expect to make all philosophers converts to our opinions? Almost every phenomenon, almost every fact in nature, seems to admit of an explanation upon more than one principle." Barton concluded that scientific authority, particularly deductive conclusions, was limited in its ability to persuade because of American's intellectual permissiveness in natural historical matters.

For American natural historians of the late eighteenth and early nineteenth centuries, what was critical was that the category of fact remained elastic. Eyewitness testimony was authoritative if the witness established credibility. To make definitive generalizations about what was, or was not possible, confined and diminished nature, equating naturalists with the very Europeans they worked so eagerly to disprove. But this epistemology resulted in a dangerous paradox: all manner of ideas about nature could exist and few, if any, could be refuted with complete assurance. Observational facts, however improbable, were far more worthy of belief than dicta derived from theoretical speculations. This definition of and this reliance upon facts, coupled with an uncertainty over what the American natural environment might contain, fostered an intellectual openness and permissiveness that allowed possibility to become the dominant scientific metaphor and outlook on American nature; yet it also created the conditions that many Americans feared in their politics: a prejudiced, vocal majority overwhelming an enlightened but less powerful minority. Careful scrutiny of nature, it appeared, had already shown that phenomena beyond reasonable belief could be found in the natural world. With European science casting aspersions on their country, Americans became politically committed to an understanding of nature that elevated possibility to new heights and practically devoted to a method of natural history study that privileged observation and testimony over theory and experiment. The debate over swallow submersion brought into relief some unsettling realities for natural historians of the new nation: the democracy of facts they helped to create was a powerful force and one they could do little to stop.

But what of the swallows? Birds, like the humans observing and discussing them, are historical actors, and historians can work to explain their behavior. Is there reason to believe or to doubt the testimonies of those who witnessed swallows plunging into the autumnal water or disengaging from the springtime mud? Is there not a natural explanation for the swallows' behavior in the spring and fall, one that might help to explain, but not employ, the unlikely theory of subaqueous hibernation and resurrection?

The species of swallows cited by early republic observers and testifiers were those that lived and continue to live in the eastern third of North America during their breeding season, the warmer months from March and

April to September and October: the barn swallow (*Hirundo rustica*), the bank swallow (*Ripara ripara*), and the tree swallow (*Tachycineta bicolor*). The cliff swallow (*Petrochelidon pyrrhonota*) now lives in eastern North America but has expanded its range from the mountain west to the east only in the last 100 to 150 years.[66] On occasion testifiers cited the purple martin (*Progne subis*), a species of swallow, as well as the chimney swift (*Chaetura pelagica*), a member of the *Apodidae* family that resembles swallows. While the northern rough-winged swallow (*Stelgidopteryx serripennis*) also inhabits eastern North America, it does not appear that those observing or writing about swallows identified it as a separate species, likely lumping it together with the bank swallow with whom it shares size, physical markings, behavioral similarities, and habitat. John James Audubon is credited with discovering the northern rough-winged swallow by accident while collecting bank swallows in 1819, a date later than most of the swallow submersion testimonies.[67]

All of these eastern North American swallow species live near or frequent aquatic habitats—the banks of rivers and creeks, the edges as well as the air over lakes, ponds, marshes and swamps.[68] All North American swallows are primarily insectivores that capture their prey in flight, though a few species will gather emerging, dying, or recently deceased insects on the ground in rare, opportunistic feeding.[69] The tree swallow is notable for its ability to digest plant material, specifically the berries from the wax-myrtle tree (*Myrica cerifera*), permitting it to survive periods of cold weather and low insect availability as well as allowing it to winter farther north and arrive earlier in the spring than the other species. Importantly, all North America swallows migrate south in the winter; the tree swallow has the northernmost range, wintering in Florida, while the majority of this species as well as all other eastern North American swallows reside in Central and South America and the islands in the Caribbean. No swallow species spends time swimming in or on water routinely; however, records exist of tree, bank, barn, and northern rough-winged swallows swimming after falling from aerial combat with other swallows, when fledglings accidentally fell from a nest, or in attempts to escape the grasp of predators in pursuit. Many of the species also gather water for drinking or bathing while in flight, giving the appearance of hitting the water. [70]

Modern ornithologists have recorded behaviors in swallows that are analogous to those witnessed by testifiers of the early republic, providing more reliable information that can help historians to solve what it was that

PLATE CCCL

Figure 3. John James Audubon, *The Birds of America* (London, 1838), 4, plate 385. Most North American swallow species frequent aquatic habitats, and some species, including the bank swallows here depicted by Audubon, make their nests in steep river banks. Behaviors common to bank swallows, such as entering and exiting their nest near water, may have deceived eyewitnesses. Courtesy Beinecke Rare Book and Manuscript Library, Yale University.

early national Americans saw. For example, the tree swallow species account in the American Ornithological Union's exhaustive *Birds of North America* describes the nonbreeding aggregation of tens of thousands of birds in trees and marshes and swirling flight behavior that recalls the eyewitness account of Samuel Dexter's informant, Judge Foster. Annually in migration tree swallows "begin gathering at roost site about an hour before sunset, gradually forming [a] dense cloud." As the numbers of birds increases they "fly in [an] enormous vortex, much like bee swarm. As darkness approaches, flocks wheel low over cattails or trees and with each pass large numbers drop quickly down to roost."[71] Could flocking behavior of this sort, swirling masses of birds that quickly descend and disappear into reeds, have been what those who saw the swallows submerge witnessed? Perhaps. Ornithologists have also established that in unseasonal periods of cold some species of swallows survive by undergoing individual and collective torpidity, a temporary hypothermia, and have been discovered clustered together inside the holes of trees and other enclosures. These birds have been reanimated by the warmth of the sun or in the hands of those who discovered them.[72] Might an individual in the early republic have stumbled across a collection of swallows recovering from an episode of torpidity inside a cavity, near the edge of a stream or lake? Probably.

Nest construction behavior and sunbathing also help to explain what early republic witnesses might have seen. The barn swallow uses an aggregation of mud pellets mixed with grasses in the construction of its nest, while the tree swallow, especially those nesting near water sources, uses mud and aquatic plants in nests. That these pellets were gathered from water's edge in the early spring may account for swallows congregating along river banks, the birds becoming dirty from their efforts and confusing observers about what it was they were doing.[73] In the early spring tree swallows also sunbathe for warmth, sometimes en masse and in tightly packed clusters; for the first species to return in early spring, such behavior might not have been uncommon when the weather can turn cold so quickly. Is seems probable that Foster and other early republic Americans observed unusual but not atypical tree swallow behavior—a collection of swallows on the ground, wings spread, their backs or bellies to the sun and lethargic from the cold—and mistook it for something that he or she was preconditioned to believe.[74] The typical and extraordinary behaviors of swallows—the roiling flocks with rapid descents into the reeds of marshes, episodes of swimming, the ability to survive sudden cold weather through temporary hypothermia, the use of gathered mud for nest construction, and the employment of en masse techniques for warming—offer clues as to what it was that early republic Americans witnessed when they observed the birds behaving in ways they perceived as odd.

Human opportunities to observe swallows closely increased in this period as some species adapted positively to greater human presence on the early republic landscape. As trees were cleared, swamps drained, and fields turned into agricultural land, many early republic commentators noted that the local temperatures were increasing, the summers warmer, and the winters less harsh; however, modern climatologists are less confident than early republic observers that these changes were as dramatic as they claimed.[75] How these local temperature changes affected swallow migration or the food sources for swallows is unclear, but overall warmer temperatures likely would have produced favorable conditions for increased insect populations, in turn fostering the conditions for larger swallow populations. Accompanying these local climatic changes was an overall increase in human habitations and buildings, and some swallow species abandoned their traditional nesting locations in tree holes and natural cavities, using instead the eaves and crannies of human constructed buildings.[76] As barn swallows, purple martins, chimney swifts, and tree swallows lived more intimately with humans, in the same buildings in fact, it stands to reason that early republic Americans might become more interested in swallows and their behaviors, especially those times when swallows left for the winter as well as when they returned in the spring. Where did they go? When did they leave and when did they return? Questions of this sort were asked and answered by early republic observers, with proponents of migration and submersion taking sides and facing off in the print culture of the period.

Yet swallow submersion stories in print appeared less frequently as the nineteenth century progressed and disappeared entirely by the early twentieth century. Two factors account for this. First, an evolving scientific practice, described in the next chapters, rendered swallow submersion stories too fantastic to be believed. Those who still argued for submersion and those who believed it identified themselves immediately as unscientific and therefore not worthy of serious consideration in any aspect of natural knowledge. Second, the results of bird banding, a practice in which metal rings are affixed to the legs of captured and released birds, established definitively that all North American swallow species migrated; banded birds were observed in other countries and birds banded one year were observed in the same area the next. John James Audubon is credited with beginning bird banding in the United States in 1803, and over the course of the nineteenth century the practiced spread and intensified. By the early twentieth century bird migration was firmly established and accepted as the norm for over 75 percent of all North American bird species.[77]

Chapter 2

Natural History and the Market Economy: The Profitability of Plants and Rocks

Much to the chagrin of American naturalists, disputes over methods, disagreements about knowledge-making procedures, and epistemological skirmishes such as those over swallow submersion were recurring features of early national natural history. The rules over what was and what was not proper conduct, proper observational technique, and sound reasoning seemed ever shifting and never settled. Yet those interested in establishing the United States as an "empire of reason"—those most invested in natural history as a truth-making pursuit and as a profession—were not incapacitated by these dilemmas, stubborn though the conflicts may have been. These naturalists—some of them trained abroad, more of them educated domestically as college and university programs took shape, and most living in or near the nation's largest cities—worked to create a practice distinguished from its undisciplined imitators by the creation and cultivation of authority and a reliance on expertise acquired through education, experience, and experiment. Like Francis Bacon two hundred years earlier, they imagined and worked to create natural history in America as a pyramid of inductive reasoning with a broad base of collectors and gatherers that narrowed to an apex of savants. Institutionally at least, their efforts to foster a disciplined natural history in the United States proved modestly successful.

The last decades of the eighteenth century and the first decades of the nineteenth witnessed the growth and establishment of natural history in United States higher education. This period saw the creation and expansion of university positions in natural history and related fields, many of these positions sharing time in medical education and medical curriculum. Students enrolled in and paid for courses and lectures in natural history defined broadly, as well as in the more specialized subdisciplines of botany, materia medica, comparative anatomy, and later, mineralogy and geology. Graduates wrote theses, published their findings, and found employment in other colleges and universities, in medical practice, and eventually, for a few, with state-sponsored geological and natural history surveys.[1] These decades witnessed as well the founding of new scientific institutions, most notably the Academy of Natural Sciences in Philadelphia in 1812 and the Lyceum of Natural History in New York in 1817, as well as the appearance of increasingly specialized scientific journals of high quality (most notably Benjamin Silliman's *American Journal of Science* in 1818) and foundational single subject monographs.[2] Even as academic natural history began to prosper, however, naturalists encountered resistance from democratic elements of the early national political climate, one permeated by anticolonial overtones and a citizenry suspicious of self-proclaimed experts.[3]

American naturalists represented themselves as loyal sons of the Revolution and friends of the new nation to overcome such suspicions, ready to assist the country with their knowledge and expertise. Like many if not most Americans, they interpreted the politics associated with colonial rule as demeaning and infantilizing. Naturalists, in turn, extended their displeasure with colonial rule to aspects of the natural history practiced by colonizing powers and imagined a new style of natural history tailored to the unique political and demographic characteristics of the young United States. Natural history conducted under British rule offered colonials entry to a transatlantic conversation about the natural world, access to exchange networks that could enrich a plant collection or family coffers, and proof positive to oneself and fellow colonials of an individual's erudition and accomplishment. But these exchanges were bounded by a complicated matrix of genteel performance, gift giving, patronage, and, above all, an intricate dance of deference. As well, these relationships were delicate; they required a subtle maintenance, and American colonists consistently played the role of collector to European patrons even if they got something in return.[4] Early national naturalists' writings record a recurring longing to be experts to their own countrymen after the Revolution, not merely provincial gatherers for Europeans and surely not emulators of Europeans who identified specimens in America. A domestic American natural history, however, posed a troubling dilemma: how to acquire information from American citizens without recreating the deferential relationships, the colonial relationships, emblematic of the colonial period?[5] In other words, how should naturalists work successfully and in the long term interests of their practice in a postcolonial nation?

American naturalists and the societies to which they belonged proposed one answer by enlisting concepts modeled on the idea of the market, one both financial and intellectual. They aimed to substitute the less tangible rewards of the patronage system with the more transparent incentives of fee for service. In circular letters from scientific academies, public broadsides, newspaper articles, magazine announcements, and private correspondence naturalists encouraged ordinary Americans to submit to them plant and mineral samples, thus ensuring naturalists a flow of information vital to a vibrant natural history practice. Without strong institutions to lend them credibility, durable and august organizations akin to the Royal Society or the Académie des Sciences, naturalists hoped that a market-based exchange would also work to establish their much-coveted position as experts and enhance the prestige of their scientific academies; naturalists reckoned that these moves could overcome another burden that they faced in the eyes of their countrymen.

If it worked according to plan, individual collectors would submit specimens (plants, minerals, and so forth) and would be compensated with information—in theory, definitive, incontrovertible identifications—that could be useful for identifying these specimens for trade or sale. There were hints that correspondents would be rewarded publicly too; perhaps their names might appear in print and they would be given credit for the submission and the discovery. If natural history of the colonial period was the quiet pursuit of the genteel and disinterested, then early republic natural history, some of its architects seemed to suggest, was to be the public province of the interested—those curious about the natural world and those with something to gain by it assisting in the collection and making of that knowledge.

This market-oriented approach to natural history did not work as designed, however. In fact, it is arguable whether it worked at all. Evidence suggests that the reformulated practice naturalists imagined—an approach that would profit everyone pursuing natural philosophy and history—was Pollyannaish. Fewer Americans than expected responded to the calls for samples issued by naturalists. When they did, the archival record suggests, naturalists wrote back with the identifications less often than they promised, if at all. It appears that naturalists and ordinary Americans were not entirely willing to participate in the give and take that a market-oriented natural history demanded. Misunderstandings about what naturalists were requesting, conflicting interpretations over what possessed value, and a general confusion over the goals of taxonomic natural history characterized these exchanges. In not responding or backing away from the exchange that they invited, naturalists were not being stingy, unhelpful, or greedy. Instead, they were acting cautiously and in their own long-term interests and those of their practice for two reasons. First, neither most naturalists nor the institutions with which they were affiliated had the means to recompense or employ collectors around the country. Second, and of equal importance, the authority of natural history and of naturalists was fragile in early national America, as the controversy over swallow submersion shows. It was in the interest of naturalists to consolidate and establish a firm foundation on which to grow the practice and establish their expertise. Closely aligning and subjecting naturalists' influence, their identifications, and their judgments to the manipulations and misinformation that ruled the marketplace could, and did, become a dangerous, potentially self-defeating proposition. Therefore, naturalists abandoned this democratic, market-oriented natural history almost as soon as many had issued calls for it to begin, falling back on tried and true methods. Correspondence with individuals one knew to be trustworthy and already versed in natural historical methods would be more rewarding and efficacious, many naturalists reasoned, than would a haphazard, fee-for-service correspondence with an unknown correspondent or frontier resident. It proved more reliable to exchange letters and specimens with those whom one knew and could vouch for—established naturalists, former students, or those one sent on collecting expeditions—than to rely on the vagaries and interestedness of ordinary Americans. Longer than their propaganda might suggest, established naturalists replicated the patterns and epistemology of the colonial era, one heavily reliant on gentlemanly protocols. For all their promises about a new natural history, diffusely democratic and responsive to its citizenry, naturalists with visions of an empire of reason turned out to be begrudgingly conservative, not dynamic and creative. They did not, as some post-revolutionary rhetoric suggested, turn natural historical practice on its head; rather, naturalists followed old practices and called them new. Instead of the promised American natural history revolution, this was American natural historical evolution, a sleight of hand from patronage to patrician. Early republic naturalists complained about slow progress and the sorry state of American natural history, blaming it in part on ordinary Americans who failed to engage their stubbornly hierarchical practice. Ordinary Americans were either not aware, not willing, or not interested in sharing information with naturalists to the extent necessary for a vibrant exchange; and naturalists did not press the issue as they abandoned a fee-for-service, democratic natural history as inimical to their goals. But even in these fumbled exchanges both naturalists and ordinary American agreed on one thing: there was a wider market in natural history to be exploited.

Since cooperation and correspondence failed to yield a rich harvest, naturalists and some ordinary Americans with an interest in nature became aggressively entrepreneurial in natural historical matters. Some evolved into speculative collectors, assembling cabinets for sale and for public display, both of which could be lucrative if one could find someone to purchase the collection or an audience to view it. Other naturalists struck out on their own to collect the specimens that they wanted, selling their natural historical expertise along the way where they could. Whether they appear to moderns as itinerant peddlers, midway hucksters, or the ancestors of modern science, early national Americans with an interest in nature, intellectually and financially, began to see a wider consuming public as their audience, one with a capacious appetite for nature and a distinctly American natural world.

Early republic American naturalists, the botanically inclined especially, were a cautiously optimistic lot. They imagined themselves uniquely and advantageously placed at the center of a network of North American plant cultivators, gardeners, and collectors. They traced a web that stretched from the urban centers of Boston, New York, Philadelphia, and Charleston to the ever-expanding frontiers of the American west in the Ohio and Mississippi valleys, and, for a few, into the Caribbean and across the Atlantic. After the Revolution, American naturalists continued a vigorous correspondence with one another in much the same fashion that they had before the Revolution when they communicated with one another and a few served as provincial correspondents and collectors for Europeans.[6] Specimens continued to exchange hands and informational letters containing queries regarding classification and discussions of discoveries, as well as gossipy letters, were unabated.[7] But a sense of urgency animated those who wished to jump-start American botany since many naturalists considered botany, more than any of the other natural historical subdisciplines, to be the sci-

ence upon which the United States might establish its economic independence.

Manasseh Cutler, the Ipswich, Massachusetts, minister and botanist,
gave voice in 1785 to the sentiments of many of his colleagues when he
implored a more active investigation into American plants. The "economical uses of the vegetable kingdom are exceedingly numerous; not only fur-
nishing food for man and beast, materials for agriculture, and various
forms of arts and manufactures," he wrote, "but it supplies important articles of commerce, and, in some countries is the greatest source of internal
wealth."[8] Cutler's call for greater attention paid to plants was typical of the
era, yet his enthusiasm was tempered by the near-constant lament from
naturalists that there was a "total lack of botanical enquiries" among the
American populace, owing to the fact that "the subject has never been
taught in any of our colleges." More important, Cutler thought, was the
"mistaken opinion of [botany's] inutility in common life."[9] An even rudi-
mentary comprehension of botanical classification would show, Cutler
believed, that plants of various class, order, and genus share characteristics.
Knowledge and training along these lines, he thought, would lead to more
efficient identification of potential food sources, potential export commodities, and potential resources for manufactures.

Cutler and those calling for the addition of botany to college and university curriculums could feel pride and a sense of accomplishment; rather
quickly, botany expanded into the curriculums of many, if not most, of the
nation's universities and colleges. The University of Pennsylvania, Harvard
College, Bowdoin College, Williams College, and Yale College as well as
many others added it to the course of study and by the 1820s botany had
become a mainstay of most university and college curriculums.[10] When
botanical study is expanded to include materia medica, the body of knowledge devoted to medicinal herbs and plants, it is beyond doubt that univer-
sity-level botany instruction was healthy and growing inside academe. As
well, those calling for botany study were heartened by the establishment
of botanical gardens, for study and for pleasure, in some of these same
institutions.[11] While the results of increased botany instruction in colleges
would take time to bear fruit, naturalists like Cutler worked to disabuse the
public of its botanical ignorance. They imagined a two-pronged solution:
first, develop a vibrant taxonomic botanical practice by cultivating a
national network of specialists sustained by research and publication; sec-

ond, work toward more general education of the American public in the practical and efficient identification and use of its plants.

In this first goal, early republic botanists experienced their greatest accomplishment: taxonomic botany began to flourish during these years and American naturalists and botanists took their place as the preeminent interpreters of North American flora by the end of the second decade of the nineteenth century. Communities of botanists clustered in Philadelphia, New York, Charleston, and Boston around the colleges and universities as well as the private and botanic gardens under cultivation. Much to early national botanists' frustration, the earliest general floras about North America—general botanical texts—were published by Europeans. André Michaux, a French naturalist who traveled from Florida to Hudson's Bay and westward to the Mississippi, published *History of the Oaks of America* in 1801 after returning to Paris. After André Michaux's death in 1803, his son, François-André, continued his father's work and published a general work based his father's collections, *North American Flora*, and his own three-volume *History of the Forest Trees of North America* in 1810.[12] Frederick Pursh, a German botanist whose travels had been subsidized in part by Benjamin Smith Barton and sustained by the Philadelphia community of botanists, published in 1814 his two-volume *Flora Americae Septentrionalis: Or, A Systematic Arrangement and Description of the Plants of North America*, a general botanical treatise that included accounts of specimens collected for Barton (which he never used) as well as descriptions of plants collected by Lewis and Clark.[13]

Irritated and chastened that they had been beat to press by Europeans, American botanists quickly made their mark on systematic, taxonomic botany. Thomas Nuttall, also a beneficiary of Barton's assistance, published his well-received two-volume general flora *Genera of North American Plants* in 1818; it was followed quickly by his *Journal of the Travels into the Arkansas Territory* in 1821. William P. C. Barton, the nephew of Benjamin Smith Barton, penned his own flora of the Philadelphia region in 1818 and a two years later a three-volume general text, *A Flora of North America*. Stephen Elliott began bringing out successive numbers of his *Sketch of the Botany of South Carolina and Georgia*, published between 1816 and 1824, and in Boston Jacob Bigelow published his *American Medical Botany*. Amos Eaton, then a professor at Williams College, published the first edition of his benchmark textbook *Manual of Botany* in 1817 (the first of eight editions before 1840), and Eaton's student, John Torrey, contributed *A Flora of the*

Northern and Middle Sections of the United States in 1824.[14] These texts established American botanists as those most expert in cataloging and describing the botanical contents of North America. Except for Eaton's *Manual*, however, these were writings for other botanists or those with specialized interest in botany. The works were dedicated largely to classifying and describing briefly the characteristics of individual species and genera: modes of vegetation, geographic distribution, and brief remarks about species' relationships to their environment; they were not texts written for the general reader. As he wrote in a letter to Torrey, Eaton considered himself no great botanist and spoke to the difference between his popular approach to botanical education. "You are made for the highest walks of science," he wrote to his student, "nice accurate investigation—new discoveries and improvements—to correct the blunders of others and to keep the ship of science in trim." He considered himself different, "made for the noise and the bustle. My forte is among the rabble." If his efforts had any merit, he concluded, "it consists in the art of simplifying."[15] To Eaton simplifying meant creating a work digestible by greater numbers of American readers, one that arranged genera systematically and described the species, to be sure, but also a text that had an eye toward practical application. Eaton carried on the second aspiration of this period's botanists— educating the public at large about the plants and trees of the United States.

Animated by nationalist and pedagogical zeal, naturalists wrote practical manuals and easily comprehensible keys to plants and trees as well as tracts aimed at improving agricultural methods; among the most popular and prominent published prior to 1800 was Humphrey Marshall's *Arbustom Americanum: The American Grove, or, An Alphabetical Catalogue of Forest Trees and Shrubs, Natives of the American United States*. Marshall, a cousin of the Philadelphia-based royal botanist John Bartram, a Quaker, and a Pennsylvania resident, offered a list of mid-Atlantic native trees and shrubs according to Linnaean classifications and later provided a description of their uses in "Medicine, Dyes, and Domestic Oeconomy." Marshall aimed for an audience both high and low. He consulted "Botanical Authors" for information but intended his book for readers without formal training. He explained to the uninitiated that botany was the branch of natural history comprising "the right knowledge of Vegetables, and their application to the most beneficial uses." Botany was an object of study that merited the "attention and encouragement of every patriotic and liberal mind," particularly those interested in the nation's welfare. His countrymen were aware that the "continual enormous expense" of imported botanical products drained the national coffers. There was plenty of plant folk knowledge in circulation, Marshall admitted, but he explained that "observations and researches founded upon, and directed by, a knowledge of Botany" would meet a degree of success higher than what Americans "may gain by tedious experience, or stumble by chance upon . . . respecting the uses and medicinal virtues of plants." The "more general knowledge we obtain of the character and appearance of plants," Marshall wrote, "the more likely we shall be also to encrease our knowledge of their virtues, qualities and uses." Aware that his readership would be more "embarrassed and confused than profited" by technical language or terms, Marshall adopted the "most plain and familiar method . . . to render the work as generally useful as possible." He was a popularizer and his vernacular guides to describing plants and trees were designed to make botany more inviting to the residents of the new republic. Whether Marshall's efforts were successful is, of course, open to interpretation. One measure by which success can be determined is to what extent Marshall's method and style reflected or influenced writings that followed. Marshall's plain style and his emphasis on applied knowledge of plants can be seen in a number of the publications that followed *Arbustrum Americanum*.[16] Bernard M'Mahon, an Irish émigré friend of Marshall and a seed collector and nurseryman in Philadelphia, published in 1806 *The American Gardener's Calendar*, a book devoted to kitchen and flower gardening, orchards, vineyards, fruit trees, as well as hothouses and forcing frames; his book was coordinated to each month of the year, "useful in every state of the Union," and, he hoped, aimed "to induce an association with the science of Botany with practical horticulture, without which the latter can never be so advantageously conducted."[17] Samuel Deane, author of *The New England Farmer*, combined natural history instruction and new techniques for improved agriculture. His collection of alphabetically listed, accessible entries offered advice on efficient tilling and tips for identifying useful plants commonly found in New England.[18] Marshall's and Deane's dual attention to botanical classification and utilitarianism characterized much of the period's botanically oriented natural history literature—theirs was a practice that aimed toward edification and improvement.

These initial forays into utilitarian natural history notwithstanding, enthusiasts and advocates considered the subject barely begun. "It is our duty to study [Nature's] ways, in order that we may know what is meant for our particular benefit," Charles Willson Peale told listeners as he outlined his philosophy of natural history in a public lecture. The study of natural history should be, he cajoled, "not only interesting to the individual," but a national priority. It held the potential to propel the nation toward economic independence, every citizen and profession benefiting from the pursuit.[19] To maximize these benefits and to understand their country more fully, natural historians cataloged locales, some as small as the countryside surrounding a city, others as large as individual states.

Thomas Jefferson's *Notes on the State of Virginia* served as the template for these natural histories of place. In Queries 1 through 7, Jefferson described Virginia's boundaries, rivers, ports, mountains, "cascades," animals, vegetables, minerals, and climate. Jefferson plodded though subcategories of navigable and nonnavigable rivers, caves containing or without minerals, and plants sorted by their uses: medicinal, "Esculent," ornamental, and those "Useful for fabrication."[20] These lists provided evidence of Virginia's natural bounty and suggested that the state, and by the extension the nation, could support itself on its own natural resources. When Jeremy Belknap turned his attention to New Hampshire, he followed Jefferson's form and wrote successive chapters describing the state's boundaries, mountains, rivers, lakes, and streams. He listed its quadrupeds, birds, fish, plants, and trees; he noted its climate, the variations in temperature between summer and winter, and the amount of annual precipitation. "Few persons in this country, have studied natural history as a science . . . to the extent which is desirable," Belknap wrote. With so much of America poorly understood, "it would be unpardonable not to take notice of its natural productions." Belknap considered his knowledge of natural history "imperfect" but undertook an attempt to catalog the "ample field of inquiry," a list of vital importance to the state and the nation.[21] Stephen Williams, a former mathematics professor at Harvard, described the Vermont landscapes and climate. He enumerated Vermont's animals, lavishing attention on the beaver and its importance in trade. Williams, like Jefferson and Belknap, considered an examination of the natural resources vital to the success of the young nation, natural history a means through which to decipher the instructions for nature's use.[22]

The overwhelming majority of early national publications on botany—be they pedagogical texts such as Barton's *Elements of Botany*, Amos Eaton's *Manual of Botany*, or less technical writings found in newspapers or magazines—stressed the need for greater study of plants and the importance of new botanical discoveries to the building of the nation. The botani-

cal literature of the late eighteenth and early nineteenth centuries, much of
it published in newspapers and literary magazines, worked to distinguish
itself from information about plants and trees found in herbals, almanacs,
or collections of folk knowledge, these genres a haphazard assemblage of
unconfirmed facts and conventional wisdom retold. Advocates depicted
botany as a novel and superior practice to other approaches and stressed
its distinctiveness; thus, botany was part of a quiet campaign to eradicate
popular misinformation and alternative epistemologies. Botany texts that
worked to bridge the divide between technical and popular—among them
Eaton's *Manual of Botany* and Almira Hart Lincoln Phelps's *Familiar Lectures on Botany*—instructed reader in the very basics of plant identification
and preservation, including the creation of herbaria for careful examination
outside the field.[23] According to its proponents this introduction to botany
was an extended exercise in identification and classification, not as ends
unto themselves but as a means for self-improvement as well as a superior
method for identifying useful items for food, manufacture, and medicine.
Botany, as depicted for an audience enthusiasts imagined as a national one,
was also a democratic, utilitarian practice that would aid the new nation
and its citizens.

Samuel Latham Mitchill, a New York City physician, editor of that city's
preeminent medical journal *The Medical Repository,* and co-founder of the
Lyceum of Natural History, captured this spirit in a address to students at
Columbia College. The "true object" of the botanist, he argued, was not the
"parade of literature and pomp of science" but instead "the development of
such properties as may some way be serviceable to man . . . in short, whatever can lessen the wants, or increase the happiness of the human race."[24]
Recast with a utilitarian, universal gloss, botany would aid the individual as
well as the country, each person at a time. Botany would develop and refine
character, he promised; it would teach discipline and patience and hone the
skills of observation. (It would likewise steer its practitioners away from
indolence, luxury, and vice.) Finally, botany would assist the nation by
identifying new locales of valuable resources, both medical and economic.
Botany, as depicted by authors writing in this vein, was a literature and
practice of individual self-improvement and collective national development.[25]

Such heady, optimistic, and inclusive rhetoric was part of an attempt
by botany advocates to reorient the practice in the minds of most Americans, away from its associations with elite and polite society, its esoteric

rules and narrow taxonomic disputes, and toward a more diffuse foundation. Recent scholarship has shown that botany particularly and natural history more generally offered colonial Americans access to a genteel and learned transatlantic conversation about nature.[26] American nature enthusiasts created and fostered valuable connections in the metropole through these exchanges, cultivated epistolary friendships, traded specimens, and worked diligently to establish a reputation for erudition among correspondents local and abroad. Provincial American naturalists—among them such botanical luminaries as John and William Bartram, Cadwallader Colden and his daughter Jane Colden, Alexander Garden, and other less famous individuals—used and displayed a knowledge of natural history and botany to create and reinforce a cosmopolitan identity, a sense of self that allowed them to overcome the insecurities and anxieties associated with living on the peripheries of learning, of knowledge making, and, indeed, of civilization itself. These colonials were curious about nature to be sure, but natural knowledge was also instrumental in fashioning an imperial, transatlantic identity. For them, natural history was as much about performance as it was about knowledge; and these individuals performed natural history to distinguish themselves from their more vulgar neighbors. A working knowledge of botany's rules, its language, and its conduct signaled a cosmopolitan awareness. The ability to converse in its specialized tongue became a sign of one's admission to, and membership in, a transatlantic elite of polite society, connoisseurship, and taste. Botany and natural history became proxy discussions of discernment, refinement, and pleasure in the hetero-and homosocial parlors and salons of the colonial and early national elite.[27]

Thus, recasting botany as a communitarian, nationalist endeavor helped advocates to disaggregate botany and salon culture, natural history and an exclusive cosmopolitanism. Such nationalist repackaging also allowed naturalists cover to propose and formulate a different relationship between savant and the ordinary collector. For all the participatory delight and information afforded provincial naturalists under British rule, colonial naturalists remained worried that, at base, they were little better than errand boys for European patrons of science. The links they cultivated afforded them information, books, scientific equipment, and some modicum of celebrity; yet naturalists could not shake the anxiety that they were not enjoying the full benefits of these exchanges. These relationships were subject to vagaries, determined by personal reputation, and conducted through

letters from afar. Because they seemed to control so little, colonial naturalists expressed concern that the permeable rules of conduct that governed
deference and patronage were rules that Americans did not understand
or were unable to exploit. In this perceived inequality of exchange, the
Philadelphia virtuoso Benjamin Franklin began to sense and describe a
dichotomy between a European science associated with "rhetoric, showi-
ness, fancy, unnaturalness, idealization, invention, deception, and indolence," as one historian writes. He contrasted this to an "American" science
that represented itself in terms of its honor, its reasoning and "demonstra-
tion," its "accuracy of description involving an attention to particulars,"
and its attention to "Nature" itself without adornment and without art.[28]

Thus, early republic naturalists seized the opportunity afforded by
the anticolonial political climate of the new republic to lambaste as
demeaning the relationship dynamic of colonial natural history and to
reimagine how information sharing could be conducted. One method naturalists' employed was to link a sense of patriotism and the needs of the
fledgling nation, to recast the practice as more inviting for participation by
ordinary Americans. More than one naturalist agreed with Nicholas Collin,
a Lutheran minister and member of the American Philosophical Society,
that although they might be "citizens of the world," American natural historians were duty-bound "to cultivate with peculiar attention those parts
of science, which are most beneficial to that country in which Providence
has appointed their earthly stations." They may be curious about plants and
animals in foreign lands, Collin wrote, but "Patriotic affections" required
attention to objects closer to home.[29] Cursory examinations, anecdotal
reports, and two centuries of European colonization convinced Collin and
native-born Americans that North America possessed the resources necessary to support and to sustain the new nation economically.

So in the decades that followed the American Revolution, botany enthusiasts repeatedly attempted to enlist and encourage the assistance of domestic naturalists as well as physicians, military men, travelers, nurserymen,
and gardeners as collectors or informants for their own projects—anyone
with exposure to plants of which they were unaware. Through encouraging
conversations, private letters, and public calls, American botanists
requested samples of plants from throughout the new nation. Part and
parcel with this exchange, collectors could expect a correspondence and
would be compensated with classificatory identifications and suggestions
for potential uses, and should a new discovery be important enough, the

discoverer might be credited with its location, thus granted a form of immortality.

Naturalists and ordinary Americans followed a similar correspondence and pattern of participation when the subject extended to minerals and precious metals. Most Americans knew little about geology or mineralogy and contacted natural historians to have deposits or discoveries assessed and categorized. Since there was little anecdotal speculation about rocks and ores in circulation (it was easier to say with assurance if a lump of coal was the genuine article for example), naturalists judged themselves able to establish an authoritative voice on these matters. One such writer was Charles Creswell, a resident of western Pennsylvania. In 1809 he wrote the American Philosophical Society to solicit their "deliberations and judgment on a matter that has excited a Curiosity." After heavy rains, Creswell wrote, "a large mist resembling in appearance and smell of a coal pit" would rise from the earth. The mist was likely gas escaping from a naturally occurring oil deposit and Creswell wondered how he might exploit it. Likewise, a Mr. Brown wrote Barton from Camp Legionville, Pennsylvania, in 1792 to report the discovery of iron ore and "black lead" in a hillside that "appears to have suffered a violent degree of heat," indicating, Brown thought, larger subterranean deposits. He asked Barton's advice as to whether the find might yield more iron. In 1808, D. R. Patterson of Virginia wrote to Barton, "I own the quarry of Marble which Mr. Jefferson has described in his *Notes*." The only marble deposit in Virginia and never "worked," its quality was "infinitely superior to any American marble hereto discovered." Patterson claimed that "several good judges say it is equal to the Egyptian & Italian marble." He contacted Barton because a "Gentleman" sought to purchase it, but Patterson claimed ignorance of its value. He asked Barton to inform him "of the value of the quarries in your neighborhood, or the prices at which they usually sell, from which I could estimate the value of mine."[30] Whether Barton answered Patterson, Brown, or Cresswell is unclear. Still, in cases such as these, it appears that some Americans were turning to naturalists to predict the viability of various mines and resources, fulfilling naturalists' aspirations that natural knowledge would be used to establish the economic foundation of the young nation.

Natural historians welcomed as well the opportunity to authenticate claims of lucrative gold deposits, specifically one requested by those with stakes in North Carolina, the location of the early republic's first gold rush. William Thorton, a physician from Washington, D.C., and an individual who owned "very extensively" in North Carolina, was of the "opinion that my Purchase contains an immensity of Gold." In 1805 he wrote the American Philosophical Society with an account of his mines, hoping they would assure him as well as potential shareholders that he was "without any danger of deceiving myself or others" that his stake possessed "incalculable value." Thorton enclosed a pamphlet from the North Carolina Gold Company that described the geologic characteristics of the area and awaited the society's assessment of his deposits. Likewise, Joseph Richardson transmitted "statements of the quality of some native gold found in the State of North Carolina" for the society to consider. He wished to learn from them any information concerning the quality of future excavations. He was concerned that a "large piece being inferior in quality to the smaller grains" indicated that "the larger lumps are not so pure as the smaller grains." He hoped that the society could confirm that this was a "groundless suspicion." Thorton and Richardson worked to legitimize their value claims by relying on the geologic expertise of natural historians; thus, they enlisted the authority of natural history to stabilize the volatile and speculative market economy surrounding gold. Natural historians, in turn, welcomed such solicitations. They could at once perform and authenticate their expertise on matters of natural resource value by providing solicitors detailed information about the geology of regions unknown to them.[31]

From this kind of correspondence and individual initiative grew natural histories of place—of cities, neighborhoods, and states—which were perhaps the most famous of early republic natural history texts. In these state and local natural histories, such as Jefferson's *Notes on the State of Virginia*, Belknap's *History of New-Hampshire*, and others, authors drew on accounts provided by fellow residents, soliciting and receiving information about areas unknown to them. Typically, authors scrutinized and then included, with qualifications if necessary, descriptions of animals, plants, minerals, and trees. Reports that came from men of established authority were included with little or no comment. By contrast, anecdotal reports that were unverifiable or related by those who had "interests"—financial or otherwise—in the stories were treated with some degree of caution. Such skittishness extended to information, generally botanical, that was collected from Indians. Nearly all naturalists with an interest in botany recognized that Indians possessed an unparalleled knowledge of North American plants and their uses; however, the discourse that accompanied the inclusion of information obtained from Indians placed it at a distance—Indian testimonies were always mediated by white writers.[32] More often as not, reports of Indian knowledge of plants and their use were dismissed as superstitious and ineffective, and often as representing knowledge already lost, "the combined effects of warfare, civilization, and amalgamation with the whites" having diluted and cast doubt upon Indian materia medica and materia alimentaria. In short, reports from Indians were treated as "vulgar." Reports of plants' medicinal properties should be investigated but were to be doubted. Those individuals who swore to the properties described were, to naturalists of the time, easily identifiable as "credulous people" and easily ignored.[33]

These reports on individual states and other locales provided a foundation for a catalog of American natural resources, but the most energetic advocates of natural history still called for greater effort from the across the spectrum of American citizens to catalog the American natural world. "Little [attention] is paid to the study of nature in the United States," Barton wrote in his 1799 *Fragments of the Natural History of Pennsylvania*. Whereas there was reason to hope that natural historical education was improving, Barton complained that educators still spent precious time on "languages which are withered or dead." He lamented that natural history was not considered an "indispensable branch of polite or useful knowledge." Were it pursued "with a portion of that innocent and useful zeal with which it is cultivated in Europe . . . in less than twenty years, the animal, vegetable, and the mineral productions of the United States would be pretty well investigated." Instead, the "pursuit of gain" occupied the majority of the American people; natural history was left to the "labours of two or three individuals, unaided by the public, and trammeled by professional engagements and pursuits."[34] Faced with discouraging prospects for natural history, practitioners emphasized forcefully the commercial benefits of their practice. Barton and others aimed to meet those interested in gain on their own terms.

To facilitate that process, scientific societies solicited natural history samples from ordinary Americans, coaxing information with lucrative promises. Philadelphia's short-lived Linnaean Society issued a public notice for Americans to send "any plants, ores or any mineral substance whatever" to their organization, where they would be examined by the "botanical and mineralogical departments of the society." The organization believed that their knowledge would "assist in obtaining a full knowledge of the medicinal and dying drugs indigenous of our soil." It would "expedite the discovery of useful metals; to aid the manufactures of their country," all the while removing "the inconveniences and disadvantages of individuals, not possessing an acquaintance with natural knowledge." In return, the examination results would be communicated to the individual transmitting the specimen, "together with such information relative to its nature and uses."[35] Whether any individual submitted specimens to the Linnaean Society is uncertain; its records no longer exist. Other natural history organizations made similar appeals—among them, Philadelphia's American Philosophical Society, the Lyceum of Natural History of New York, and Boston's American Academy of Arts and Sciences. The lofty goals of these appeals contrasted with the recorded results because ordinary Americans either misunderstood what the solicitors sought or differed over what commodities possessed value.

A typical example of an exchange that such appeals engendered was a letter sent to Benjamin Smith Barton by H. B. Trout, a resident of western Pennsylvania, asking him about the viability of raising opium poppies. Trout, a correspondent unknown to Barton, praised Barton's 1803 botany textbook, *Elements of Botany*, "wherein it is stated that the *peiparer sommiferum* might be cultivated in the countries of the Unighted-States with much pecuniary profit." Trout asked Barton for seeds, directions for their cultivation, and gardening tips in time for the following season: "What climate of the Unighted-States would be most favourable to the growth of the poppy—what sort of manner would be best calculated to put on the ground in which the poppy is to be sowed?" Trout, it appears, thought that he might capitalize on a growing American demand for opium, a narcotic frequently utilized by physicians and imported at great expense. Taking his lead from Barton's suggestion that the United States needed more domestic poppy production, Trout saw the plant's cultivation as his ticket to entrepreneurial wealth.[36]

Later that year Barton received another letter about poppies, this from George Washington Trout.[37] The second Trout wrote to Barton that he was "charmed with the display of your patriotism in recommending to the people of the United States the culture of the poppy; and its manufacture into opium." Trout recognized the plant's economic potential and sought advice to sow his crop successfully. To induce a response Trout distanced himself from what might appear crude financial interest and instead appealed to Barton's "eminent dignity" as a man of science whose purpose was the "general diffusion of knowledge." If men "avail[ed] themselves of the gifts of nature" monetary profits were secondary to the "increase [in] the Stock of Science," he wrote. His request, therefore, was not "an unparalleled act of presumption" but an inquiry whose "principal stimulus" is the "Desire of Utility." Should Barton communicate this valuable information, it would confirm Trout's belief that Barton was indeed a "lover of science" and "friend of mankind."[38] There is no evidence that Barton answered these letters.

It appears that some Americans saw these invitations as a way to satisfy their curiosity about objects that they had discovered or as a means to begin a correspondence with a naturalist. One Gabriel Crane submitted an account of a grub to the American Philosophical Society. He reported that he had found a worm in a "state of vegetation" and that his examination had caused the worm's destruction; moreover, his theory was that the worm was the sperm of a much larger animal. Crane related his discovery after "having seen an advertisement containing a general invitation to make communication to the American Philosophical Society."[39] Members of these organizations regarded requests such as Crane's, among them submissions of beans with "unusual qualities," worms pulled from inside children's ears, and a treatise purporting to overturn Newton's "Theory of Universal Gravitation," of little value to the process of nation building.[40] Still, these submissions suggest the degree to which early republic Americans differed over the interpretation of natural history. Some early republic correspondents sought to make their objects of curiosity known, but the naturalists reviewing the submissions appear to have considered them anomalous and unimportant. Naturalists likely imagined themselves using their skills and knowledge to make the natural world predictable, determine patterns, and locate sources of national wealth; they were not interested in identifying curiosities.

American natural historians of the late eighteenth and early nineteenth centuries had embraced the European recategorization of intellectual and emotional responses to wonders. Like their European counterparts, they pushed curiosities to the margins of natural history practice and collection and concerned themselves more with representative samples and objects illustrative of larger groupings.[41] American natural historians' cataloging efforts were part of this shift, though disputes and individual episodes of strange phenomena demonstrate that curiosities and wonders continued to occupy their minds. Still, natural historians doggedly pursued an intimate knowledge of America's landscape and its contents, particularly in those regions where one might find plants and minerals essential to national prosperity. More than one early republic natural historian lamented that fellow Americans have "as yet but little taste for Natural History," even the "most simple observations," one investigator wrote, "leaving but few traces upon their minds."[42]

A persistent interest in unique objects and unusual natural processes dominated the correspondence of those writing to the elite naturalists. The divergent emphases in the understanding of natural history practice help to explain the persistence of early republic curiosity stories and unique objects. It also suggests why natural historians so infrequently responded to stories of magical beans or frogs found inside rocks: this was an epistemology and practice they were attempting to eradicate, each submission forcing natural historians to admit the remoteness of success. Conversely, what those who wrote natural historians hoped to gain is difficult to determine. Likely they expected a more complete understanding of the objects they possessed, legitimization of their efforts to preserve them, perhaps a valuation of their object, and confirmation of their role in the larger cataloging effort. In all probability, solicitors received no response, natural historians dismissing these requests out of hand.[43]

Coal, ores, and gold were certainly valuable to nation building. Nonetheless, in his *Collections for an Essay towards a Materia-Medica of the United States* (1798), Benjamin Smith Barton wrote that the "man who discovers one valuable new medicine is a more important benefactor to his species than Alexander, Caesar, or an hundred other conquerors." "All the splendid discoveries of Newton," he continued, "are not of so much real utility to the world as the discovery of Peruvian bark, or of the powers of opium and mercury in the cure of certain diseases." Barton urged young physicians, naturalists, and gardeners to search for new materia medica; the prospect for its discovery was "particularly happy." Barton wrote that "the volume of nature lies before you: it has hardly yet been opened: it has never been pursued." Botany and, more specifically, materia medica he called "the *punctum saliens* of science in our country," and he encouraged his students and his countrymen to explore the fields and forests of the North America for discoveries that would result in the "happiness of one's country" and "add luster to your names."[44] Specifically, Barton encouraged the search for New World analogs to Old World medicinal plants used in the tonics and emetics to treat yellow fever and other fatal epidemiological diseases.

Few medicinal plants received more attention in early republic America than American colombo. The colombo root, an expensive import from Asia, was an emetic and purgative important to the dispensaries of all physicians. Rumors emanating from the trans-Appalachian west convinced Barton that the New World possessed an analog or an American colombo. However, as Barton and others quickly became aware, more than one plant was masquerading as the American colombo, eventually classified as *Frasera walteri*. Two others, *Hydrastis canadensis* and *Zanthorhiza apiifolia*, were also said to be the American colombo root. Excitement over American colombo was linked directly to its purported uses. Among western residents colombo was used "in the heat of the summer, [to] put a stop to a wide and fast spreading gangrene"; it was also rumored to be used by Cherokee Indians to treat cancer. Some used it to alleviate inflammation of the eyes; others told of its use in cloth dyes.[45]

Identifying the American colombo frustrated a number of its investigators. After receiving a small specimen of *Zanthorhiza*, a plant thought "less pure than the Columbo," Barton believed that it was "in certain cases, to be preferred to that celebrated bitter." The *Zanthorhiza apiifolia,* commonly known as the parsley-leafed yellow root, grew commonly in the Carolinas and Georgia but rarely, if ever, in the Ohio Valley. *Zanthorhiza* was a species often conflated with *Hydrastis canadensis*; the fact that the latter was often called "Yellow-root" in the vernacular undoubtedly added to the confusion. But *Hydrastis* grew in "various parts of the United-States; particularly in the rich soil adjacent to the Ohio and its branches, in the western parts of Pennsylvania and Virginia; and in Kentucky," the region being settled by Americans most rapidly in the period. Barton considered the *Hydrastis* a "powerful bitter: perhaps not less so than that of the *Zanathorhiza*." Initial research into the plants' utility was promising, and Barton urged Americans to search out and to send him examples.[46] Individuals answered his request, transmitting specimens accompanied by urgent pleas to identify their submissions. More than one correspondent was eager to be the first to harvest the root and reap the material rewards. Frontier Americans anticipated finding and harvesting the colombo, becoming local if not national heroes, and receiving the material rewards consistent with the discovery. Barton's rulings on these matters disappointed most, however, dashing their hopes of quick wealth.

John Beatty of Cambridge, Ohio was frustrated to learn from Barton that "the root I sent you is called *Frasera*[,] a term I don't understand nor

Table 35

Fig. 1

Fig. 2

Fig. 3

Drawn from Nature by W. P. C. Barton.

Tanner, Vallance, Kearny & Co. Sc.

FRASERA WALTERI.
(American Columbo.)

Figure 4. William P. C. Barton, *Vegetable Materia Medica of the United States, or Medical Botany* (Philadelphia, 1818), table 35, *Frasera walteri*. American colombo, reclassified as *Frasera caroliniensis* but labeled in this image as *walteri*, was one of the most eagerly sought plants during the early years of the republic. Courtesy New York Public Library.

Figure 5. William P. C. Barton, *Vegetable Materia Medica of the United States, or Medical Botany* (Philadelphia, 1818), plate xii, *Zanthoriza apiifolia.* Parsley-leaved yellow root, or yellow wort, was commonly confused with the American colombo. Courtesy The Huntington Library.

can I find any Doct[or] that does." (Unbeknown to Beatty, he had located American colombo). Undeterred by the discouraging information, Beatty wished Barton to be more precise: was his "the real Columbo or not?" He tried to cajole a rapid reply, "as now is a good time to gather it." Should Barton think it colombo root, "pray let me know [how] much it is worth a pound as I intend to gather and cure a quantity if I find it [and] turn it to my advantage." One of the best doctors in the western country told Beatty that his sample was the "true Columbo." However, with misinformation swirling and sharp dealers ever present, "I depend more on your judgement," Beatty wrote. In a postscript Beatty once again underscored the urgency: "be explicit about the root as it is a good time to gather it now the tops are just showing above ground as my son was that way and brought me some."[47]

In the years surrounding Beatty's letter, Barton was one of a few naturalists engaged in an effort to determine whether various roots growing in the Ohio valley might be the lucrative colombo and part of a larger effort to categorize the materia medica of the United States. Yet records show that rumors, exaggerated stories, and confusion characterized and impeded that search. One correspondent enclosed "seeds of the plant found in the Western country which is said to posses the vertues of the Columbo root." The writer found it in "swamps" but also "on the tops of hills." Paradoxically it grew both "in the richest bottoms and on the poorest ridge," and he observed that it "grows best in rich loose soil, & that no animal will eat it." The writer wished Barton to give his opinion and awaited a reply.[48] There is no record that Barton responded to this correspondent, but confusion waned for metropolitan naturalists once specimens replaced anecdotal reports. Still, distance and a dearth of trained naturalists in the west could do little to reduce frontier uncertainty over plants.

Richard Brown, a former medical student of Barton's who lived in Louisville, Kentucky, sent Barton a specimen "of what the people of this neighborhood call the Columbo root. It grows here in great abundance." He described what he knew of the plant but admitted that he had never seen one himself and apologized that "my entire ignorance of botany renders it impossible for me to give you a better description." The people of the region asked him frequently to identify the root and to authenticate their finds. Unfortunately, Brown had been "obliged to answer doubtingly," not possessing the skills to say whether it was or was not the true colombo root. "It would give me much pleasure to hear your opinion of it," he wrote. He enclosed a packet that contained a specimen he believed to be *Orybanche virginiana*. The people of Kentucky, Brown wrote, "call it the cancer root and Beech drop" and used it to treat various diseases. Again he asked Barton if he would "do me the favor to let me know your opinion of these points. They have excited a great deal of enquiry in this country and I should be happy in having it in my power to pronounce an opinion respecting them with confidence." Though he was a physician, Brown admitted that "it is subject of great mortification to me that I have never studied botany." The western country "is such a field for research" that knowledge of the science, Brown mused, "would be to me a source both of profit and pleasure."[49]

Brown, like many others in early republic America, embraced the fusion of natural knowledge and economic profits proposed by natural history advocates. He and his neighbors in Kentucky looked to the fields and forests as landscapes where natural knowledge and entrepreneurial zeal could blend seamlessly. For some of those who gathered plants, fossils, and ores, the location of lucrative resources resulted in financial windfall. For others, success proved more elusive, confusion rather than clarity characterizing the transactions over putative discoveries. Stories such as that of the colombo root suggest that appeals to the most prominent adjudicators on these matters were only one means to determine the identity of plants; and evidence suggests that these prognostications were often disregarded or manipulated, raising questions and possibilities about the efficacy and limits of botany and natural history that surely troubled their advocates. These moments of dispute, perhaps imagined as the optimum opportunity to establish epistemological authority, instead made manifest how tenuous was botanists' ability to settle these controversial matters. The authority of natural knowledge, Barton and others came to realize, was compromised and challenged by the authority of the early republic marketplace—an economy that was rapidly transitioning toward capitalism even as older forms of exchange persisted. If a purported root sold as "true Columbo," natural historians could do little to dissuade the possessor that he purchased something other than the authentic article. Local knowledge, putative medicinal efficacy, and faith that a plant was what one believed it to be were powerful means of shaping belief. Misinformation, misunderstanding, and manipulation came to typify early republic natural history transactions as natural historians faced the results of so closely aligning their practice

with commerce. Suspect botany bolstered by the authority of the marketplace was an alliance difficult to undo.

Naturalists were frustrated but circumspect about this state of affairs.
They continued to preach the economic, utilitarian benefits of botany, especially for Americans living in an acquisitive society. An individual who
could identify lucrative trees and plants was more likely to succeed economically than a neighbor who could not; the marketplace prompted and
reinforced this equation. With the worth and value of some commodities
resting in part on natural historical valuations, those with broader botanical
knowledge could better judge claims of worth, ignoring competing claims
when they believed the information to be wrong. But naturalists' authority
was limited in early republic America, a historical moment when a hierarchical natural historical practice encountered a postcolonial society in
which unbalanced relationships in politics and governance were increasingly challenged and unwelcome. Certainly, naturalists received information about American nature and disseminated their techniques and
epistemology throughout the continent; eventually, their taxonomic identifications located plants that were useful to the nation and to the world.
But frontier Americans were hesitant to establish and to accept patrician
relationships with eastern naturalists if no personal benefit was obvious to
them. Ordinary Americans might correspond with naturalists but they were
unwilling to provide them samples without compensation, whether informational or fiduciary. Early republic Americans were acutely sensitive to
the inequalities of colonial relationships and ordinary Americans were
unwilling to permit themselves to be manipulated by elite naturalists. When
they sensed that their knowledge was to be used by others for financial
gain, early republic Americans wanted to share in the promised profits of
American nature.

Naturalists and botanists confronted a society of artisans and farmers
who sought economic and political freedoms at odds with the dreams of
their social betters and who possessed their own ideas about plants derived
from experience, gardening, folk knowledge, and local usage. Individuals
such as H. B. Trout looked to botany and to botanists to settle matters of
local dispute as well as for economic advice; they were interested in the
national flora catalog but ambivalent about becoming unpaid collectors for
eastern elites. If fortunes could be made from the landscape—and the
promises of naturalists suggested that they could—then those who pos-

sessed the land containing the plants should garner the rewards, ordinary Americans thought, rather than distant naturalists with specialized knowledge. In short, botany enthusiasts encountered a democratizing republic reluctant and at times resistant to adopting a hierarchical botanical practice.

In books, literary magazines, newspapers, broadsides, and personal letters, natural historians appealed to individual acquisitiveness and economic nationalism to generate interest in their practice. Characterizing North America as a continent of unrealized profits, they expanded on preexisting assumptions concerning nature's potential, portraying its imagined limitless resources as an individual's springboard into prosperity. If the intoxicating admixture of aspiration for wealth and confidence in natural plenty enticed ordinary Americans to practice natural history, the utility and efficacy of natural history and botany were demonstrated and reinforced as the practice proved a reliable economic predictor for a few commodities. When its prognostications turned lucrative, natural history's authority increased. In a few cases, individuals who located objects of extraordinary value were catapulted into local and national celebrity, generating for the discoverer social capital as valuable as the money received. However, many more Americans appear to have questioned the natural historical enterprise when its assessments challenged botanical folk knowledge, when it resisted settling matters of local dispute, or when it failed to confirm the scientific importance of curiosities or wonders. The easy calculus of natural knowledge leading to individual and national wealth foundered as botanical and mineralogical determinations exposed economies operating on different terms: a local economy of traditional medical practice, folk knowledge, curiosities and marvels, and a broader, rapidly maturing capitalist economy determined by the desire for reliability and consistent supply. As a result, the intimate association between natural history and natural resource commodification embroiled the authority of natural history in disputes over the definitions of worth and conflicting ideas about value. Naturalists saw their empire of reason corrupted in practice and in the minds of ordinary Americans, too closely aligned with the market and its dynamics, buffeted by individuals they did not know and agendas they could not control.

Chapter 3

The Perils of a Democracy of Facts:
Interpreting American Antiquities

A few years prior to 1819, Dr. James Overton, then professor of medicine at Transylvania University, presented to John Clifford, a transplanted resident of Lexington, Kentucky, and a proprietor of one of the town's storefront antiquarian museums, an object dug from an "ancient open temple" on the Caney Fork River from north-central Tennessee's Cumberland Plateau. That object came to be known as the Triune Vessel. The Triune Vessel was a flagon that stood eight inches high, its three hollow heads attached to a hollow stem that held approximately one quart of liquid. The object was made of clay along "with ferruginous matter and flinty particles," the faces painted with streaks and "deep blotches" of brown, red, and yellow ochre across the forehead, down the sides of the cheeks, under and over the eyes and stretching to the ears.

The Triune Vessel that Clifford described was just one of thousands of artifacts unearthed in the early republic, a period when white emigrants flooded the trans-Appalachian west as well as an era when the continent's ancient past occupied a vibrant, if contested, place in the imagination of many early republic Americans. Pioneers to the early west, prepared to settle a recently depeopled wilderness, instead encountered a landscape that demonstrated ancient inhabitation. The mound groupings ranged widely in size, in number, and in arrangement. The smallest sites contained a single mound, perhaps two or three; the largest sites such as those at Circleville and Chillicothe, Ohio, contained upward of twenty to several dozen.

These sites and the artifacts discovered in and around them elicited varied responses as to their use, who built them, and when they were constructed. Proponents of various conjectures found convincing proof in the

Figure 6. "The Triune Vessel." From the Caleb Atwater Papers, Maps and Drawings. This image of the effigy pot popularly known as the Triune Vessel was drawn by John Clifford's sister, Sarah Clifford, sometime around 1819. Courtesy The American Antiquarian Society.

low walls and tumuli of the region, their explanations bounded, it seemed, only by the limits of their imagination and their ability and willingness to borrow ideas from classical writings and ancient legends. Amid the cacophonous theories regarding the mound builders, however, Clifford's belief in the "most striking coincidences" between the "natives of Hindoostan" and those who built the mounds was far from fringe. His argument for Asian migration from Siberia to North America settled in the comfortable middle along a spectrum of explanations running from Lost Tribes of Israel, Vikings, migrants from Phoenicia, and refugees from Atlantis, to evidence supporting polygenesis, or a separate creation of human beings. His serial article employed homological arguments but relied as well on careful scrutiny of physical artifacts such as the Triune Vessel. Likewise, Clifford brought together Old and New World people through comparative linguistics, architecture, manners and customs, and physical features. His article explained the differences between the peoples who built the mounds and contemporary Native Americans; Clifford and most other early national antiquarians believed that the latter could not or did not build these structures. Most early republic antiquarians were convinced that the mound builders were expelled by violent, nomadic, and primitive bands; the vanquishers, this thinking went, were the ancestors of contemporary Indians.

In his intellectual and commercial pursuits, John Clifford was at the nexus of two interconnected phenomena in early republic natural history: debates about the origins of the mounds in the journals and publications among those who styled themselves naturalists; and the activities of those living in the Ohio Valley who incorporated the artifacts dug from the mounds into preexisting ideas about buried treasure, divining rods, money digging, and magical objects held in the earth. As these notions were brought from New England and New York to the Ohio Valley by settlers moving west, the early republic witnessing a renaissance in treasure hunting.

The promise of financial reward, particularly ancient coins and treasure, likely prompted as many mound excavations as did antiquarian curiosity about their origins. Certainly the two reinforced one another. Legends about long-ago visitors to America easily accommodated the artifacts found in the tumuli, in turn raising expectations that the mounds might hold items of greater value. The discovery of a copper coin "in the neighborhood of some ancient ruins" at Marietta, Ohio, led locals to argue that it was evidence that those who built the mounds were European and that great stores of treasure were held in the mounds.[1] A letter to the American Antiquarian Society detailed Roman coins found in Tennessee, a Spanish coin in Circleville, and an English coin in Trumbull County, Ohio. Many of these "discoveries" proved fraudulent. After "Several East Indian coins" emerged near Cincinnati, a former "captain of an East Indiaman" admitted to purposely "losing" them there.[2] Nevertheless, admissions of deception could not compete with treasure-hunting traditions that promised rapid financial gain.

More often than specie, artifacts of ancient cultures rewarded those digging in the mounds. Beads, pots, and tools emerged from the earth, many with distinctive markings. An Antiquarian Society correspondent from Alabama wrote of a rock inscribed with "enigmatical characters" that attracted the "attention of the curious not only of our own but of all the neighboring states." The writer was certain that the rock was not the "work of some person merely for the sake of exciting speculation"; rather, it was designed to answer "some valuable purpose" by those who in the vast "vortex of time, have been swept away."[3] Two clay bowls "distinctly" inscribed with the "common Arabick figures" 597 and 8 were taken from a tumulus on the Little Yellow Creek in Ohio.[4] Though not the treasure many sought, these artifacts commanded value as evidence in support of the various theories being promoted in natural history publications. Storefront antiquities museums like John Clifford's in Lexington and Daniel Drake's in Cincinnati paid excavators for their finds, creating a source of supplemental income.[5] This economy of antiquities frustrated those like Caleb Atwater, an antiquarian working in Circleville, Ohio, who were "obliged to give some thing handsome for some articles" now that they were "in the hands of avaricious men."[6] Atwater tried to dissuade those with "selfish views" to give him their found artifacts. But the early republic interest in Ohio Valley antiquities only reinforced the overtones of ancient treasure-hunting traditions. The American land was laden with mysteries, secrets, and possibilities. It held objects with the economic potential to change a life.

Origin stories blossomed as mounds fell victim to treasure hunters and farmers in the first decades of the nineteenth century. Excavated coins and artifacts pointed to any number of peoples, among them the Celts, the Druids, Scandinavian Vikings, the Phoenicians, and the Lost Tribes of Israel. The last example, that the mound builders were ancient Jews, became a cottage industry as theorists attempted to connect biblical history with the present.[7] Theorists bickered but could never settle on a single group of mound builders. Such precision seemed unnecessary. The abundance of evidence suggested that more than one group visited (and lived) in North America, leaving artifacts and traces of their inhabitation scattered across the continent.

Clifford marveled at his prize discovery, the Triune Vessel, and in a series of articles published in Lexington's short-lived literary magazine, *Western Review and Miscellaneous Magazine,* he mused about the vessel's potential for solving the mystery of how that area of North America came to be inhabited by humans. Originally from a Philadelphia merchant family, Clifford had represented the business on travels to Italy and the Mediterranean years earlier. So he could write with confidence that "although we cannot boast that the pottery of our aborigines equals the vases of Etruria in workmanship, yet much information is to be obtained from the examination of those few specimens which have been found uninjured." His eight-part serial article, "Indian Antiquities," led readers through his examination of the Triune Vessel and his researches into, and conclusions about, the American antiquities of midcontinent North America.[8]

Clifford's articles exhibited all the characteristics of a gentleman schooled in the polite learning of the time. He blended his antiquarian observations with musings on philology and numismatics, epic poetry and ancient agriculture. Armed with a bookish knowledge of antiquities from throughout the world, he offered a detailed description of the vessel and noted how it corresponded to and differed from other archaeological discoveries in the Americas. Clifford wrote that the Triune Vessel, though similar in "workmanship" to the "Mexican" style, was not created by the "nations of Anahuac" because it did not represent the "smallest ornaments" and "exact form of the various parts of the dress and appendages" that characterized Central American idols and paintings. Instead, he thought the vessel's heads were "perfectly natural" and without adornment except a small "oval prominence" that was "probably meant to represent a knot of hair." Clifford considered the faces to "display a striking resemblance to the Asiatic countenance" and believed that the painting on the faces bore a "strong resemblance to the modes in which the Hindus designate their different castes." The Asiatic features, the vessel's lack of minute embellishment, and the face painting led Clifford to conclude that the authors of the Triune Vessel and the "circumvolutory temple" in which it was found bespoke an "intercourse between Asia and the mid-continent of America" and "almost direct proof of the identity of religion between the Hindoos and our Aborigines." According to Clifford "no fortuitous circumstances or train of thought incidental to the generality of mankind" could create the "striking similarities" between the Triune Vessel and the practices of ancient Hinduism. Ancient Native Americans, he firmly believed, were the direct descendents of ancient "Hindoos" and the authors of the Triune Vessel and the mound in which it was found.[9]

Historians of archaeology, anthropology, and early America rebuke John Clifford and his ilk for looking past what seems to moderns so obvious: that the builders of the mounds were not a race disappeared from

North America but ancestors to the Native Americans of the area.[10] They accuse Clifford and his era of half-consciously fashioning a mound-builder "mythology" to assist their expansionist designs on the American continent and to assuage their guilty consciences over its corresponding racial genocide. "Men in search of a myth will usually find one, if they work at it," one historian writes, and the constitution of the mound-builder myth involved malevolent imaginative labor.[11] Early Americans suffered from cultural inferiority and longed for an ancient past on par with that of the Old World, this scholarship argues; the mounds provided the physical evidence that Americans needed to imagine an ancient history with the patina they sought. The myth "permitted a form of historical self-delusion that transferred the sins of the conquerors onto the conquered" by positing the mound builders to be the original, semi-civilized inhabitants of North America and Indians as the savage latecomers.[12] Thus, white settlers in the Ohio River Valley in this period were only the latest in a series of North American subjugators: contemporary Indians gained title to the continent through right of conquest, as did the early republic settlers who later replaced Native Americans. This mound-builder myth "took root, flourished and grew" through the nineteenth century. "Then the scientists took over from the mythmakers and hacked away the luxuriant growth of fantasies" ending an episode in bad science and a sad chapter in American race relations.[13]

This interpretation, persuasive and convincing to a point, prevails because it tells a familiar and powerful story: the triumph of an objective science and a modern reckoning of prior American racial injustice. But it predominates at the expense of a more historically attuned understanding of the early republic's engagement with the North American ancient past. Focusing on the ulterior motives for the mound-builder myth elides regional difference and rivalry, individual idiosyncrasies and personal piques, as well as important internal debates about evidence and rules of conduct in the early American antiquarian circles. It is a view that obscures as well the vital importance of artifacts and eyewitness accounts in establishing authority among antiquarians of the early republic. By focusing on the cultural logic of a putative national mound-builder mythology, scholars miss how savants such as Clifford used antiquities—the mounds and the artifacts that came from them—to establish themselves as credible interpreters of American nature and how they utilized these objects as valuable assets to remove the obstacles that barred frontier Americans from erudite, learned conversation in cities such as Philadelphia, Boston, and New York.

Scholars too quick to focus on the early republic's contributions to the myth of the vanishing Indian miss as well a significant trend: the shift of the locus of antiquarian activity from east to west over the first two decades of the nineteenth century. The late eighteenth century witnessed antiquarian research the topic of conversation in eastern scientific societies and their publications. But by 1817 when Clifford printed his pieces in the *Western Review*, the subject and its practitioners were increasingly western—Cincinnati, Lexington, and the towns of southern Ohio. Western cities had replaced Philadelphia, New York, and Boston as the major centers of early republic antiquarian research. In the second and third decades of the nineteenth century it was those living in the Ohio River Valley system who led early national investigations of the ancient American past and attempted to bring to it some sense of order. To do so, they relied on artifacts such as the Triune Vessel to distinguish their practice from conjectural history and fanciful speculation, which they believed had marred earlier research.

Late eighteenth-century white Americans understood the Indian mounds and their contents through competing intellectual traditions traveling opposite trajectories. The first and older tradition was a melange of transplanted folk wisdom, occult beliefs, and magic practices about treasure hunting and mysterious objects dug from the earth. Often overlooked by those tracing the history of American archaeology, this tradition was increasingly divorced from its early modern intentions and meanings; nevertheless, it was persistent, highly adaptable, and incorporated the mounds and ideas about them into a magical worldview about the American continent and its ancient past.[14] If this first tradition was quiet but persistent, the second was on the rise and much noisier. It was a facet of natural historical investigation dedicated to studying the peopling of America. How humans came to the New World had occupied thinkers and naturalists since the Columbian encounter, and the eighteenth-century discovery of the Bering Straits made migration from Asia among the most probable answers.[15] Antiquarians from across the globe, aided by improvements in transportation and communication, made the peopling of the Americas a prime question in ethnographic investigation by the late eighteenth and early nineteenth centuries. This increased scope and scholarly intensity bred confidence among practitioners that their efforts would determine the historical identity of the first Americans, their migration patterns, and what had become of them; the comparative techniques these antiquarians employed would only be improved by new information pouring in from around the world. These two traditions appealed to different constituencies but coexisted and shaped the ancient past in the imagination of the young republic.

If these intellectual approaches structured the investigation of objects being dug from the earth, then concern and anxiety about the future of the republic colored the meanings attached to these objects. Republicanism dominated the political discourse of the founding generation, much of it manifested in writings and discussions about the need for civic virtue, the debilitating effects of luxury, and the benefits of manufacturing versus those of agriculture. This rhetoric and discourse leached into ideas about North America's ancient past. White Americans of the early republic considered human history to be an evolutionary process from "rude" simplicity to "civilized" complexity, their beliefs derived from the French and Scottish Enlightenment. They thought societies passed through four distinct stages based on the predominant mode of subsistence: hunting, pasturage, agriculture, and commerce, each stage superseded when the population exceeded its ability to produce enough food for its people. Evidence from ancient through modern history suggested the pattern to be true. Located somewhere between the third and fourth stages, the young United States was a society on the rise. But as white Americans debated policies designed to retard or to propel social evolution, they looked to those Indians among them and to those who inhabited the Old Northwest and saw dispersed, transient groups entrenched in the first stage. From all the evidence that they chose to highlight, white Americans surmised that Native Americans had lived this way for a very long time.[16]

James Bowdoin, first president of the American Academy of Arts and Sciences in Boston, offered a standard account of this belief in an address to the organization in 1780. "Whatever relates to the aboriginal natives of America, not already noticed in history, may be comprized in a very narrow compass," he wrote. "Their want of civilization, and improvement . . . will justify the opinion, that the present race of them, in manners and conduct, differ very little from their ancestors, who lived centuries ago." Bowdoin conjectured and concluded "that the ancient and modern history of these people . . . would appear but little more than a transcript of each other; and that it would be in vain to search among them for antiquities."[17] His

logic rendered Native American society static, making contemporary Indians windows into the past, the behaviors exhibited in the present direct
analogues to time immemorial.

According to Bowdoin's thinking, the mounds white Americans
encountered east of the Appalachians were not the signs of civilization or
remnants of organized, coordinated effort. Thomas Jefferson echoed this
line of thought in *Notes of the State of Virginia*, completed in 1783. The
mound that he excavated near Monticello was little more than human
remains randomly "deposited on the common surface of the earth, a few
stones put over it, and then a covering of earth," a second layer placed over
the initial, "and so on." Thus, mounds white Americans were to encounter
could be attributed to burial practices, "their origin and growth from the
accustomary collection of bones, and deposition of them together." Based
on his excavation and what he knew of other Indian mounds, Jefferson
determined that there was "no remain as respectable as would be a common ditch" among Indian architecture, nothing that would indicate
"labour on a large scale." He concluded confidently, "I know of no such
thing existing as an Indian monument."[18]

But accounts and stories of earthen walls, massive tumuli, and mound
groupings began trickling east from the Ohio Valley starting in the late
1780s. These reports described trenches, ramparts, and "fortifications" that
enclosed numerous mounds. The most important early communiqués
came from members of the Ohio Company in Marietta, and because the
reputations of those reporting the finds were deemed reputable, the reports
aided a rethinking and a reimagining of the ancient American past.[19] Jonathan Heart, an army major in the company, responded to a letter sent him
by Benjamin Smith Barton asking for any information he had about the
mounds. Heart described mounds he had seen and related reports of others;
his letter was read to the American Philosophical Society and published in
their 1793 volume of *Transactions*. He reported that he had examined the
"works" at Muskingum in Ohio and Grave-Creek in western Virginia. In
each locale, Heart described the structures as consisting of "square and
circular redoubts, ditches, walls, and mounts, scattered, at unequal distances, in every direction, over extensive flats." He continued that the
"common mounts, or Indian graves, or monuments (for they are not
always found to contain bones), are scattered over the whole country, particularly along the Ohio [River], and its main branches." Marveling at their
extensive spread, Heart opined that he had "scarcely ever seen a handsome

situation on a high flat, adjoining any large stream, where there were not some of the above mentioned vestiges of antiquity." Heart added more of his own observations as far south as "the headwaters of the Yazoo and Mobile" and noted that travelers related to him stories of similar structures on the "low grounds of the Mississippi."[20]

Heart turned his attention to the creators of these structures. "Who those inhabitants were, who have left such traces; from whence they came, and where they are now; are queries to which we never, perhaps, can find any other than conjectural answers." In response to the then-popular theory that the structures might have been built by the Spanish explorer Hernando de Soto, Heart disagreed: "[de Soto] was not on the continent sufficient time to construct even at Muskingum" and de Soto had not traveled as far north as most of the locations of the mounds.[21] Nor were the mounds "constructed by any European, Asian or African nation since the discovery of America by Christopher Columbus."[22] Erosion and the evidence of multiple tree generations on top and around the mounds pointed to a much earlier origin.

Instead, Heart articulated a two-pronged argument that characterized antiquarian logic during the early republic. First, Heart argued that the mounds could not have been built by contemporary "Indians or their predecessors or some traditions would have remained as to their uses; and, they would have retained some knowledge in constructing similar works." (Heart maintained this position even though he related that "Chacktaw-Indians" told him of an "elevation of earth about half a mile square, fifteen or twenty feet high" in which lived the "Great Spirit" and place of origin of the Choctaw people.)[23] Antiquarians made it a point to ask various Indian groups about the mounds, and the overwhelming majority of those queried were reported to be ignorant of their use or who built them. Second, Heart employed the laws of social evolution, along with physical evidence, to establish that Indians were not the authors of these structures. Heart was convinced that the Muskingum "works" were not "constructed by people who procured the necessaries of life by hunting" as he believed most Indians did. Heart continued: a population "sufficient to carry such works never could have subsisted in that way." The coordination of labor necessary to build these structures exceeded the abilities of people locked in the lowest stage of social development. Heart deduced that "the people who constructed them were not altogether in a state of uncivilization" as were the Indians he knew. The society that built the works at Muskingum, something so vast and complicated, "must have been under the subordination of law," replete with "a strict and well governed police." Otherwise, the authors of the mounds "could not have been kept together in such numerous bodies, and made to contribute to the carrying on such stupendous works."[24] Heart's conclusions, which he admitted strayed from his "business . . . to give you facts, and not to form conjectures," recognized the sophisticated undertaking involved in constructing the mounds at Muskingum and his letter registered an admiration for the people who built them; at the same time Heart also dismissed the possibility that Indians could have built these structures.[25]

Bishop James Madison, president of the College of William and Mary, offered a castigating counterinterpretation of mounds he had observed, one as dismissive of ancient grandeur as was Heart of contemporary Indians. Madison wrote to Barton in 1803 and the letter was later printed in the American Philosophical Society's 1809 *Transactions*. He explained that his aim was "to remove error of any kind" in order to "promote the progress of intelligence." Invoking the privilege of the eyewitness, Madison took aim at "our literati," those who suppose themselves "most profound in historical, geographical, and philosophical lore." Had they visited the sites as had Madison, had "they first examined into the fact," they would have concluded, as had he, "that what had so greatly excited the *admiration of the curious*, existed only in their imaginations."[26] Madison continued: "No one was more impressed, than myself" with the opinion that the west held "regular and extensive fortifications, of great antiquity." He examined a number of sites on the Kanawha River in what is now West Virginia with an "ardent curiosity" and a "full conviction" that the mounds were the work of an advanced society "skilled in the means of military defence." Initially, their appearance was "imposing," and Madison's mind seemed to "acquiesce in the current opinion, more disposed to join in fruitless admiration, than to question the reality of those fortifications." But as he continued his observations and as he examined more sites in the area, "the delusion vanished," he reported. Madison noted that the earthworks were not located in strategic positions and dismissed any military logic in their construction. Instead, the mounds were Indian burial sites almost exclusively. In excavated examples Madison found alternate strata of bones and earth which had grown up gradually "as death robbed a family of its relatives, or a tribe of its warriors." A proto-stratigraphy suggested to him that the mound groupings were "not the temporary station of a retiring or weakened army, but the fixed habitation of a family, and a long line of descendants." The walls were built, he thought, for ceremonial purpose or to demarcate parcels for planting. Confident that his measurements and descriptions were accurate, Madison was more circumspect in his opinions of the mounds' use, admitting that his ideas were conjectural. Eschewing definitive conclusions about the mounds, he concluded that he and his fellow researchers "want here a compass to guide us" but "are left to find our way through this night of time."[27]

For many observers the most logical compass to guide antiquarian studies and determine the authorship of the mounds was also the simplest: ask the Indians of the area whether they had built the mounds. But the Indians in the Ohio Valley were consistently reported to be as ignorant about the mounds as were the newcomers. More than one commentator noted that "the oldest Indians have no traditions as to their authors, or the purposes for which they were originally intended."[28] Nor should they, it would seem. The Indians whom settlers and antiquarians queried were almost entirely relatively recent transplants to the Ohio Valley, settling there after white encroachment had pushed them west. While longer-term tribes who inhabited the Ohio Valley, including the Shawnee and Miami as well as the lower Mississippi-residing Natchez, do appear as interlocutors, more often than not the tribe that was consulted was the Lenni Lenape, and antiquarians relied heavily on the writings and research of the Delaware missionary John Heckewelder.[29] These tribes reportedly never used the mounds, nor had anyone for a long time. Trees cut from their tops were several hundred years old; evidence of rotting trunks convinced more than one witness that "there may have been several generations" of trees. The mounds were "in a state of decay for a 1000 years." So there seemed "no ground to question [the] great antiquity for these prodigious labours."[30] Since Indian traditions did not seem to shed much light on the authorship of the mounds, American antiquarians sought other sources for clues and discussed openly the ways in which antiquarians might be required to adopt a more permissive set of evidentiary rules than in other branches of natural history.

Benjamin Smith Barton signaled the methodological difference between natural history and antiquarian study. In a letter to the transplanted savant Joseph Priestley, discussing some artifacts dug from a mound in Cincinnati, Barton wrote that "[you] will sometimes find me leaving the sure road" of natural history for the "too often uncertain path of the antiquary." Barton admitted that "some uncertainty is necessarily involved" in these endeavors. Whereas natural history was based on verifiable facts obtained from trusted sources, "the light which serves to conduct [the antiquarian] is frequently extremely faint: the imagination and conjecture are, therefore, naturally called in to his aid." Barton and most naturalists fought against speculation in the practices of botany and zoology. Yet he and many others thought such leaps permissible, even necessary, in describing the ancient past; particularly in an inquiry "where the subjects of investigation have been taken from the darkness of the GRAVE."[31]

Thaddeus Mason Harris, librarian of Harvard College and traveler to Ohio, concurred with Barton's methodological latitude. Antiquarian study was a "subject where all is conjecture." It was difficult if not impossible, he thought, "to form a decided opinion." Antiquarian "truth" should therefore be founded on those conclusions that have "the most PROBABILITY in [their] favour," not those which were irrefutable. Harris's contention that the mounds were built by emigrants from Asia was an opinion that he thought had "more than the support of probability," for correspondent mounds in northeastern Asia convinced him that he was right.[32]

But the latitude that some antiquarians afforded themselves and their endeavor was met with skepticism and outright derision from those who wished for a more factual and grounded practice. Moreover, skeptics seemed to tire of the intractable but simple divide at the heart of antiquarian studies: whether or not the ancestors to contemporary Indian tribes were capable of having built the mounds and related structures. John Adams wrote to Thomas Jefferson in 1812 asking him to recommend books that offered an account of "the confused traditions of Indian Antiquities."[33] Jefferson did not recommend contemporary works of antiquarians but cautiously suggested works by James Adair, Theodore de Bry, and Joseph Lafitau. The last author, Jefferson wrote, "has in his head a preconceived theory" about ancient nations and "selects therefore all the facts, and adopts all the falsehoods which favor his theory" while eliminating those facts which work against it. Adair also speculated from fragmentary evidence: "He believed all the Indians of America to be descended from the Jews: the same laws, usages; rites and ceremonies, the same sacrifices, priests, prophets, fasts and festivals, almost the same religion, and that they all spoke Hebrew." With Adair, the reader must be "be constantly on his guard against the wonderful obliquities of his theory." De Bry's work was better regarded by Jefferson. Although "fact and fable are mingled

Figure 7. "A Bird's Eye View of the Ancient Works on the Muskingum." From Thaddeus M. Harris, *The Journal of a Tour into the Territory Northwest of the Alleghany Mountains* (Boston, 1805). Harris provided readers of his travel journal with an image of the ruins on the Muskingum River in Ohio that suggested a sense of size and proportion for the mounds found there. Courtesy The Huntington Library.

together," it was written without "a favourite system" and could be trusted.[34]

Adams's reply to Jefferson's suggestions for reading both captures his acerbic wit and registers a deeply felt frustration about antiquarian methods, one Adams did not alone share. He complained that "the various Ingenuity which has been displayed in Inventions or hypotheses to account for the original Population of America," along with "the immensity of learning profusely expended to support them," appeared to him "what the Physicians call the *Litterae nihil Sanantes* (Writings correcting nothing)." Adams continued with some jocularity that whether "Serpents Teeth were sown here" giving rise to humans, whether men and women "dropped from the Clouds upon this Atlantic Island," or whether they immigrated "are questions of no moment to the present or future happiness of Man." Neither good promoted nor evil averted "can be made in answer to those questions." Adams breathlessly mocked the antiquarian project: "I could make a system too." The 700,000 "Soldiers of Zingis," when in battle, "set up a howl, which resembled nothing that human Imagination has conceived," terrifying their enemies and prompting victory. "The Indian Yell resembles this: and therefore America was peopled from Asia." Or, the armies of Zingis "surrounded a Province in a Circle, and marched towards the Centre." Thus, "the Scotch Highlanders who practice the same thing in miniature, are emigrants from Asia. Therefore the American Indians, who, for anything I know, practice the same custom, are emigrants from Asia or Scotland." Adams dejectedly admitted, "I am weary of contemplating Nations from the lowest and most beastly degradations of human Life, to the highest Refinement of Civilization: I am weary of Philosophers, Theologians, Politicians, and Historians. They are immense Masses of Absurdities, Vices and Lies."[35] Other skeptics of the antiquarian method, such as the Pittsburgh printer Zadoc Cramer, embraced a position of epistemological humility and deemed a definitive answer difficult to determine. The antiquities of the region were "a subject often touched upon by historians and speculative writers," but both "early and late writers seem to be equally in the dark" as to the age, authorship, and "the cause of the total extinction or banishment of the settlers." But about this predicament Cramer was circumspect and he ended his observations of some mounds on the Ohio River with a quote from Alexander Pope's *Essay on Man*, exploring the limitation of "man's researches":

Say first, of God above, or Man below,
What can we reason, but from what we know?
Of man, what see we but his station here,
From which to reason, or to which refer?
Through worlds unnumber'd tho' the God be known,
'Tis ours to trace him only in our own."[36]

Adams's deeply felt frustrations and Cramer's ambivalence did little to deter or retard antiquarians from engaging in speculative connections. Such leaps of logic not only allowed those interested in the ancient American past an opportunity to overcome the hardship of fragmentary and elusive evidence; they also enabled them to see their way past a troubling possibility: namely, that if the authors of the mounds were the ancestors to Indians, then environmentally driven cultural degeneration might be a plausible explanation as to what happened to those who built the mounds. Early national Americans were aware that societies could fall as well as rise; the annals of the past and the laws of social evolution demonstrated this to be the case. In his longest writing on antiquities, Benjamin Smith Barton instructed his readers that history taught that "civilization has been constantly preceded by barbarity and rudeness." Yet it also suggested the "mortifying truth, that nations may relapse into a rudeness again; all their proud monuments crumbled into dust." Those who scoured the ruins of past societies in the present might themselves become "savages, subjects of contemplation among civilized nations and philosophers."[37] What caused societal degradation was a matter of vigorous debate in the early republic, and the rise and fall of peoples as well as empires was a subject of intense debate—consider the reception of Thomas Cole's painting series *The Course of Empire* in 1836.[38] But the European derision of the American climate persuaded early republican antiquarians to characterize the downward cycle of history as driven by human, not natural, factors. Had they not, a plausible if not entirely persuasive argument could be made that the Indians were the degenerated descendants of the more advanced mound builders, an argument already advanced by Europeans dismissive of the United States.

A reading of the historical record suggested to American antiquarians that temperate, relatively dry climates were considered the most advantageous for the progress of human societies. From the Fertile Crescent to Egypt, from Greece to Rome, warmth, semi-aridity, and climatic regularity

characterized the locales of historically advanced civilizations. Eastern
North America did not fit this mold, it would seem. It was wetter than Asia
Minor or the Mediterranean; the summers were much hotter and the winters much colder. Constantin François de Chassebœuf, Comte de Volney, a
French philosophical traveler to the United States, lambasted the "fluctuat-
ing" and "capricious" climate of North America. Volney characterized
North America, in particular the Ohio Valley, as swampy, laden with a foul
air that bred fever, fostered disease, and rotted teeth.[39] The "most striking
feature of America is the rugged and dreary prospect of an almost universal
forest," he wrote. The land is "sterile and rough, or encumbered with the
fallen and decaying trunks of ancient trees. Clouds of gnats, mosquitoes,
and flies hovered beneath the shade, and continually infested my peace."
Such "is the real state of these Elysian fields." This climate, he argued,
prevented Indians from advancing beyond the first-stage of human development and thus the mounds he thought were no great monuments of
antiquity. Prior to his trip to the United States, Volney surveyed the ruins
of once great civilizations in Egypt and Syria. A self-styled expert of the rise
and fall of societies, Volney did not expect great things from America.[40]
Because of the insalubrious climate, Volney hinted that over time future
Americans would appear more akin to their Native American predecessors
than their European forebears.

American natural historians labored to prove Volney wrong by demonstrating that areas cleared of trees warmed, the climatic variations between
summer and winter becoming less severe. Those living in a cultivated
American landscape "enjoy a large proportion of fine and moderate
weather; with more days of sunshine and serene sky, than perhaps, any part
of Europe." The winters were cold, they admitted, but they "brace and
invigorate the bodies of the people: and the genial warmth of our summers
increases the generative principle." Careful attention to temperatures and
precipitation, they argued, showed that no latent degeneracy lurked in the
American soil once the land was brought under cultivation. There was no
climatic evidence to suggest that America could not support an advancing
civilization.[41] From this finding, antiquarians were quick to conclude that
Indians had not degenerated either. Though Native Americans had not
advanced up the ladder of social development since arriving in America—
they remained stubbornly in the first stage of social development—neither
had they fallen down its rungs. Evidence supported their arguments, antiquarians thought, and worked to counteract skeptics such as Bishop Madi-

son who regarded Indians as the "degenerated branches of the nations who erected these works."[42] With Indians among the least likely of possible candidates, antiquarians looked for the most probable builders of the mounds. Exemplifying the permissive logic of natural historical possibility, scholars of ancient America found answers in Indian legends, comparative linguistics, Central American histories, but most importantly in the artifacts that continued to emerge from the west.

Antiquarians cobbled together scraps of disparate evidence, weaving them into a series of speculative narratives about the origins and fate of those who built the mounds of the Ohio Valley. For example, the Indian missionary John Heckewelder, first in personal correspondence with naturalists and later in print, related a legend that figured prominently in many of the theories of the mound builders: according to the Delaware Indians, their ancestors came from western part of North America. When they crossed "the Namaesi Sipu or Mississippi River," Heckewelder reported, the Delawares allied themselves with the "Mengwe, or Iroquois." The Delaware and Iroquois made war upon and drove away a people they called the "Alligewi" who were settled in the Ohio basin. The Lenni Lenape told Heckewelder that the Alligewi were a "wonderful people, of gigantic stature, building fortifications and burying their dead in holes, over which they threw mounds of earth." The battles took place over a number of years after which the Alligewi emigrated to the southwest and never returned.[43]

Early national antiquarians connected this legend fragment with another drawn from the Aztecs. According to Abbé Clavigero, an eighteenth-century historian of Mexico, the Aztecs dated their arrival in the country of Anahuac, a province of Mexico, in 648 C.E. Aztec oral history and hieroglyphics attested to a northern, ancestral emigration by a people, the Olmecs.[44] Early national antiquarians fused these legends, concluding that modern Mexicans were formerly the Alligewi. Evidence from early exploration accounts suggested that when the Spanish settled New Orleans "they discovered the Natchez and Nagatoch Indians on the Mississippi and Red River to be of the same race as those of Mexico." The Natchez had "made similar progress in civilization and possessed the like religion, being worshippers of the Sun and sacrificing human victims to their deities." Thus, many antiquarians could feel as confident as John Clifford that "we possess indeed both historical proof and tradition that the Aborigines of this country were a different race" from the Indians.[45]

Evidence from comparative linguistics lent credence to these conclusions or at least did not directly dispute them. Early national scholars with interest in philology modeled their method on that of the French Jesuit traveler and missionary Father Pierre François Xavier de Charlevoix, who recorded his thoughts on Indian languages from the 1720s in his *Journal of a Voyage to North America*. Charlevoix eschewed studying Indian manners and customs, religions and traditions because he was convinced that such an investigation would produce "a false light, more likely to dazzle, and to make us wander from the right path, than to lead us with certainty to the point proposed."[46] Nonliterate nations such as Indians could not sustain a collective memory, he thought, and those institutions that depended on memory—law, religion, civil government—would be obliterated by time.[47] Nations unable to preserve distinct institutions were also equally unlikely to experience refinements or radical changes in their speech; this meant that Indian languages were, the thinking went, transparent windows into the past. While Thomas Jefferson—one of foremost early national compilers of Indian vocabularies—thought that Indians' diversity of language suggested a long residence in North America, the view that came to be more widely adopted in the early nineteenth century was that such diversity was largely superficial, prior investigators having mistaken dialects for languages. Barton authored what came to be the standard view on Indian language: that "that in all the vast countries of America there is but one language . . . referred to one great stock, which I call the language of the Lenni-Lennape or Delawares."[48] Barton's views assumed a correlation between mental and linguistic development that ultimately concluded that Indians and their lack of social development were not a product of their environment but of distinctive mental and cultural biases.[49] As more trees fell to the axes of white settlers and a chain of mounds interspersed from the Great Lakes to Louisiana emerged, the deficiencies that many assumed to be characteristic of Indians did not appear to apply to those who built the mounds.

The mounds grew in size but decreased in age and evolved from rounded to flat-topped when viewed north to south. Unlike contemporary anthropologists who divide these midcontinent structures into the expressions of distinct cultures, early republican antiquarians largely considered these mounds the work of a single culture built over a number of years as their builders proceeded from northeast to southwest. Though different antiquarians quibbled about the details, most thought that the mound-builder culture demonstrated advancement up the ladder of societal advancement, their conclusion evidenced by the construction of larger mounds when viewed from east to west. Henry Marie Brackenridge, the western author and politician, wrote to Barton in 1813 that since childhood he had been interested in mounds, visiting "almost every thing of this kind, worthy of note on the Ohio and Mississippi." Through a combination of examination and reflection, "something like hypothesis, has taken the place of the vague wanderings of fancy." Brackenridge regarded the mounds as "traces of a population far beyond what this extensive and fertile portion of the continent is supposed to have possessed." Articulating what was becoming a standard antiquarian interpretation, he thought that the North American midcontinent exhibited "traces of two distinct races of people, or periods of population, one much more ancient than the other." The first and more ancient period was "marked by those extraordinary tumuli or mounds" while the second, more recent period was denoted by an Indian architecture that demonstrated a persistent decline since the arrival of Europeans to North America. Brackenridge believed that when the mounds were constructed "there existed on the Mississippi, a population as numerous as that which once animated the border of the Nile, or of the Euphrates, or of Mexico and Peru." Grounding his hypothesis on an examination on the dramatic ruins near St. Louis, at Cahokia, he wrote: "I am perfectly satisfied that cities similar to those of ancient Mexico, of several hundred thousand souls, have existed in this part of the country," before the people who built the Cahokia mounds migrated south into Mexico.[50]

Brackenridge, who drew on descriptions by Clavigero and relied heavily on the travel accounts of the German naturalist Alexander von Humboldt, detected resemblance between the mounds and the teocalli, Aztec religious structures.[51] The mounds at Cahokia were "evidently constructed with as much regularity as any of the Teocalli of New Spain, and [were] doubtless chased with brick or stone, and crowned with buildings but of these no traces remain," he lamented, the stones, gradations, and steps reduced because of erosion. That the structures were oriented to the cardinal points, that they possessed several platform stages, that some mounds were dramatically larger than others, and that the large mounds were surrounded by smaller ones symmetrically arranged was no accident, Brackenridge argued. It was a sign that "Mexicans" and those who built the Ohio mounds practiced the same "arts and customs," the distance from the mounds on Red River to the nearest in New Spain close enough that "they might be considered as existing in the same country." With the Mexicans reportedly possessing "imperfect traditions of the construction of their Teo-calli," and Indians supposedly ignorant of the mounds in the Mississippi basin, Brackenridge concluded that the mound builders of the Ohio and Mississippi valleys were ancestors of those who built the monuments in Mexico.[52]

Brackenridge's letter to Barton, published in 1818, was the last sustained writing concerning antiquities to appear in the American Philosophical Society's *Transactions*. Benjamin Smith Barton's death in 1814 brought an end to the American Philosophical Society's sponsorship of such writing. Until his death, Barton and the American Philosophical Society had served as the leading collector and centralizer of antiquarian information—though other institutions such as the American Academy of Arts and Science in Boston and the New York journal *Medical Repository* reported occasionally on antiquarian matters, as did individual authors and a few literary maga-zines.[53] Barton's death left antiquarian studies, already a fragmented collec-tion of enthusiasts, without a clear patron and a defined center. Westerners such as John Clifford saw an opening to wrest away from the east a subject that largely concerned the west. It was a conversation in which western antiquarian enthusiasts hoped to make important interventions, which they did, simultaneously raising antiquarian empirical standards by emphasizing the importance of artifacts and attempting to police out of the practice those who adhered to less stringent methods. Clifford positioned himself well to spearhead these changes—there is reason to believe that he was preparing to publish his "Indian Antiquities" articles as a book—but he died unexpectedly in 1820 a month after the final installment of his series appeared.[54]

Caleb Atwater, an antiquarian working independently of Clifford but emulating his method and findings, staked his claim as an expert on the basis of his long-time residence near the mound sites and on his careful eyewitness study of their form, arrangement, and contents. Through the War of 1812 the majority of publications on the mounds had been written by travelers or short-term residents in the Ohio and Mississippi valleys. By contrast, Atwater, who settled in Circleville, Ohio, in 1815, distinguished himself from those travelers "who riding at full speed, had neither the industry, the opportunity, nor the ability to investigate a subject so intri-cate."[55] In his 1820 book-length article "Descriptions of the Antiquities dis-covered in the State of Ohio and other Western States," Atwater made sure to single out the antiquarian writings of those he wished to emulate; he

Figure 8. "A View of the Pyramid of Cholula, Near Mexico." From Caleb Atwater, "Description of the Antiquities Discovered in the State of Ohio and other Western States," *Archaeologia Americana: Transactions and Collections of the American Antiquarian Society* 1 (Worcester, Mass., 1820). Atwater linked the mounds of the Ohio Valley and those in the central Mexican highlands. Courtesy The American Antiquarian Society.

praised New York governor De Witt Clinton, Cincinnati physician Daniel Drake, and Henry Marie Brackenridge, "men of exalted talents both natural and acquired, who have attempted to describe only such works as they have carefully examined."[56] Atwater also complimented the work of Thaddeus Mason Harris and the Marietta, Ohio, physician Samuel P. Hildreth, who described "with great accuracy" the antiquities of Ohio. Such writers, Atwater flattered, "like the great luminary of day, give a steady light . . . whilst the common herd of scribblers on this subject resemble the ignis fatuus [the will o' the wisp], which as the poet says, 'leads to bewilder, and dazzles to blind.'" Atwater identified as his foundation the cautious and skeptical writings of these physicians and politicians; upon them he would build and offer his analysis of the mounds, "examine[d] with care, and describe[d] with fidelity."[57] A lawyer by trade as well as the postmaster of Circleville, Atwater was convinced that he could contribute to the antiquarian conversation and he worked tirelessly to get his writings into print, eventually finding a welcoming venue in the recently formed American Antiquarian Society in Worcester, Massachusetts, and their first issue of transactions.[58]

Born in North Adams, Massachusetts, and a graduate of Williams College, Atwater stressed his shared heritage with members of the Antiquarian Society and he recommended himself for inclusion in the organization.[59] Atwater worked to parlay these affinities and his position into an arrangement that would promote himself and his work, as well as boost the prestige and antiquities holdings of the Antiquarian Society. The correspondence between Atwater and the society, while dealing in large measure with the details surrounding his article, stressed his eyewitness testimony, the empirical facts he possessed, and the artifacts that came from the mounds; these artifacts, in contrast to the unverifiable accounts and speculations of previous authors, would distinguish Atwater's contributions and help to establish the AAS as the leader in this field he promised. In a letter from the summer of 1818 he explained that he was amassing a "small cabinet of curiosities calculated to throw some light on our path leading through the dark ages of Antiquity." He indicated that he already had "several articles in my possession, and through the kindness of my friends in various parts of this Western country I am almost daily receiving additional ones." He hinted that one day he hoped to give the society these artifacts, along with an "an essay more full, and I would fain hope, by far more satisfactory than the hasty ones which you have seen" on antiquities. Atwater probed the society's enthusiasm for his work when he wrote that "nothing but poverty prevents me from making an accurate survey of all these ancient remains and describing them, accompanied by diagram sketches" and that publication of his work in full would cost seven thousand dollars; to induce a response to his letter he noted obliquely that the governor of the Michigan territory, Lewis Cass, had urged him to form his own antiquarian society in Ohio, a potential rival to the Worcester society.[60]

Atwater's negotiations with the American Antiquarian Society intensified in 1819 when he asked for two hundred dollars to defray incurred expenses and indicated that some of his writings would be appearing shortly in New York's *American Monthly Magazine*.[61] (Atwater attempted to publish his work by subscription—it was advertised in the *American Monthly Magazine*—but it appears that he found few, if any, subscribers.)[62] More importantly, Atwater began to manage the society's expectations regarding his cabinet of artifacts and his promise to send it to the society. He explained to Isaiah Thomas, founder and president of the AAS, that a market—literal and intellectual—for ancient artifacts was taking shape in the Ohio Valley and hinted that his interests and those of the American Antiquarian Society might be diverging. Since Atwater had last written, "a society in Cincinnati has been formed for the purpose of collecting antiquities by Mr.[John] Clifford who had previously been engaged in collecting every relick of antiquity." More than "$10,000 is raised for this express purpose and they are offering large sums for every thing." But Atwater intimated that as much as a community of antiquarians and a market for their finds was taking shape, so too were rivalries forming and machinations emerging. He explained to Thomas why he had not availed himself of this lucrative opportunity: "Not having the funds and several severe essays having been written & published against my collecting to send away articles of this kind—these things have operated against me, except among my personal friends."[63] Atwater explained that he had received letters from "gentlemen in Philadelphia . . . remonstrating in strong terms, against my sending articles out of this country." In the meantime, Atwater suggested that the society might contact Clifford, who "writes me, that he has 3000 specimens assorted, labeled and now opened free of expense to visitors, in a large room fitted up for the purpose." Even with his intentions ultimately unclear, Atwater assured Thomas that he hoped to send his small cabinet in a year.[64]

Atwater's feverish correspondence with the Antiquarian Society contin-

ued throughout 1819 and 1820, but as the essay was readied his mood dark-
ened and he began to express anxieties about its reception and a defiant
attitude about fact-checking questions from Thomas.[65] Asked about the
locale of Clifford's Triune Vessel, an artifact that figured prominently in his
article, Atwater assured Thomas, "I have all the proof of its being found
where it is said to have been . . . and little or no doubt remains on my mind
of its being manufactured near the spot where it was found." Anticipating
critics and skeptics alike, Atwater explained: "*I wish not to multiply proofs,
where I have amply sufficient already. After having grown grey at the bar, I
have learnt that maxim.*" He elaborated: "If writers attack me, my rebutting
testimony is ready, is ample on every point, as to facts. The 'Triune idol'
and the late discoveries at Marietta are realities, which all the world cannot
do away." He had seen them and the accounts he gave of them were true.
He complimented Thomas for his abundance of caution on these matters
of fact, adding, "and I assure you that I duly appreciate your motives in
suggesting caution to me—I am so cautious that I have left out not a little
that most people would have inserted." But Atwater sensed that controversy was coming—his word would be challenged, his character would be
questioned—and explained to Thomas that "if I am attacked by any body,
it will be the authors of mutilated accounts of our antiquities, or travelers,
whom I neither fear, nor wish to please." He was, he explained, "ready to
meet them in combat, *when* & *where* they please." Atwater promised that
he could marshal the editors of newspapers and journals to vouch for his
character should such necessity arise.[66]

Atwater felt passionately enough to send another letter to Thomas two
days later qualifying and explaining his preemptive aggrievement at the
hands of his imagined critics. "If readers want anything more," he wrote,
"I cannot help it, at present. I have done *all* I could except fabricate something out of nothing." The burdens of the antiquarian were overwhelming:
there were no histories, no epic poems, no images, and no printed records
upon which to draw. "All we have," he explained, "is a few fragments of
history which have fortunately been saved from the deluge of time. The
mighty ocean of history has swallowed up the rest." Whatever his essay's
faults, whatever its shortcomings, he thought that his efforts should be
praised, not criticized. He warned, "What is left undone will soon, be too
late forever to do." Every "vestige" of the ancient culture was endangered
Atwater argued; all of it "will soon be destroyed by the present generation
and leave not a wreck behind." His aim in collecting and writing about

antiquities was "to snatch from the destroying, ruthless hand of man" as many artifacts as he could muster and "bear them to the place of deposit, which your enlightened liberality has erected, there to remains for the inspection of future generations." He might have saved only a few, Atwater admitted, but he had to contend with a "mighty host—millions of people, who are daily destroying them, in every part of the country, from Erie's southern shore to the Mexican Gulph, from the western foot of the Allegh- any, to the western bank of the Mississippi."[67]

Initially, at least, Atwater's concern and pique seemed unfounded; his essay delivered what he promised. It offered a nearly exhaustive survey of the known mounds in Ohio Valley accompanied by twelve engraved plates and numerous drawings of artifacts, some of the first images of mound arrangements and their contents.[68] Like those antiquarians he hoped to emulate, Atwater was careful in his analysis: he disaggregated American antiquities into three categories to reduce confusion—those of the ances- tors of contemporary Indians, those of Europeans or of European origin, and those of "that people who raised our ancient forts and tumuli."[69] The first half of the study comprised largely sober descriptions of artifacts and surveys that emphasized the dimensions and the arrangement of the Ohio mounds. But the second half represented a sharp break, which Atwater titled "Conjectures, respecting the Origin and History of the Authors of the Ancient Works in Ohio." This section and the remainder of the work repeated the origin theory promoted by Clifford, that those people who built the mounds were descendents of the "Hindoos." Like Clifford, Atwater felt confident that his use of excavated artifacts made a stronger case for the affinities between Old and New World and he based his conclu- sions on the evidence in his hands, which he supplemented and bolstered by the writings of naturalists who had traveled or lived in Asia and Central America.[70] He acknowledged that in doing so was straying from the empiri- cism and he dismissed critics who "require proofs amounting to mathemat- ical certainty." People who insist on such exacting standards "need not give themselves the useless labour of perusing the remaining part of this mem- oir." He argued to his readers that the nature of antiquarian study "does not admit of such proof." But if "absolute certainty be not attainable," it appeared to Atwater that "reasonable [certainty] is." Atwater concluded that his comparative technique was empirically grounded, based on the artifacts, and would reveal "whatever belonged to [the mound builders] in

common with any other [people], either now or heretofore inhabiting this
or any other part of our globe."[71]

If Atwater hoped that his article would move the antiquarian conversation forward and establish him as an authority, he experienced disappointment almost immediately. Atwater's empirically based conclusions were
contradicted within the same volume of *Transactions* by the New York physician and naturalist Samuel Latham Mitchill, who concluded, on the basis
of the same empirical standard, that mound builders were Malay. Mitchill
wrote that a Mr. Gratz of Glasgow, Kentucky, had sent him specimens of
cloth taken from the wrappings of a mummy found in Mammoth Cave.
The fabric found on the mummies had "a perfect resemblance to the fab-
ricks of the Sandwich, the Caroline, and the Fegee islands." This Mitchill
determined after examining the fabric sent by Gratz and examples brought
to him by sailors returning from the Pacific. They showed "marks of a
similar state of the arts, and point[ed] strongly to a sameness of origin in
the respective people that prepared them." The "similitude" of the fabric
led Mitchill to argue "that colonies of Australians, or Malays, landed in
North America, and penetrated across the continent, to the region lying
between the Great Lakes and the Gulph of Mexico. There they resided, and
constructed the fortifications, mounds, and other ancient structures." They
were later overtaken by "the more warlike and ferocious hordes that
entered our hemisphere from the northeast of Asia." These "hordes" conquered and expelled the Malay mound builders to Central and South
America.[72]

Atwater's article and the whole of the *Archaeologia Americana* did not
receive the response that he and the Antiquarian Society might have hoped
for—very few magazines and newspapers reviewed the publication. Moreover, Atwater's article was singled out for lengthy criticism by an anonymous review (later revealed to be C. S. Rafinesque, enigmatic professor
of natural history at Transylvania University) in the *Western Review*. In it
Rafinesque obliquely accused Atwater of borrowing without attribution the
work and opinions of Clifford as well as other antiquarians; he nitpicked
Atwater's measurements and his engravings; most brazenly, he disparaged
Atwater's prose style and corrected his grammar.[73] Atwater responded to
this review with a scorched-earth campaign against Rafinesque that
included damning letters to Thomas, Samuel L. Mitchill, Benjamin Silliman, and Transylvania University president Horace Holley. In one of them
Atwater promised that he would "take care, that [Rafinesque's] true name,

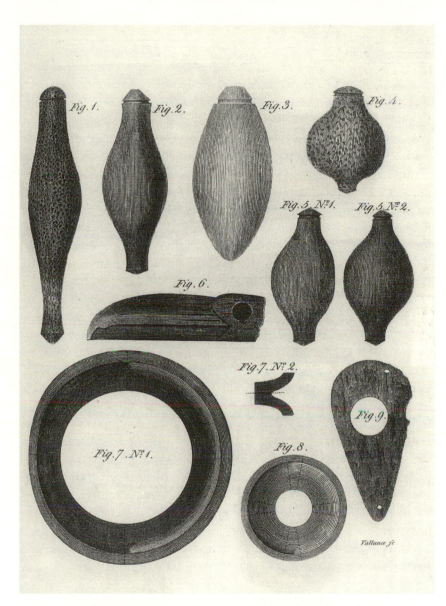

Figure 9. "Engraving of American antiquities by John Vallance." From Winthrop Sargent and Benjamin Smith Barton, *Papers relative to Certain American antiquities* (Philadelphia, 1796). This plate depicts some of the excavated objects sent east from the Ohio Valley and described in Sargent and Barton's text. Courtesy The Huntington Library.

real character, and private history shall be well understood," and he worked
hard to prejudice those in the antiquarian and natural history community
against Rafinesque. (Atwater did not have to work especially hard. Rafinesque was disliked by many members of the American natural history community, possessing few if any advocates when his behavior got him in
trouble.) To Thomas, Atwater complained of Rafinesque as "abusive . . .
self conceited, overbearing, and hateful" and claimed that Rafinesque was
demanding publication of his antiquarian writings as a appendix to *Archaeologia America.*[74] Atwater's efforts proved successful; he built on Rafinesque's already tarnished reputation among naturalists, and Rafinesque's
writings only once more appeared in any of the leading scientific journals.[75]
But the antiquarian controversies and a dispute over his royalties proved
too much for Atwater; within a year of the article's publication, he
informed Thomas that he was resigning his position as Ohio counselor to
the society and withdrawing from all antiquarian and geologic research.

Atwater's combustible personality and his rapid departure from antiquarian studies militated against his invocation of empiricism and his reliance on artifacts in dramatically changing the predominant antiquarian
method. Though seemingly more reliant on artifacts than before, more
demanding of precise measurements, and less willing to trust secondhand
testimony, most antiquarians continued to combine empiricism and speculation, artifact and conjecture about the authorship of the mounds. Atwater's most enduring contribution to antiquities research was his eventual
deposition of many of his objects discussed in his essay with the Antiquarian Society, a move which helped to establish it as a viable organization and
likely the center of antiquarian studies in the 1820s. Its members established
contacts with antiquarians around the world, seeking information from
likeminded individuals and institutions with which to determine probable
links between ancient European and Asian peoples and those of ancient
North America. Descriptions and images of artifacts they possessed were
sent abroad. In return, the society received drawings, maps, and descriptions of artifacts and mounds from Germany, Scotland, France, Scandina-
via, British India, the Pacific Islands, and Central America.[76] With them,
members proceeded much as had Atwater. They drew parallels between
contemporary "primitive" cultures or the remains of ancient societies and
the people who they suspected built the mounds.[77] Frequently, the analogies
or parallels they drew between cultures blurred from similarity into homol-
ogy; the mound builders not only exhibited similar traits to present or past

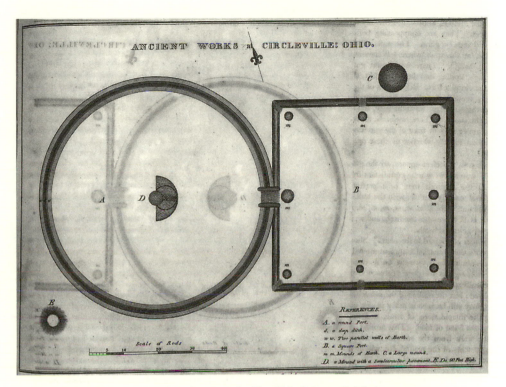

Figure 10. "Ancient Works at Circleville, Ohio." From Caleb Atwater, "Description of the Antiquities Discovered in the State of Ohio and other Western States," *Archaeologia Americana: Transactions and Collections of the American Antiquarian Society* 1 (Worcester, Mass., 1820). Courtesy The Huntington Library.

societies, they were the same people.[78] Ironically, the probabilistic method employed by American antiquarians in concert with their foreign contacts admitted more possible links than it eliminated. Antiquarian "truth" then became inseparable from personal discernment—a matter less about certainty than about individual choice.

The editors of American scientific journals, caught in the antiquarian crossfire coming from the Ohio Valley, scaled back on publishing antiquarian articles in the early 1820s. Of those that did make it into print, editors appear to have expected stricter evidentiary standards than personal whim. If an older style of antiquarian writing comprised description followed by conjectures (often enough just conjectures), then the newer form confined itself to what could be known with accuracy. Antiquarian articles published in scientific journals after 1820 were more cautious, restricting themselves to measurement almost exclusively. One of the few antiquarian articles published in the *American Journal of Science* described a mound excavated in Virginia. After giving precise measurements and a description of its form, the author refused to offer more. He conceded that the mounds were used sometimes as "repositories for the dead," citing as evidence the decayed bones he had located. "Otherwise we have no certain data; no historical facts to guide us in our enquiries into this subject . . . All we know of them is derived from a very few obvious facts, the rest is speculation drawn from slight probability."[79] Such epistemological caution characterized a distinction that editors began to draw between antiquarian studies and that which would be considered science.

Though the subject disappeared from scientific journals, articles and books about antiquities flourished during the 1820s and into the 1830s. Largely uncontested by an antiquarian community that had quit, died, or no longer wished to participate, texts that dealt with ancient America began to acquire breathless, even fantastical characteristics that earlier antiquarian writings lacked. John Haywood, the former attorney general of North Carolina, who relocated to Tennessee, wrote *The Natural and Aboriginal History of Tennessee* in 1823, drawing heavily from the writings of Atwater and Clifford. But in his chapters that concerned the ancient history of the region Haywood included myriad and unverifiable accounts of individuals excavating relics, discovering coins, and positing their own theories as to what these objects were and what they meant. Whereas Haywood played fast and loose with evidence, Clifford and Atwater were careful with facts. They ensured that readers understood that ancient, Indian, and European artifacts indicated nonoverlapping period of inhabitation or exploration of the region. Haywood and those individuals he included in his *History* collapsed these distinctions: the discovery of Roman coin was not a hoax or evidence that Romans could have visited North America after the mounds were built but "proof" that the Lost Tribes of Israel had visited or settled in North America.[80]

The popular antiquarian literature that flourished in the 1820s and 1830s resembled in form if not content the more empirically grounded antiquarian writings by compiling references among similar works to reinforce their truth claims. But authors embellished artifact finds to distinguish their books. In the place of scientific caution they filled in the gaps between data and desire. William Pidgeon, in word and image, depicted epic battles between the mound builders and the Indian "hordes." Pidegon wrote of an interlocutor, Dee-coo-dah, the last of the Elk Nation, who told him of North America's ancient past and the Elk's history of mound building.[81]

Josiah Priest's wildly popular *American Antiquities and Discoveries in the West* gathered evidence to support visitations from ancient Egyptians, Greeks, and Romans, among dozens of other groups. Edmund Flagg and Ira Hill saw evidence of multiple immigrations and settlements by ancient Phoenicians.[82] And Constantin Rafinesque described North American colonization by the Atalans and Cutan people, who were later expelled by the more savage Iztacans.[83] In the hands of these authors, North America looked less like a New World and more an extension of the Old.

Novelists and lecturers capitalized on the early republican interest in topics antiquarian. Cornelius Matthews wrote of the "behemoth," a mastodon that terrorized the ancient population of North America, forcing them to build mounds and walled cities to protect themselves.[84] Montrose Wilson Dickeson, a Philadelphia physician and antiquarian, profited from his successful excavations in the Mississippi Valley by offering public lectures on American antiquities. Later Dickeson would commission and travel the country with a 320-foot-long moving panorama depicting mounds from Ohio to Mississippi, the work painted by the Irish émigré artist J. Egan.[85]

Against this backdrop of romanticized tales, however, a desire for a more precise method persisted. The American historian William H. Prescott thanked Thaddeus Mason Harris after reading his unpublished "Researches into the Origin of the Indigines of North and South America." "Your hypothesis of a primitive population from Malay stock," Prescott wrote, "will not be easily disproved, now that the traces of this population are so completely swept away." But Prescott was uneasy: "For the same reason, I should suppose it would be difficult to satisfactorily establish it." Prescott appreciated reading the "Researches" but thought it of little use. It "embraces a discipline, indeed, somewhat foreign to my proposed subject, in which I shall confine myself to what is actually known"—historical facts. Harris's "inquiries necessarily extend from what is known into the region of speculation."[86] Prescott aligned himself with a growing number who thought that speculative antiquarian study had run its course. Scholars such as Prescott as well as many others were willing to wait for new approaches

ANCIENT AMERICAN BATTLE-MOUND.

(See Note, page 29.)

Figure 11. "Ancient American Battle-Mound," frontispiece to William Pidgeon, *Traditions of De-coo-dah: and Antiquarian Researches* (New York, 1853). Courtesy The Huntington Library.

to the ancient past that would reveal less debatable findings. Through the first decades of the nineteenth century, a reluctance to engage in speculation and conjecture characterized individuals who wised to distinguish themselves from an equally powerful and more popular approach to the young nation's ancient past. But speculative antiquarian stories persisted, even flourished. As one group of antiquarians became increasingly silent on the matter, waiting for more precise information, another group filled in the space they left open. The theories generated by those digging in the western mounds increased in volume and prominence now that fewer and fewer voices were available to contradict them.

Consequently, to understand the early republican interest in antiquities, it is essential to understand the complicated rules of evidence. Antiquarian truth existed on a continuum, the scientifically inclined adhering to the most stringent rules, those heirs of treasure-hunting traditions the most relaxed. Anxieties over the cyclical nature of social development faded to more hopeful aspirations of universal progress as the founding generation, those most empirically-inclined, gave way to the more imaginative inheritors; with them vanished concerns over climate-induced degeneration. Although the different constituencies disagreed over methodology and particulars, the early republican interest in antiquities played a starring role in an emerging and powerful version of history, a vision captured in the frontispiece to the Smithsonian Institution's first publication, *Ancient Monuments of the Mississippi Valley*. The 1848 volume is an extensive investigation of all known mounds, surveyed and classified by apparent use as well as artifacts and prevailing theories as to their construction and authorship. Edited by the institution's first secretary, Joseph Henry, the volume is credited by many contemporary scholars as the beginnings of American professional archaeology. In it, the Native American's role in an emerging and powerful version of American history is codified and captured. No longer players in their writing of their own history they would be at the pushed very edge of the frame, to the margins of historical consciousness. The Indians were once the conquerors of the moundbuilders but now they were vanquished; the aboriginal period of American history was over. Early republican America built its version of itself not on scattered remains and artifacts of those whom it viewed as barbarous and savage; rather, it fashioned an exciting and fictional history for itself on the ruins of a more mysterious and more heroic foundation.

Figure 12. "Ancient Works, Marietta, Ohio," frontispiece to E. G. Squier and E. H. Davis, *Ancient Monuments of the Mississippi Valley: Comprising the Results of Extensive Original Surveys and Explorations* (Washington, D.C., 1848). Courtesy The Huntington Library.

Chapter 4

Disciplining the Democracy of Facts:
A Theology of Nature

In September 1823 Edward Hitchcock, a newly ordained Congregational minister and later one of America's leading geologists, addressed the recently organized Lyceum of Natural History in Pittsfield, Massachusetts. To this audience of natural history enthusiasts Hitchcock offered words of encouragement and support, hoping to bolster the lyceum's fragile prospects for success. Like other natural history advocates since the American Revolution, Hitchcock stressed natural history's benefits to the individual and the nation. His talk emphasized the intellectual and social improvements the student of nature could expect. He stressed natural history's potential to refine morals and keep the young away from vice. Excursions into the natural world, he promised, would invigorate the sedentary body and refresh the distracted mind. Natural history tends "to increase, in its votaries, a love of country," he argued. The landscapes explored by one versed in it "will always be dearer to us than any other fields, any other vallies, or any other mountains." He cited commercial benefits, adding, "Were there time, I might exhibit the numerous ascessions that are often made to a nation's wealth, strength and glory, through the agency of natural history." But Hitchcock had other topics to cover and moved to what he thought the most important result of scientific study.[1]

Natural history, he wrote, will "unfold to the Christian, a minute and thorough knowledge of the works of his heavenly Father, and disclose ten thousand new and unthought of beauties and glories." Hitchcock thought that natural history students "can scarcely avoid inhaling a portion of that warm and holy incense, which forever rises toward heaven from the altar of nature." Nor could they "refuse to join in that ceaseless song, which is chanted by creation in full concert, without a discordant note, to the praise of Jehovah." For Hitchcock and many of the period's natural historians, the individual, social, and economic benefits of natural history study walked hand in hand with the religious. Like others, he blurred the sacred and the scientific. Hitchcock began his address with an Old Testament story of King Solomon's wisdom, which "consisted in a knowledge of natural history." Just as the patriarch met with "mementos" of the "perfections of God" through the study of natural works, so would contemporary Americans find "fresh fuel to feed the flame of devotion" as they observed the natural world. To study nature using natural historical methods, Hitchcock argued, was to examine the very essence of God.[2]

Hitchcock advocated more than a casual appreciation of God's hand in the natural order; he was promoting serious and careful study of natural systems not as knowledge qua knowledge but an inducement to examine something grander, something more evanescent, something transcendent. Hitchcock saw opportunities for a new awareness of the divine intelligence to be accomplished through the collective project of science. Knowledge of nature and knowledge of the God were inseparable; while it was imperative to possess a "particular acquaintance with the minutest parts of creation" to see God's hand in the order of nature, even the untutored and the unscientific would already be aware of that relationship. Hitchcock added that it would be impossible to observe nature carefully and "not be struck with obvious marks of divine wisdom, power and goodness." However, Hitchcock proposed an examination that went beyond the "Creators' works one by one," a mere collection of natural facts. He advocated the study of nature's "mechanism, relation and object." What "makes the deepest and most abiding impression on the memory and the heart" are the affinities between animals and plants, rocks and mountains, not rocks or animals in isolation. The generalist "whose eye takes in at once the heavens and the earth has a confused and indefinite sense of magnificence, variety and beauty," Hitchcock argued. But the individual possessed of a systematic understanding, the individual "who examines the physiology of an individual animal, or plant, is astonished and delighted at the marks of contrivance, design and benevolence he discovers." A sophisticated and careful study of natural objects, their systematic arrangement, their interconnections, and their relationship would edify and excite the soul.[3] Within Hitchcock's blend of natural history and theology lay the foundation for a transition from an observation-and fact-based endeavor to a pattern-driven practice of organizing natural knowledge. What Hitchcock and those like him were describing was an admixture of natural history and nondenominational Protestant theology that played a positive role in reining in and tempering the excesses and enthusiasm within the democracy of facts. The devotional approach to natural history Hitchcock traced established limits and boundaries regarding hard-to-believe natural facts and phenomena; instead of treating the truths about nature as uncertain or provisional, possibly or probably true unless an isolated fact militated against it, Hitchcock stressed order, established patterns, and fixity. Hitchcock's nature behaved according to laws, patterns established by God but available for study and appreciation by humans

Hitchcock's fusion of Protestant Christianity and natural history is characteristic of the much natural historical writing during the period. This union, often termed "natural theology," can be found to varying degrees in many early republic natural history texts. Yet as much as historians know about early republic religious culture—denominational politics and enthusiastic revivals in particular—they know less about American natural theology, its logic, and its uses. One reason may be that natural theology, in the strictest sense, is based on the exercise of natural reason alone, without reference to revelation. Certainly present in early republic America, natural theology was not a major theological tradition. A theology of nature, however, better describes the cluster of theological and scientific beliefs about the meaning of the natural world and God's relationship to it.[4] Early republic Americans were avid creators and consumers of a theology of nature, an approach that explained and explicated the natural world through divine creation and design, an easily embraceable and fluid discourse that offered a safe religious meeting ground for all Americans in times of denominational strife.[5] While white Americans might argue over doctrinal and denominational matters—which they did vigorously and vociferously in the early republic—they seemed to agree about the devotional value of nature to demonstrate divine magnificence and the wisdom of the created order. Within this theology of nature are perspectives less understood that reveal how Americans treated natural history and religion; how this relationship promoted the spread of scientific ideas through American culture; and how the theology of nature fostered the authority of naturalists by working to replace a natural history epistemology more welcoming of patterns, more willing to pursue system-building, and more comfortable with expertise and the concept of an expert.

The theology of nature did not teach strict Christian doctrine. Instead, it established the affective and emotional parameters through which scientific findings could be, and should be, understood and made comprehensible. The theology of nature added emotional depth to the factual descriptions of animals, plants, and natural phenomena in natural history writings. It asserted that wonder, awe, appreciation, and gratitude were the proper emotional responses to nature, praise due God for the fascinating, interesting, and marvelous natural world creations. The theology of nature taught reverential responses as well as devotional exercises. If natural history was an epistemology and method that suggested how to examine, how to categorize, and how to arrange and bring order to nature, the theology of nature taught Americans how to respond; it suggested how people should feel. In word and image, this theology established the contours of affective response and provided the emotional rhetoric as well as a gestural vocabulary with which Americans shaped and practiced a devotional approach to the natural world.

The theology of nature was forged in print. It taught natural history and nondenominational theology in equal measure through a combination of text and image. Yet the works that detail this theology have received less attention from historians than they deserve One reason may be that the leading scientific journals of the early republic generally avoided outright references to God, religion, or design; as a result, the theology of nature has escaped the strictest historians of science. For example, the pages of Philadelphia's *Transactions of the American Philosophical Society*, Boston's *Memoirs of the American Academy of Arts and Science*, New York's *Medical Repository*, Philadelphia's *Medical and Physical Journal*, and New Haven's *American Journal of Science* are largely devoid of theological reasoning or references to the divine. This absence of religious reasoning has led historians to conclude that science and religion of the period were separate enterprises; natural theology they leave to others scholars.[6] While a few American naturalists may have considered science a secular pursuit, evidence suggests that these journals did not include discussions of religion because their intended audience might have found it jarring or off-putting. The *Transactions of the American Philosophical Society*, the *Memoirs of the American Academy of Arts and Sciences*, and the *American Journal of Science*, long considered barometers of scientific progress, were also the journals aimed at an international audience, at least in part. Hoping to supersede religious conflicts, these organizations avoided as much as possible any references to religion or religious reasoning.[7] Those journals aimed at an American audience, however, *Medical Repository* and *American Journal of Science*, were more willing to admit religious explanations into their pages, though they did so infrequently. These remained largely sober and serious publications.

The theology of nature in print is underappreciated because it blends genres and refuses to fit into recognizable, established literary categories. Invocations of the theology of nature are ubiquitous and they can be found seemingly everywhere in early republic print culture, from offhand remarks about science as the handmaid to religion to explicit treatments of science as illuminating evidences of God's handiwork. However, they can be found most explicitly in works of natural history and science aimed at a wider audience than naturalists. This literature took many forms: textbooks, the Harper publishing house's famous "Peter Parley" series, encyclopedias, periodical articles, sermon collections, botanical guides, and devotional calendars, to name just a few.[8] Works like these are by no means strictly natural history. At the same time, they cannot be considered theology, either. A prime example is the three-volume work by Henri Bernadin de Saint-Pierre, *Studies of Nature*. Benjamin Smith Barton edited and translated from the French a Philadelphia edition published in 1808. The second and third volumes contain literary pieces on history and literature; the first is devoted to science and religion. The books contain the most current information on zoology, ornithology, ichthyology, botany, and other natural history subjects, setting this information within a diffuse theological framework. The first volume is arranged according to the Linnaean classificatory rules and provides sketches and plates. Extensive footnotes by Barton provide explanatory elaboration for an American audience possessing a less sophisticated understanding of natural history, as well as adaptations to make the text attuned to the particulars of American nature. Fact-based and containing little systematic conjecture, this work reinforced prevailing natural history techniques and avoided speculation. Theology of nature authors viewed conjecture and systems in terms similar to American naturalists: to be avoided because it was presumptuous to define nature.[9]

If naturalists considered conjecture and system the result of poor methodology, theology of nature authors considered speculation an unwarranted use of human reason, one that constricted divine wisdom. Systems and theories "within which we circumscribe the Supreme Power," Saint-

Pierre wrote, "far from determining its bounds, only mark the limits of human genius." He added that systems acted the "part of the tyrant of Sicily who fitted the unhappy traveler to his bed of iron: he violently stretched, to the length of the bed, the limbs of those who were shorter, and cut short the limbs of those who were longer." Briefly, he suggested, systems fit unimaginable natural complexity into arrangements humans could understand, whether they were correct or not. "When so many trivial laws of Nature are, under our very eyes, unknown, or misunderstood," Saint-Pierre continued, "how dare we presume to assign those which regulate the course of the stars, and which embrace the immensity of the Universe?" He excoriated "Algebraists," "Geometricians," and "Chymists" for their use of "methods and systems." The "revolutions which their opinions, though intolerant in the extreme, undergo in every age" were evidence that a total explanation of nature was a foolhardy exercise. Instead, Saint-Pierre wished the observer of nature to "confine [oneself] to notions the most universally admitted, and supported by the highest authority." These notions or "natural truths" are those "with which every peasant is acquainted."[10] These simple truths were that God created the universe and arranged it according to divine will because its complexity was too vast for humans to understand or to explain.

Instead of elaborate scientific systems that obscured more than they illuminated, Saint-Pierre advocated an acceptance and celebration of human intellectual limitation, sentiments that resonated with the anti-intellectualism associated with the democracy of facts. He proposed a simple, almost childlike approach to nature. "Nature is of unbounded extent, and I am a human being, limited on every side. Not only her general History, but that of the smallest plant, far transcends my highest powers." He wrote that his advocacy of explanatory resignation should not be regarded as a lack of effort but that the order of the universe was too vast to understand. Instead of frustration, one should celebrate the mysteries of the natural world, each a window into the magnificence of the Godhead. There was purpose to natural complexity, Saint-Pierre reasoned: "It is from a regard to our happiness that [Nature] has concealed from us the laws of her Omnipotence." It would not be "possible for a being so feeble as Man to embrace infinite space" without forcing it to suffer. Consequently, ignorance of the master design but reverence for the particulars was what God intended. Humans could demonstrate devotion in the acts of observation and examination. Moments that resulted in awe and wonder are the "the emanations from her beneficence."[11] Since the construction of elaborate intellectual architectures tended to befuddle, to confuse, and ultimately to misrepresent nature, Saint-Pierre advocated observation and description, acts that had the double benefit of producing correct natural history and the right emotional tenor through which viewing nature would be a devotional experience.

A restriction of human reason and celebration of simple observation are predominant themes that run through natural theology literature. Authors frequently provided engraved images to represent and to reinforce this predominant message. In Thaddeus Mason Harris's *Natural History of the Bible*, the reader is presented with an idealized scene of the Garden of Eden. Adam is portrayed at the moment of naming, fulfilling a divine mandate to observe and to identify all animated nature.[12] This image validates simple descriptive natural history and draws a parallel between Adam's example and current natural history practice. The text offers a list of natural history objects mentioned in the Bible. Plants, animals, and phenomena named in the various books are explained in modern natural history language. "The Book of Nature and Revelation equally elevate our conceptions and incite our piety," Harris observed. Nature and revealed religion "mutually illustrate each other; they have an equal claim to our regard, for they are both written by the finger of *the one eternal incomprehensible GOD*." Though human striving might wish to understand nature's design, it was beyond human capacity to know. The theology of nature suggested that it was better to emulate Adam performing descriptive tasks than attempt to know something outside the bounds of human intelligence; better to wonder at nature than circumscribe it with meager human attempts.[13]

The frontispiece from Saint-Pierre's *Studies of Nature* depicts wonder and awe at the majesty of divine creation and introduces the theme of experience instructing youth. The aged figure offers to the children the entire landscape of nature in its grandeur. In the theology of nature, instructing youth in awe and wonder was essential to inculcating the proper blend of learning and reverence. More than one author argued that parents should aim "to connect [children] with the thoughts of God so evidently and indissolubly" that even as adults they "must live under an habitual sense of the presence of God, and act up to his pleasure and commandments, even amidst his worldly occupations."[14] One of the most important subjects is the ability to "make observations upon the various causes of Nature," skills that will "rouse [children's] imagination, and fire their

Figure 13. Frontispiece to Thaddeus Mason Harris, *The Natural History of the Bible: or a Description of All the Beasts, Birds, Fishes, Insects, Reptiles, Trees, Plants, Metals, Precious Stones, &c. Mentioned in the Sacred Scriptures. Collected by the best Authorities, and Alphabetically Arranged* (Boston, 1793). Courtesy The Huntington Library.

bosoms to noble pursuits."[15] Once implanted, natural history in a religious context would provide an appreciation for the divine miracle of creation throughout life. The theology of nature directed toward young people can be found in untold numbers of books and articles across various genres, including didactic conversations between parents and children about nature, lengthy descriptions of individual seasons and observations of the daily changes, sermons about the goals of various natural history disciplines, and calendars of devotions. Divergent in the particulars, these works united over the importance of educating young people in the divine origin of nature and implanting in them a reverence for it.[16]

These themes have not gone unnoticed in the historiography of the early republic. Historians of nineteenth-century American culture have studied the creation of an American sublime intimately connected to the American landscape. An emotional, aesthetic, and religious response inherited from Europe and adapted to America, histories of the sublime are sensitive to change over time and issues of nationalism, gender, class, politics, and technology. Focusing on natural wonders such as Virginia's Natural Bridge and New York's Niagara Falls, these histories demonstrate how such sites became invested with religious overtones by pilgrims, overtones carried into print and image. Human figures are often shown below or atop enormous natural features, the juxtaposition of human scale and grand expanse creating appreciation for the enormity of the divine intellect.[17] Yet the sublime, by definition, is an emotional and intellectual response to an object and experience out of the ordinary, at which the viewer is simultaneously awed and terrified.[18] While important to cultivating an appreciation of the immensity of God and the lack of importance of humans, sublime experiences were moments of rupture. They were not part of daily routine. Indeed, most early republican sublime sites were often great distances from settlements, their inaccessibility enhanced since leisure travel was a luxury not available to the majority of Americans. The sublime, consequently, was neither a common nor a sustainable category through which communion with the divine could be established. Natural theology writers sought to inculcate an easier relationship with the natural world. They proposed that in the quotidian aspects of the natural world could be found the evidences of the divine intellect necessary for proper devotion.

Perhaps the most enduring theme in the theology of nature is that every aspect of the natural world—each flower, each animal, each rock—contained an imprint of God and an entry-point into contemplation of the

Figure 14. Frontispiece to Bernardin de Saint-Pierre, *Studies of Nature* (Philadelphia, 1808). Courtesy The Huntington Library.

divine. It would be impossible to walk outside and not find one. "Let us adore God in his wonderful works," one writer implored, and "admire his power and wisdom in each of his creatures." Rather than waiting for moments of revelation to appear or the sublime to occur, the theology of nature suggested a regular and constant relationship to nature. "In every season of the year, his goodness, and tender mercies towards every being on earth" are revealed, one author wrote. The result of careful attention to the minute and dramatic seasonal changes "makes us not only happy but virtuous; for if we have God and his works continually in our sight, with what love and veneration shall we not be penetrated! with what confidence shall we not resign ourselves to him! with what zeal and transport shall we not sing his praise!"[19]

The theology of nature stressed the ease with which every American could approach the natural world. "Nature offers to all her children," an author wrote, "the first, the most innocent, the least expensive, and most universal of all pleasures." This author stressed that nature study was available to all members of society, regardless of economic wherewithal or social standing. It would be impossible not to encounter pleasure "in the contemplation of nature . . .the poor as well as the rich may indulge in it." The low cost of nature appreciation, ironically, "is what lessens its value." Americans were "foolish" not to prize what all could share; "if we were reasonable, nothing should give more value to a blessing than the thought that it makes the happiness of our fellow-creatures, as well as our own." Authors contrasted the pleasures received from nature with the competitive world of commerce, enticing Americans away from the marketplace and the pursuit of gain. One author wrote, "How trifling and vain are those far-fetched magnificent amusements which the rich obtain with so much trouble and expense, which leave a certain void in the soul, and always end in ennui and disgust! Whereas nature, rich and beneficent, presents us continually with new objects." The artificiality of art and markets are pleasures "of short duration, and vanish like a dream, the charms and illusions of which are lost at the moment of waking. But the pleasures of contemplating the works of God, are solid and lasting, because they open to us an inexhaustible source of new delights." The sky, the earth "enamelled with flowers," bird songs, "the various landscapes and prospects one more delightful than another" promise to "furnish us with new subjects of satisfaction and joy." If Americans were insensible to the beauties of nature, "it is certainly our own fault; it is because we behold the works of nature with an inattentive and indifferent eye." But with a proper balance of scientific study and placement within the divine orientation, nature would provide a continual source of intellectual enjoyment and spiritual fulfillment.[20]

The frontispiece to *Beauties of Nature Delineated* shows this appreciation in practice. The female figure exemplifies the theology of nature. She is surrounded by nature and poised contemplatively, the multitude of natural forms rendered into peaceful order for an appreciation of daily and seasonal rhythms. "On whatever part of the creation we turn our eyes we every where find something, which intersects either our sense, our imagination, or our reason," the author wrote. All of nature is formed "to afford us numberless pleasing objects . . . our love of variety is constantly excited and constantly gratified." The daily practice of nature contemplation leads to an interior state of humility—nature's infinite variety and magnitude chastening even the hardest heart. Not just enormous mountains or natural wonders but "even the smallest worm, a leaf, a grain of sand, present us with objects of admiration." Study of the everyday rhythms of the natural world would reward the contemplator. One author summarized, "We shall find that there is no satisfaction more heartfelt, or more lasting, or more conformable to human nature, than the calm pleasures which the contemplation of the works of God affords."[21] Tranquil contemplation of nature was as much a means of devotional reverence as it was an approach to the study of the natural world. Americans were constantly reminded of this message by print culture and the natural world around them.

In his address to the Pittsfield Lyceum, Edward Hitchcock employed theology of nature rhetoric and logic. He argued for natural history as a set of powerful skills and analytical techniques that allow its users to consider and to understand the divine in infinite new ways. However, Hitchcock also emphasized the vastness of creation and stressed the relationships between various objects within nature. Devotional feelings, Hitchcock admitted, were not the "infallible concomitant of zeal in natural history." Experience showed that a man may "traverse the whole globe and to spend his whole life among the works of God that are sublimely great or elegantly little, and yet his icy heart never feel one thrill of devotion, nor any sense of the Divine Presence or Goodness." These individuals were "Uzziahs in the temple of nature—unconsecrated priests" to whom there "cleaves a moral leprosy"; such examples "do not evince that the study of nature's works tends to foster skepticism and pride," he wrote. Rather, these people demonstrate "the strength of prejudice, the power of selfishness, and the obduracy of

Figure 15. Frontispiece to Christoph Christian Sturm, *The Beauties of Nature Delineated; or, Philosophical and Pious Contemplations on the Works of Nature, and the Seasons of the Year. Selected from Sturm's Reflections by the Rev. Thaddeus M. Harris* (Charlestown, 1800). Courtesy The Huntington Library.

the human heart."[22] Even so, Hitchcock considered God-less natural history
a threat. To counter free-thought and rationalist natural historians, Hitchcock shifted the emphasis of the theology of nature away from an examination of single objects to contemplate, study, and comprehend the complex
relationships in nature. More radically than those authors who celebrated
a naive appreciation of nature and the divine, Hitchcock pushed natural
history and the theology of nature to embrace conclusions based on invisible evidence, theoretical arguments, and reason-based conclusions. Hitchcock and those naturalist authors coming of age in the second and third
decades of the nineteenth century began to push natural history and the
theology of nature away from its embrace of the democracy of fact and
toward a theological approach to nature that resembled in practice and
prescription an empire of reason.

Hitchcock's writings also assumed a sophisticated audience, one familiar with scientific practices beyond natural history. He drew on natural
history, astronomy, and geometrical progression to make his points. To
explore the magnitude of creation, for example, Hitchcock invoked the
heavens and the planets. "This globe, amid the unnumbered world that fill
the universe, is but as a grain of sand on the sea shore: Yet we have reason
to believe that every portion of the universe is equally interesting with that
which we inhabit." Hitchcock estimated that roughly thirty thousand species of animals and over forty thousand species of plants had been discovered and described on the earth, "and in each individual animal, not to say
plant, are not much less than a million of parts." Hitchcock speculated that
the universe contained "2000 millions of habitable worlds." He suggested
that one "take now an anatomical survey of an individual animal or plant
and proceed to dissect in imagination the countless millions found on this
globe." Imagine another world containing an equal number of organized
beings. "Advance thus from world to world until you have reached the last
of the 2000 millions! And after all this is done, recollect that you have just
entered the threshold of creation! What imagination does not sink under
an effort so mighty, and feel an overpowering sense of the wisdom and
glory of Jehovah!"[23] Awed by the immensity of contemplating the nearly
infinite, Hitchcock urged his listeners to consider the association between
objects and from it to conclude that divine intelligence, not chance, had
designed this world and the worlds beyond.

Hitchcock's reliance on speculative conclusions and emphasis on connections within nature represent a subtle but important shift in the use of

the theology of nature to explain and justify natural history and the maturation of the practices with which it shared so much. Hitchcock was part of
a second generation of natural historians practicing after the Revolution, a
crop of naturalists less anxious about their tenuous hold on authority in
society and more confident in their ability to interpret and make sense of
the natural world. His efforts to push the discipline of natural history and
the public's understanding of it toward a systematic comprehension of the
natural world, one in which it was possible to understand cause and effect,
was indicative of a much larger movement among his cohort of naturalists.
Hitchcock thought that enough facts had been collected to sustain attempts
at drawing conclusions about nature in contrast to naturalists practicing
after the Revolution.

Yet Hitchcock and others like him needed to demonstrate that the
methods he espoused and the conclusions he offered were not unwarranted
impositions of human reason onto divine order; nor did the theorizing he
advocated contradict the factual foundation of natural history. Hitchcock's
efforts to accomplish this goal are observable in his determined campaign
to explain and validate geology and geological reasoning. Some early
national Americans deemed the enterprise of geology intellectually foreign,
religiously suspect in the least, heretical at worst. Aware of the controversies
surrounding geology, Hitchcock suggested to the lyceum audience that
geology was benign, nothing more than the projection onto the past of
present, observable, and verifiable natural processes and phenomena. Consequently, geology and geological reasoning could not be heretical.[24]

Still, Hitchcock noted that the history of geological methods and theories was far from august and failed to inspire confidence, littered as it was
with abandoned theories and systems. "The marked extravagance of former
theories of the earth adopted by geologists," Hitchcock wrote, "have produced a strong prejudice against every thing on the same subject." Critics
of geology cited the endless and confusing debates between Neptunists
(those who thought water shaped geologic features), Vulcanists (those who
thought the prime agent in geologic change was volcanic activity), and Cat-
astrophists (those who argued for sudden, short-lived, violent episodes) as
the first among many reasons to ignore geology particularly and theoretical
approaches to understanding nature generally. Yet Hitchcock carefully distinguished himself from these former theorists and their extravagances by
enlisting familiar antitheoretical natural history arguments and rhetoric.
Unlike past individuals, Hitchcock and geologists who shared his approach

were "men of a very different stamp—men whose grand object is the collection of facts, and who are extremely cautious of hypothesis; adopting none, except such as seem absolutely necessary to explain appearances." The hypothesis that Hitchcock advocated, one he believed the evidence supported, was that the creation of the physical earth was "obviously a slow process, a work of much time, frequently suspended and renewed, and could not possibly have resulted form a catastrophe so violent and transitory as the Noachian deluge" alone. In adopting this stance, Hitchcock was aligning himself with the uniformitarian school of imperceptivity slow geological change.

Hitchcock did not cite the "original and regular strata constituting the crust of the globe" when making his case for his theoretical conclusions, as did most prevailing explanations for geology. Instead he focused upon the evidence left by the processes at work: as he put it, "the accidents those strata have subsequently experienced, the abrasion and excavation of their surface, and the dispersion of the fragments thence broken off and rounded by attrition." Hitchcock argued that the gradual deposition of dirt, sand, and rocks punctuated by sporadic episodes of violent upheaval determined almost all landforms on earth. He suggested that all Americans should become familiar with these natural processes. Personal observation with erosion or sandbars, for example, should convince Americans that the land was constantly changing, Hitchcock thought. Massive earthquakes and volcanoes proved that such change could happen rapidly and dramatically.

Hitchcock's address attempted to convince his listeners that geological reasoning was not a radical break with the fact-collecting epistemology of natural history but rather a logical extension of it, a next step. The uniformitarianism Hitchcock described fit well with an observation-based natural history.[25] Just as natural history in the democracy of fact relied on the quotidian observations of ordinary Americans, so Hitchcock's campaign for the acceptance of geology relied on similar democratic appeals. Everyone had witnessed the damage wrought by rogue water and floods, for example: the erosion, the deposition of sand and rocks in new locations, perhaps even the redirection in the course of a stream or river. Instead of averring that cataclysmic events explain the earth's features, uniformitarianism proposed thousands of small accretions and erosion. Canyons were the result of years of erosion; dunes were formed by years of windblown sand. Hitchcock's adoption of uniformitarianism did not preclude divine intervention or miracles, he noted, but it did distinguish him from other geologists who offered alternative systems to explain earth history in this period, and it made him one of the earliest American naturalists to adopt these new philosophies.

Hitchcock's geologic timeline necessitated a longer duration than the creation story put forth in Genesis, requiring thousands of years in contrast to the Bible's six days. Hitchcock answered critics by offering that one need not accept at face value the creation story. It was possible to read its language figuratively rather than literally. For those who have "adopted as unquestionable truth the common exposition of the first chapter of Genesis," Hitchcock wrote, his views "may seem the result of a hasty and dangerous criticism." Hitchcock admitted that a reconciliation between his proposed approach with "the Mosaic account is the problem the Christian geologist has to resolve."[26] Hitchcock calmed the potentially frayed nerves of his listeners by invoking themes of philosophical modesty and epistemological patience, an approach utilized by naturalists throughout the era and familiar to the general public. From an epistemological standpoint, seemingly irreconcilable facts would eventually be rendered coherent, once enough verifiable evidence was collected. In the case that Hitchcock was describing, if the Genesis account and geology appeared at odds or contradictory, this was the result of poor understandings of either geology or biblical interpretation, he reasoned. In the near or not too distant future, Hitchcock implied, human understanding would come to terms with the relationship between divine creation and the practices of geology and a systematic natural history.

Hitchcock attempted to demonstrate that geology was not a challenge to religious teachings by suggesting various approaches through which one could square new evidence from geology with the Mosaic account of creation. He offered his listener three theories then circulating in geological circles. The first, he admitted, "has met with the fewest advocates," at least among practicing geologists. It proposed that the "space between the creation and the deluge, being more than 1600 years, afforded sufficient time for the occurrence of all those changes and depositions we discover in the crust of the globe." The second theory suggested that "the periods of creation, called days by Moses, are not literal days of twenty four hours, but periods of indefinite and considerable length, during which the secondary rocks were deposited." This theory was determined by a figurative reading of the creation story, and Hitchcock cited other biblical passages where metaphorical language is used. Not wanting to abandon a literal interpretation, Hitchcock advocated a third theory. Many Christian geologists supposed that when the Genesis author described the "fundamental fact of the original formation of all things by the will of God," he did not write of the "long intermediate state" between that event and the six days when God "arranged the world we now inhabit." In short, God created the earth and all it contained in six sunrise-to-sunset days, as described in Genesis. What the author of the text did not happen to mention was the long time between the seventh day, when God rested, and the resumption of the text, which introduces the story of Eden. It was during this period that the organic remains found in rocks were deposited, later followed by violent earthquakes and floods that gave the earth its present appearance. How long that time span was, Hitchcock did not specify, but he suggested to his audience that it may have spanned thousands if not millions of years.[27]

Unsure of how this interpretation would be received, Hitchcock aligned himself with his former teacher and the most celebrated American naturalist of his day, Benjamin Silliman, a professor of chemistry at Yale College, who advocated a similar interpretation and approach to geology. In his lectures to Yale undergraduates and public audiences, Silliman neutralized and smoothed over the interpretive troubles between geology and Genesis by relying on the familiar theology of nature discourse. Silliman emphasized that he doubted neither geological facts nor biblical teachings. Moreover, he would be the last person to "force moral and religious topics into an unnatural association, with physical subjects." But Silliman considered that natural history existed in "an indissoluble connexion with the Deity." And in tracing the "secondary causes" displayed in nature, he believed that he was simultaneously studying the "First Cause," or God. Silliman continued that geology's primary object "is to trace the operation of the Creator's laws" in studying the "arrangement of the crust of the planet." Figured as a devotional exercise as much as an intellectual and scientific endeavor, geology could not possibly be heretical. Instead, to Silliman, Hitchcock, and geology advocates like them, the discipline presented a powerful tool through which to contemplate the divine. If in grandeur geology fell "short of astronomy, and what physical science does not," Silliman admitted, it had as its ultimate subject of study "the power and wisdom and sustaining energy, of the omnipotent Creator and Governor."[28] Silliman hoped to assure the American public that geology was not a heretical attack on the Christianity and the Bible but a window into the underlying structures of nature, the foundation laid by God, available for study by those who wished to know not only the history of the earth but the divine though a new lens of appreciation.[29] Silliman and Hitchcock, so confident that geology and religion were not antithetical, went so far as to entice potential students to study geology with religious incentives. The more one knew about earth history, they argued, the more one would understand God and the human place within the natural order: geology would assist the search for answers to existential questions.

Hitchcock's and Silliman's elision of a theology of nature and geology also allowed them to reassert the role of the naturalist and geologist as experts. But in contrast to prior generations who could offer only their credentials as naturalists and as elites in making a case for expertise, Hitchcock (and Silliman to a lesser extent) could argue for it from a position as expert in both geology and theology. Trained for the ministry as well as for natural history and geology, Hitchcock could offer assurance that geological study and the labors of naturalists were not infringing on established theology, just as he could explain from a position of authority that the empirical inquiries of natural history and geology were exercises in devotion as well as the accumulation of knowledge. Hitchcock was able to articulate a modified vision natural history and geology for the general public, one that overcame the tensions of elites versus the democracy of facts, and theorizing versus fact gathering. Instead of an empiricism that eschewed theorizing, a search for facts without a system in which to fit those facts, Hitchcock offered both: the incentive to discover facts and the system in which those facts would fit. Facts were facts that made sense with each other, he suggested, because they made sense as part of God's design. If the facts did not appear to jibe, it was because of human frailty, either in observation or in poor creation of the system, not because facts contradicted God's creation. According to Hitchcock, Americans could explore the natural world comfortable in the belief that their observations and acquired natural knowledge would lead them to a closer communion with God and safe in the conviction that their efforts would not lead them into apostasy, skepticism, or disbelief. They knew this because Hitchcock the naturalist, the man who understood nature on its own terms, and Hitchcock the minister, the man who understood scripture, told them so.

Not all Americans were persuaded by the arguments advanced by Hitchcock and Silliman, particularly theologians threatened by geologists posing as interpreters of scriptures. Yet opposition to geology is difficult to gauge. It appears that only a few voices in the United States, albeit strident ones, gave any sustained attention to the subject. This muted reaction to geology stands in contrast to that in the United Kingdom, where the controversies geology generated were more vibrantly debated in public discourse. Moses Stuart, professor of sacred literature at Andover Theological Seminary, attacked Hitchcock and Silliman for their reading of Genesis. Specifically, he directed his complaint at the use of geology instead of philology to interpret the Bible, not at geology as a methodology or practice. Stuart argued that the author of Genesis designed "to set forth the facts, that God was both the original and subsequent maker and disposer of all things in heaven and on earth; that he performed this great work in the period of six days." The "exegesis of some geologists interferes substantially with this instruction." While rocks may seem to admit of an ancient origin, Stuart was concerned that geologists' theory about their creation over thousands of years "annihilates the force of the appeal in the fourth commandment," that on the seventh day God rested. The intrusion of geologists into biblical interpretation, therefore, "becomes a serious matter." As illuminating as geology might appear, Stuart posed a vexing accusation to all geologists: "Why do you wish to interpret Scripture so as to make us skeptics?" Stuart's sensitivity and concern stemmed more from an undermining of traditional literary techniques to interpret the biblical text: "Where is the interpreter of Scripture to go for his maxims and rules in order to interpret an ancient writing? Is he to resort to recent science, in order to explain what was written some 4000 years ago?" All people "must see that this will never do; and therefore philology cannot concede the right of geology to put a meaning on the words of Moses."[30] Likewise, he was concerned that geology, unlikely to turn Hitchcock or Silliman into heretics, would not be understood by the majority of Americans. Stuart thought the subject too complicated and his countrymen too unsophisticated to understand its nuance. Instead of illuminating the sublime intricacies of divine order, geology would be misunderstood or misapplied, producing hordes of freethinkers and rationalists, or planting and sowing the seeds of doubt and skepticism. One need only look to the case of Thomas Cooper, the notorious agnostic, who was removed from the presidency of South Carolina College for his religious and political views, his skepticism, he admitted, fostered in part by his embrace and teaching of geology.[31]

These challenges aside, Hitchcock and Silliman helped to transform Americans' understanding of geology and natural history as a practice by recasting them as devotional exercises. Naturalists promoted a redefined practice aimed at experiencing wonder and awe as much as it was about categorizing nature. In this process, Hitchcock, Silliman, and other geologists prompted a shift in emphasis from contemplating a single object to an examination and search for the relationships between objects. Instead of individual rocks, for example, geology studied how rocks were formed and how landscapes shaped. This shift represented, however seemingly small, a transformation for natural history and the theology of nature, one that was welcomed and embraced by naturalists and the wider public. Natural history continued unabated and geology continued to attract adherents. The frequent reprinting of geology texts and broadsides advertising public geology lectures confirm that while some Americans may have been uncomfortable with some of the long-term implications of geology, that did not sway them from learning more about the investigation of earth history.[32]

Contrary to the prevailing historical arguments about geology and its place in challenging Protestant Christianity, the practice may have supported an orthodox interpretation of Genesis rather than undermining it. In the minds of many Americans, geology lent scientific and historical proof to Genesis rather than dismembered it, particularly in regard to evidence for the Noachian flood. The confirmation of an ancient global deluge "is sufficiently proved, by the vestiges left upon the globe, and geologists are generally agreed in admitting the fact," Silliman wrote. The introduction of scientific support for the flood's historicity more readily created an environment in which a literal interpretation was possible. The upshot was that geology propelled a literal reading of the book of Genesis, rather than the opposite.[33] While a more sophisticated and noisy opposition to geology did develop in the 1840s and 1850s, this opposition was gradual, beginning in earnest years after Silliman's and Hitchcock's propositions helped to harden literal interpretations of the Genesis account.

As an expansive and diffuse cluster of arguments and approaches to the natural world, the theology of nature worked to discipline the excesses in the democracy of facts. It was also powerful enough that it helped to propel changes in the way that ordinary Americans viewed natural history and geology. This it accomplished by neutralizing religious challenges to science through the revalorization of wonder and awe, and through prescribing a simple process to guide individuals in the investigation of individual facts, a process that moved from the contemplation of a single object to an appreciation of the intricate arrangements and underlying processes that composed the natural world. Theoretical and conjectural arguments, anath-

ema to the dry, fact-based epistemology American naturalists advocated in
the first decades of the republic, were reconfigured by this second generation of naturalists. Rather than pitting facts and naturalists against one
another in public forums, as was the design in the democracy of facts, these
naturalists aimed for a natural history practice that fostered consensus,
dampened controversy, and generated cultural authority. Because the overriding answer to natural historical questions when coupled to a theology
of nature was always the same—God is magnificent, God's wonders are
incomprehensibly intricate—nearly all Americans could find agreement in
its conclusions. Hitchcock, in association with geologists and naturalists of
this second generation, repositioned natural history in ways that allowed it
to become more theoretical, with individual practices incurring less skepticism and the individuals who devoted their time to the subject accorded
more cultural authority. They portrayed epistemological changes as
improvements, all eventually leading to a better comprehension of nature's
complexity, as well as a more thorough understanding of the divine.

Naturalists succeeded in harnessing the theology of nature for their collective benefit, and their practices were treated in the second and third
decade of the republic with less hostility and more legitimacy. In part that
is due to the manner in which some naturalists engaged the public. Hitchcock did not stress difference; he did not advocate conflict. Hitchcock and
those of his generation assumed their authority, unlike earlier naturalists
who worked to create legitimacy for their practices and for themselves.
In part this confidence came from ready access to formal training, better
professors and teachers, and a stronger community of naturalists on which
to draw. Part of it came from a lessening of the hostilities between elites
and ordinary Americans over nature, as open combat between facts and
class tension was replaced by cooperation. Finally, naturalists of the era
could also take pride in their practices as they found themselves, finally,
being asked to fulfill the promise made by naturalists after the Revolution:
assisting the nation by helping to build the state.

Making Natural History Credible: Geological Surveys and the Utility of Republican Science

William P. C. Barton, nephew of Benjamin Smith Barton and, like his uncle, professor of materia medica at the University of Pennsylvania, regarded the Corps of Discovery (the name assigned the Lewis and Clark expedition of 1803–6) with ambivalence. His assessment of it formed a portion of the introduction to his 1817 *Vegetable Materia Medica of the United States*, Barton's effort at a comprehensive catalog of all known plants in the nation that might have medicinal or pharmacological utility.

Barton lambasted what he thought to be Lewis and Clark's meager natural historical accomplishments: he condemned their amateurism, lamented the opportunity lost for the advancement of science generally, and hinted at the expedition's injurious role fostering an affiliation between the federal government and the early republic's community of naturalists. "The travels of Lewis and Clarke," he wrote derisively, "have put us in possession of the Indian names of many native dietetic articles, and these names have occasionally been accompanied by imperfect description." But not much more "than conjectures," he continued, could be expected "to arise from such informal and unscientific account; and indeed, little else has resulted, on this subject, from the rich opportunities of that governmental expedition." Barton reminded his readers that "it is well known, that no botanist or naturalist accompanied those travelers" (he did not regard either Lewis or Clark as skilled in natural historical studies), and while it was neither his "intention, nor my province, in this place, to make any animadversion on the direction of that undertaking . . . we are warranted in the belief, that a very splendid harvest might have been reaped, had any competent botanist accompanied the party."[1] Barton quickly summed up his thoughts for the reader: "The travels of Lewis and Clarke led to high expectations in every branch of science . . . Unfortunately however for science, this information is not communicated in such a way, as to enable the botanist, the physician, or the agriculturalist, to draw very efficiently upon the extensive sources of knowledge they present."[2] Barton believed that in terms of natural history generally and botany particularly, the expedition of Lewis and Clark was a bust.[3]

Barton's text expresses the frustration of an individual with disappointed expectations, sentiments shared by many American naturalists who, during the first fifty years of the early republic, unsuccessfully lobbied federal, state, and local governments for patronage and sponsorship of their labors. From the inception of the republic through the 1840s, naturalists and the politicians who favored natural historical projects devised plans for the various governments to support the practices. On the rare occasions when funding requests were fulfilled, monies went to individual, discrete projects: for example, short-term support of a scientific society, organization, or a museum; start-up funds for an initiative such as a botanical garden, seed money for the endowment of a university teaching position. Government at all levels lacked the financial wherewithal and, as importantly, the political will to fund natural history thoroughly and consistently. The only source of long-term government appropriations for natural history, itself episodic and haphazard, came from within the United States military: a closed, competitive community from which the overwhelming majority of American naturalists were excluded.

Yet the results of the military relationship were dramatic and successful: the western exploring expeditions that included the Barton-maligned peregrinations of Lewis and Clark as well as the expeditions led by Zebulon Pike, Stephen Long, and the United States Exploring Expedition in 1838–42 and the various projects of the United States Army Topographical Bureau, the Army's Corps of Engineers, and the United States Coast Survey.[4] These endeavors succeeded in providing descriptions of new plants and animals, records of anthropological and dramatic encounters with Indians, and descriptions of regions with unrivaled natural beauty. The publications and reports that emerged from these expeditions galled those like Barton who expected more; still, these expeditions, the reports, and the scientific servicemen who staffed these endeavors became the benchmarks against which those naturalists aiming for governmental support measured themselves.

Naturalists' relationships with government began to change in the 1820s and accelerated in the 1830s when individual state governments appointed naturalists, those with geological expertise in particular, to conduct geologic and natural history surveys of their jurisdictions. During these two decades, maturing state government bureaucracies and natural historians found a mutually beneficial symbiosis of interests. States began surveying their lands for internal improvement campaigns—road and canal building, land assessments, and railroads—and natural historians labored to make themselves essential and indispensable to those projects by offering their expertise (once again) to assist in the description of the geological character as well as the botanical and zoological content of these locales. States hired naturalists and geologists as well as parties of surveyors to explore regions for valuable commodities and resources—ores, forests, mineral deposits—and to determine the most efficient, least costly, and most lucrative routes for roads, canals, and rail lines. Such relationships provided—in the short term—training and experience to the individuals within these naturalist teams as well as a source of modest income.

Yet it was the secondary aspect of this relationship that proved most powerful and most enduring to the naturalists of this period and beyond. Working on behalf of the federal and individual states in surveying and assessing geologic and natural historical content worked to establish naturalists as authorities on nature, in part by disciplining their fields of investigation to those of state interests, turning their general, desultory set practices into specific, identifiable, concrete forms of knowledge making. This relationship narrowed naturalists' generalized expertise, still regarded by the general public as a wide-ranging and cacophonous investigatory spectrum, toward practices that provided valuable information critical to the economic development of the individual states and, by extension, the nation. In short, it brought into alignment the increasingly specific skills and interests of naturalists and those of state and federal government and its constituents.

Naturalists attempted in the earliest years of the republic to generate support for their practice and establish legitimacy for their method by appealing to the desires and whims of a democratic populace in a vibrant print culture, their authority derailed in part by the democracy of facts they helped to engineer. They undermined their practice because they failed to rule definitively (or their rulings went unacknowledged) on natural historical disputes, establishing uncertainty as the public's default position toward nature. Their efforts to acquire specimens from ordinary Americans failed because they promised monetary compensation and aligned their practice too closely to the market. But naturalists began to establish surer footing by turning a critique into an asset: they employed the theology of nature to answer challenges to their fact-based epistemology, reminding critics that facts alone seemed inadequate to explain the complexities of nature because they were only small parts of a grand design. Naturalists gained authority in the eyes of the public, paradoxically, by admitting their own limitations when it came to understanding the totality of nature.

Governments capitalized on the naturalists' economic promises in ways that individuals did not, and naturalists acquired authority from the states more concretely than they had from the public. States wanted a sense of their economic health and potential, a survey and an accounting of the natural resources they possessed within their boundaries. Yet such an accounting did not mean that legislators wished to harvest those assets immediately or even in the near term. Their botanical, zoological, and min-eralogical wealth was to be treated as the state's nest egg, assets that might be sold or leased from time to time but essentially preserved as wealth to be banked and drawn upon as needed. Thus it was in a state's interest to get an accurate and unassailable assessment of its natural bounty; hence states permitted naturalists to take their time, squabble among themselves, and determine with confidence each asset and its extent. Individuals, by contrast, regarded naturalists' identification of their natural resources within a constellation of enticements to sell their commodities (the colombo root is a case in point). Certainly an accurate identification of a plant or a mineral would be preferable; but an inaccurate one would not be dispositive to selling one's wares, nor would an attempt to pass off a counterfeit as the genuine article. Seeing only peril in a close association with individuals and the marketplace, naturalists turned their attention to state governments, hopeful of a different outcome.

The state-sponsored natural historical and geological projects of the third and fourth decades of the nineteenth century winnowed naturalists' investigatory responsibilities and invested their practices with new prestige in statehouses and in the general public. These surveys and the aligned state and natural historical interests they represented suggested to the public that naturalists were valuable, essential even, to the functioning of the civil government, a vibrant and growing economy, and an enlightened populace. These geologic and natural historical surveys accomplished for naturalists something they could never do for themselves: they made natural history credible.

But credibility was not without a price. The more intimate relationship between natural history and the state, the more formal and bureaucratic links between science and government further hastened an evolution within the naturalist community. It shifted the balance of prestige away from gentlemanly generalists toward those with more specialized skills—away from those who had a broad-based, individualistic knowledge of nature, in short, polite learning, to those who acquired it through classroom education, specialized training, and field experience. On one hand, these changes heralded the beginning of the professionalization of American science: the specialized demands of the state begat an increasing specialization of the part of those scientists in its employ. With stronger credentials, and more confident in their abilities and their accomplishments than the prior generations, scientists in the 1830s and 1840s established new institutions to house their activities, most notably the American Academy for the Advancement of Science and the federal government–sponsored Smithsonian Institution. On the other hand, the credibility of these state-supported activities hastened the marginalization of natural history as a general practice, investing geology with new import while relegating natural history to an avocation and pleasure pursuit for those with a less disciplined interest in nature. While by no means the only factor in bringing this change, the first stirrings of the modern scientific state in the 1830s and 1840s lowered the volume from the democracy of facts so that only those scientists wishing to listen could hear it.

Through the 1820s the alliance between natural history and government at all levels resembles the rise and fall of a general early republic enthusiasm for local, state, and federal government-sponsored internal improvements. When governments were fiscally capable and willing to fund improvement projects, natural history could fare well; when the economic or political climate made the funding of such projects unfeasible or unpopular, natural history fared poorly. In the years immediately following the Revolution, for example, those gentlemen who advocated for government sponsorship of natural history activities were of the same class, general background, and disposition as those who believed that government should vigorously pursue canal and river improvements that would that would connect the interior regions of the new nation with the Atlantic trading communities.[5]

Couched in the rhetoric of broad public interest and national uplift, the pleas of the elite, those whom George Washington called the "monied gentry," saw a prominent role for natural history in service of the republic's success: the security of the union, the preservation of the government, and the prosperity of their fellow citizens. But state and federal governments appear to have received these requests for natural history funding with the same indifference and suspicion as they did requests for funding canals and roads, regarding them as selfish projects of little benefit to the greater public, thinly disguised efforts by those with a financial interest to use public funds for individual gain. So a petition for general financial support from the American Philosophical Society to the General Assembly of Pennsylvania went unfulfilled even as the petitioners stressed that the "Labours & Researches" of its member would contribute to "important Discoveries," particularly the location of commodities "which we have hitherto been accustomed to import from other Countries."[6] Just as those individuals frustrated by government's unwillingness to sponsor internal improvements formed private corporations to pursue their own internal improvement projects, so the American Philosophical Society found subscribers to fund a transcontinental natural history expedition to be headed by the botanist André Michaux in 1792, an effort that ended nearly as soon as it began when Michaux was recalled after becoming entangled in an effort to destabilize Spanish Louisiana and return it to France.[7]

Throughout the first decades of the republic, those who petitioned government were gentleman, elites within their communities who extolled the civic utility of natural history generally and the benefits of their particular endeavor to the body politic. Those were the gentlemen who had requested that ordinary men and women send them samples and specimens and had encouraged the collective enterprise of natural history. Charles Willson Peale, for example, unsuccessfully lobbied the General Assembly of Pennsylvania for funds to support his museum throughout the 1790s. During his campaign Peale stressed the museum's capacity to disseminate "useful knowledge" of great importance to the city and the state. In an episode of brinksmanship, Peale even threatened to leave Philadelphia should no legislative aid come his way. He was granted use of the State House (Independence Hall) in 1802 as an exhibition space and capitalized on this stamp of approval by publishing a circular advertising his museum as a benefit to the city and the nation. He also raised the price of admission to the museum. A showman as well as a naturalist, Peale was an easy target for opponents in the city's newspapers.[8] David Hosack, professor of botany and materia medica at Columbia College, pursued a long campaign for monies to establish, develop, and maintain a botanic garden for the students of the college and the medical community of New York. In his repeated and largely unsuccessful efforts at securing funding for the garden, he interlaced arguments about a garden's central role in medical and botanical education, its potential for the advancement of a more efficient agriculture and husbandry, how it could broaden an understanding of indigenous as well as exotic plants, and the signal the establishment of a scientific garden would send to the rest of the country and abroad about New York's maturation as a city and a state. Stretching over the first decade of the nineteenth century, Hosack's petitions were well received by various committees within the New York legislature, only to fail because of inaction or postponement. Undeterred, Hosack purchased at personal expense land for a garden, developed the facilities and improved the infrastructure, imported and cultivated plants. He then began a series of petitions for financial aid for the garden, and after the financial burden of maintaining the garden proved too great, he offered it for sale to the state at "a fair and equitable valuation." After a few years of wrangling and assessments by the Land Office and other botanists, Hosack sold the garden to the state of New York for $74,000.[9]

Controversy ensued, leading Hosack to publish a nearly sixty-page pamphlet in 1811 defending himself and "correcting many errors which have prevailed, and continue to prevail . . . through the medium of public papers and other channels of information" that he had profited handsomely for operating and then selling the Elgin Botanical Garden.[10] Aware that rumors circulating in New York characterized him as a profiteer, Hosack laboriously detailed his personal expenses and concluded his narrative by explaining that though he was paid a large sum by the state when it assumed ownership of the garden, his personal expenses on the garden cost him in excess of $28,000 above the purchase price.[11] Skeptics of public aid to natural history came to regard the Elgin purchase as a boondoggle, for without Hosack's stewardship the garden quickly fell into disrepair and disuse by the middle part of the next decade.[12] In critics' eyes individuals like Peale and Hosack were gentlemen profiting at the public's expense, individuals who used their connections inside government to support their private endeavors and to profit from natural history pursuits of dubious value and short duration. Not opposed to natural history if individually funded, critics of public outlays found an abundance of easy targets, as most early republic natural history endeavors appeared to fail or stall more often than succeed.

Even an example with the full backing of the federal government was not immune from a bumptious fate. In 1807 the United States Congress, in response to a recommendation from Thomas Jefferson, authorized the creation of the United States Coast Survey. Its purpose was an accurate mapping of all coastal features, including islands and shoals, within twenty leagues of the Atlantic shore. With maritime commerce, safer navigation, and military considerations of vital importance to the economic success and security of the nation, Congress approved the measure and instructed the president and the superintendent of the Survey to determine the Survey's course of action and its parameters. The latitude Congress gave the Coast Survey permitted it work in natural history and geology if it could show that work in these areas would assist the completion of accurate coastal charts and so long as these investigatory tangents remained "subservient" to the commercial interests of the nation.[13] An advisory commission headed by the vice-president of the American Philosophical Society and director of the United States Mint, Robert Patterson, appointed Ferdinand Hassler, a recently arrived Swiss surveyor in Philadelphia, to lead the organization. Hassler seemed an astute choice since he was trained in the techniques of trigonometric and geodetic surveying, skills necessary for the production of precise navigational charts.[14]

But problems with Hassler quickly arose. Though established by law in 1807, actual work did not begin on the survey until 1816, after Hassler taught for two years at the military academy at West Point, one year at Union College in New York, and then spent four years in England and France overseeing the construction of astronomical and surveying instruments. Hassler's plans also proved to be very expensive. He urged Congress to build two permanent observatories, one in the northeast and one in the southwest, which it did not approve. He also demanded a substantial annual salary of $3,000, as well as $2,000 annually for expenses. More daringly, he also requested independence from accounting oversight by the Treasury Department, a position that he softened, when the final contract was struck, to quarterly inspections per year. Hassler and a team of Army and Navy officers and enlisted men as well as twelve members of the Corps of Engineers began the survey in New Jersey in 1816 and continued through the spring of 1818, when the work came to an abrupt halt.

Congress modified the law authorizing the Coast Survey by excluding civilian employees, including Hassler, deeming his work too expensive and too slow. Away from Washington and near his fieldwork and with few Washington allies to aid him, Hassler was outmaneuvered by the Navy chaplain, Cheever Flesh, who convinced Congress that he could manage the survey more efficiently and economically than Hassler. For the next fourteen years, the Survey was headed by members of the Army and Navy who accomplished little of value. In 1828, the secretary of the Navy told Congress that, in his opinion, the work accomplished by the Survey had been done by "incompetent men and with incompetent means." He regarded the maps they produced "unsafe, and in many instances, useless and pernicious." Hassler was reappointed to head the Survey in 1832, at which time work resumed, but a quarter century after its inception and the expenditure of tens of thousands of dollars, the United States Coast Survey's accomplishments appeared meager.[15]

Though only marginally successful with the United States Coast Survey, the federal government continued to invest in science by bolstering the Army Corps of Engineers with a Topographical Bureau in 1818, the purpose of which was the enhancement of geographical knowledge through the performance of surveys for internal improvement campaigns and the exploration and rationalization of American lands and waterways. Squabbles inside the Corps of Engineers hindered the Topographical Bureau's accomplishments, though the expedition led by Stephen Long from 1819 to 1821 through the American west offered hints that such investments could succeed, even if modestly or incompletely. Long's expedition surveyed the Platte, Arkansas, and Canadian river systems and was accompanied by the naturalists Thomas Say, William Baldwin, Edwin James, the artist Titian Ramsey Peale, and the geologist Augustus E. Jessup. As a geographical expedition of discovery, Long's expedition added information about the Canadian River and Long's Peak, relatively minor achievements, according to his contemporary and subsequent critics. That the expedition never published an official account or narrative likewise contributed to its negative assessment; the *Account of an Expedition from Pittsburgh to the Rocky Mountains* by the expedition's botanist Edwin James in 1823 thus became the endeavor's unofficial narrative. For all the money the federal government spent on surveying and expeditionary science, it had little to show. Save expenditures to maintain ongoing topographical and engineering projects, the federal government avoided expenditures on naturalists until the late 1830s, when it authorized the United States Exploring Expedition.[16]

Naturalists' skill set would find a steadier and more welcoming partner in state governments starting in the 1820s and continuing into the 1840s. The primary and most important fusion of naturalists and state governments was with geological surveys primarily and natural history to a lesser extent, which most of the eastern and midwestern states contracted during this period. After watching the federal government's limited investment in science reduce to a trickle in the 1820s, state governments warmed to the idea of sponsoring their own initiatives for natural history and geology for a variety of reasons. First, legislators in the individual states jealously regarded the success of New York's Erie Canal, a project whose financial burden had been shouldered by taxpayers of the state, and one from which New York began profiting handsomely after its completion in 1825.[17] Second, hope for federal government–sponsorship of improvements within the individual states seemed unlikely during the first few decades of the republic. While there existed enthusiastic advocates and constituencies for national funding of initiatives that would bind the states together through development and infrastructure—Albert Gallatin, John Quincy Adams, John C. Calhoun, and Henry Clay among the most prominent—these visions and programs were rejected by James Madison in 1817 when he vetoed the Bonus Bill that would have funded a series of canal and road projects; and the election of Andrew Jackson in 1828 put an end to visions of coordinated internal improvements directed by the federal government through the 1830s.[18] Finally, advocates for the funding of state natural history and geological surveys were bolstered when gold was discovered in Georgia in 1828.[19] A thorough and fine-grained knowledge of the mineralogical and natural historical content of an individual state no longer seemed a luxury; expert knowledge of a state's nature was an economic requirement, advocates argued, a small sum expended for a potentially large return.

The motivations behind these investigations and the methods used to implement them were multifaceted: of European and imperial derivation and modeled, in part, on eighteenth-century state-sponsored geographic surveys. To those traditions American naturalists added the techniques of the newer geological survey, a practice developed by the Edinburgh geologist James Hutton and the English geologist and mapmaker William Smith.

Both men were intimately involved with the development of geological methods and geologic practice, but they were also active participants in domestic internal improvements campaigns, canal building particularly. They took advantage of the opportunities afforded by the excavations of canals, a process that lay bare the strata and layers of rock, revealing an area's mineralogical character as well as offering clues to explain the process of rock formation and the age of the earth.[20] Early republic state geological and natural history surveys also took as their precedent the state natural history surveys of the 1780s and 1790s, those written by Thomas Jefferson, Jeremy Belknap, and Stephen Williams. But the surveys of the early nineteenth century differed from earlier examples in that they included no secondhand testimonies; they offered only direct testimony from those who did the surveying, oftentimes identifying by name the individual who made the observations. They were to concentrate on the mineralogical content of the state and how best those resources might be utilized. Attempts were to be made toward an exhaustive listing of the known flora and fauna and whether those animals and plants were common or rare. In short, these surveys should be considered as part of a state-sponsored drive for internal improvements in particular, more efficient agriculture, improved land utilization, and the identification of untapped mineralogical, botanical, and zoological resources.[21]

The domestic nineteenth-century template for the state geologic survey was that of Rensselaer County, New York, made by Amos Eaton in 1820 at the behest of the patron Stephen Van Rensselaer III.[22] Eaton's survey had a defined agriculture based economic purpose—Van Rensselaer was the largest landholder in eastern New York and wished to know how to make his land more efficient. Thus, in addition to making a geological description, Eaton noted the kinds of soil, the most suitable crops to be sown on that soil, and the best methods of cultivating them—all matters of concern to a landowner wishing to rent lands as well as the tiller of the soil. A year later and again under Van Rensselaer's patronage, Eaton made a similar survey of the entire route of the recently excavated Erie Canal. The cutting of the canal had left the strata neatly exposed, giving Eaton an unprecedented opportunity to examine the geological profile of the majority of the state of New York. His findings, published in 1824, gave a textual and visual cross-section of the rock formations from Williamstown, Massachusetts, on the east, to Buffalo on the west (Eaton's report was supplemented by a section made by Edward Hitchcock across Massachusetts).[23] Eaton's surveys and reports represented a watershed for the persistent campaign by natural-ists that their methods would have economic value. However frustrated they might have been that few individuals or institutions took them at their word, naturalists from the Revolution through the 1820s never abandoned their belief and their proselytizing that, in addition to their ability to offer identification and descriptions of rocks and minerals, they could also locate and evaluate mineral and soil resources that might be exploited as sources of wealth to individuals and to the state. As Eaton's surveys were being undertaken, state legislatures began to consider that naturalists might be right.

Two early surveys which attracted considerable attention were con-ducted in North and South Carolina in the early 1820s. Denison Olmsted, professor of chemistry at the University of North Carolina (and recently graduated from Yale College, where he was a student of Benjamin Silliman), was responsible for the first of these efforts. At the end of the second decade of the nineteenth century, the legislature of North Carolina, as in most other states, was turning its attention to internal improvements particularly by dredging rivers and digging canals, and in 1819 it created a Board of Internal Improvements to prepare plans and surveys. As a testament to the controversial nature of pursuing internal improvements with state funds, the board was secondarily charged to justify its existence by making a rec-ommendation on whether there would be sufficient economic advantage to justify the cost of an extensive canal network. Olmsted believed that he might be able to answer such a question and wrote to the board suggesting "the advantages that would result from investigating [North Carolina's] geology." Making his case plainer, Olmsted wrote that he could offer an "account of the various useful productions of the mineral kingdom" which had already been discovered "or which may, from certain well-known indi-cations, be reasonably expected to be found hereafter." These included but were not limited to stone used for building, soils such "gypsum, salt, coal, marl, potters clay," all important components of agriculture and "domestic economy"; Olmsted also promised to report on any beds of substances used in painting, metallic ores, and mineral springs. Olmsted pitched his service as part of improved transportation routes, arguing that with "free naviga-tion" provided by a more extensive network of canals and roads, "many things of which we are now in actual possession, might be turned to much more profitable account." Olmsted reminded the board that "many valu-able minerals now lie neglected" in the state but suggested that "geology furnishes rules for discovering useful minerals by certain known indications, derived from other minerals in the neighborhood, from the general structure of the country, and so on." In other words, Olmsted assured the board that his was not a philosophical exercise, an expensive boondoggle that might benefit only him and other "philosophers," but a practical inquiry and one that, guided by a rational and rulebound geologic practice, would preclude "fruitless researches." He cited the work done in Great Britain and Eaton's surveys in New York as evidence that such projects were both possible and worthwhile.

Olmsted sought an appropriation of $100 to pay "for hire of a horse and servant and the charge of traveling" while he made a geological survey during his summer break from teaching at the university. He confessed that he would profit personally from the survey but cast any benefits that might accrue to him as part of a loftier purpose. He suggested that such a journey would supplement his mineral collection to "illustrate my lectures" to university students and his efforts more generally would lead to the "promotion of science, by which the natural history of the State may be better known and appreciated, both at home and abroad."[24] His request was forwarded to the general assembly but was never acted upon. Olmsted renewed his appeal in 1823, at which time he was awarded a sum of $250 annually for four successive years by the Board of Agriculture.[25] The four reports that Olmsted filed between 1824 and 1829 were distributed free "by means of agricultural societies, to the people of the State" in an attempt to diffuse this knowledge as quickly and as widely as possible. It is unclear how the government of North Carolina or its citizens capitalized, if at all, on these reports though it is notable that one enduring effect of the Olmsted reports was the appearance of public notices about gold deposits in North Carolina in New York's *Medical Repository* and New Haven's *American Journal of Science*.[26] These reports detailed the locations of the deposits as well as the means by which an individual might dig or sluice for the gold. An article by the émigré mining expert Charles E. Rothe suggested that the owners of many of the deposits were naive about what they possessed; this article and others like it helping to establish and intensify a gold rush under way in North Carolina in the later 1820s.[27]

The following year, Lardner Vanuxem, originally from Pennsylvania and then professor of chemistry and geology at South Carolina College, received from the General Assembly of South Carolina $500 for "making a geological and mineralogical tour during the recess of the college and furnishing the specimens of the same." The act of the legislature continued in greater detail, informing Vanuxem that it was "under the most sanguine expectations that the day is not far distant when the bowels of the earth will be found to contain the means of increasing the fertility of its surface," and that he conduct his researches "not only for the benefit of those who are to be instructed in academic pursuits, but also for the promotion of agricultural prosperity." [28] Similar in scope, Vanuxem's and Olmsted's surveys provided useful information for state agencies and had a dramatic propaganda value. Edward Hitchcock, reviewing Olmsted's reports in the *American Journal of Science* in 1828, pointed out that they revealed the existence of mineral riches previously unknown to the citizens of North Carolina and offered them as models to be followed by other states. "What an accession would be made to our resources, and to the knowledge of our country," he wrote, "were a thorough examination to be instituted into our mineralogical, geological and, even botanical, riches!"[29] Sentiments such as Hitchcock's—that natural history was useful and beneficial to the states—anticipated the arguments of state survey promoters for the next decade, arguments that could be joined now with demonstrable proof that natural history and geology did, in fact, create valuable new knowledge.

Following the precedents set in the Carolinas—the North Carolina surveys ended in 1828—the next state-sanctioned geological survey was that of Massachusetts, authorized by its legislature in 1830 and begun under the direction of Edward Hitchcock the following year. The Massachusetts governor, Levi Lincoln, proposed to the General Court that they add a geological and natural historical survey to a recently approved general trigonometric survey. Lincoln argued that "much knowledge of the natural history would be gained" including the extent of the commonwealth's quarries and valuable ores "so essential to internal improvements, and the advancement of domestic prosperity." He suggested that such an undertaking would cost very little and would capitalize on the expertise and labor of "some eminent professors in our colleges. He suggested that the proposed undertaking would be an excellent opportunity for their "generous labors thus far, be secured to the State." The General Court adopted the plan and the governor appointed Hitchcock in June of 1831. Hitchcock conducted the geologic portions of the survey and was assisted by at least eight colleagues in cataloging flora and fauna.[30]

In short order Hitchcock began traversing the state. By the time a reauthorized survey ended ten years later, Hitchcock had traveled ten thousand miles by his calculation—"not with railroad speed, but with a geological, which is nearly synonymous with a pedestrian pace"—and collected some five thousand specimens. He reported that he was delighted by the way his mission was received by the individuals he encountered; a "universal disposition," he wrote, "I have found in every part of the Commonwealth, to forward the objects of the survey . . . yet have I everywhere met with a hospitality that has supplied all of my wants, and with intelligence enough to and appreciate, and a disposition to forward, the objects of my commission."[31] Having met so many individuals in his travels, Hitchcock was well aware that the public eagerly awaited his findings so he released a preliminary report, subtitled *Economic Geology*, in 1832. A short treatise of only seventy pages, *Economic Geology*, located and described the classes of rocks that lay under the soil, emphasizing rocks and minerals that were "useful in the arts": building stones, slates, clays, marls, peat, coal, graphite, and the ores of lead, iron, zinc, copper, manganese, silver, and gold. Hitchcock's title astutely encapsulated his report, at long last fulfilling the promise naturalists had been making: to locate and describe specimens for the growth and economic development of the individual states and the nation. His report made manifest the link between natural history and economic growth, the association between natural knowledge and the nation's fiscal health.[32]

Hitchcock's final report, published the following year, was an elaborated seven hundred pages, accompanied by a map and engravings; it was the most extensive report of its kind yet produced in the United States. It was a detailed, if at times dry read, and in line with the requests of the state, it was oriented particularly to the utilization of "objects of pecuniary importance."[33] The section on "useful rocks and minerals" elaborated on the information contained in *Economic Geology* and detailed the locations of known quarries of granite and limestone, soapstone, and coal, noting the purposes for which they might be best used. Hitchcock described where and of what quality one could locate lead, copper, and zinc. He concluded his section on economic geology by lambasting the "credulity and superstitious ignorance" of the Massachusetts populace with regard to finding gold and silver, whether by chance or by a "belief in the mysterious virtues of the mineral rod."[34] He observed that while other states may have some minerals or ores of greater value than those in Massachusetts, he doubted that any state in the nation had as many different varieties of useful rocks and minerals and in such "inexhaustible" quantities. In his belief, from an economic standpoint the commonwealth was uncommonly blessed.

The second section of his report considered the topographic geology of Massachusetts and detailed the geologic character of various features such as Mount Holyoke and the Connecticut River Valley. The topographic writing served readers as a guidebook to the most famous geologic features of the Massachusetts landscape and was intended "to direct the attention of the man of taste to those places in the State, where he will find natural objects particularly calculated to gratify his love of novelty, beauty and sublimity."[35] He gave descriptions of mountains, of autumnal scenery, of rivers, of the view from the Boston statehouse, accompanied by moral and political contemplations. The third section, easily the largest at some 425 pages and titled "Scientific Geology," was a de facto textbook on geology with field examples. In it Hitchcock labored to explain the geologic history of the various regions of the state, offering explanations for the formation of "stratified" and "unstratified" rocks, their mineralogical character, and theories for the composition of rocks. This section also offered casual explanations and geologic theory drawn from his own researches as well as foreign authorities: the reasons why veins of coal were located where they were, theories for why certain areas of the state had experienced the uplift of strata while others had not, and the evidence that could explain the geologic processes that created important geographic features such as Boston Harbor. Fulfilling another part of his mission (though one not part of the authorizing resolution of 1830), Hitchcock made a collection of 1,550 specimens of rocks and minerals, which he transmitted to the Boston Society of Natural History for display. In addition to this collection, Hitchcock also created collections of 500 specimens each for Amherst, Harvard, and Williams colleges.[36]

The final section of the 1833 report on the botanical and zoological characteristics of the state amounted to little more than a long list of the animals and plants of the commonwealth with their Latinate binomial, their common name, and the accreditation of their first describer. Though involving the collective labor of many individuals, the zoological and botanical section was, paradoxically, the most spare. When the General Court authorized a renewal of the survey in 1837—with the primary consideration being a more detailed effort at the discovery and investigation of coal, marl, and ores—the body instructed that in the zoological and botanical sections the authors should "keep carefully in view the economical relations of every subject of your inquiry." Those instructions qualified that the General Court did not intend that the investigator should depart from arranging his report according to "scientific order, method, or comprehension"; rather, "that which is practically useful will receive a proportionally greater share of attention than that which is merely curious: the promotion of comfort and happiness being the great end of all science."[37] In situations where the descriptions previously given were incomplete, unsatisfactory, or contained in books not easily obtained by the public, the instructions urged the investigators "to redescribe or make additions" as warranted.

The naturalists involved in this botanical and zoological investigation took their charge seriously, and after negotiating a delay on the filing of their report, they submitted to the General Court six separate reports, published independently of the one on geology—on invertebrate animals, insects injurious to vegetation, herbaceous plants, quadrupeds, fish and reptiles, and birds—that totaled some seventeen hundred pages.[38] Accompanied by plates, drawings, and engravings, the reports did conform to the instructions. In the case of the text dedicated to the commonwealth's botanical riches, Chester Dewey explained that except for "necessary systematic arrangements, I have laid aside, to a great extent, the technical language of Botany" since its use would contradict the "popular object of the Survey." Scientific descriptions had already been published for those who considered themselves botanists; his descriptions were designed for the "mass of intelligent citizens."[39] The Massachusetts surveys were the most exhaustive of the period in the numbers of investigators employed and the extent of publication. They served as the model for other states and it was with some amount of pride and surprise that Hitchcock noted, in the preface to the 1841 report, that "no less than eighteen other States of the Union have commenced, and are now actively prosecuting, or have compiled, similar surveys."[40] Hitchcock also flattered the governor and the General Court that their investments were well made, adding that the governments of Great Britain and the United States were also following the Massachusetts example, though it is not clear to which surveys he was referring.

Prior to the Panic of 1837, most of the northern and midwestern states authorized surveys that resembled that of Massachusetts, though the investigatory parameters and content of each varied to a small degree. A general pattern does emerge, however: all of them included a geological component, one oriented toward economic considerations predominantly, and it was not uncommon for a state to allocate funds for a geologic survey exclusively, making no provision for the survey of a state's botanical or zoological content. Connecticut did just this when it authorized a survey in 1835 elaborating the many ways in which geological knowledge would aid the state and its citizenry: "as a guide in the examination and selection of routes for railroads and canals and internal improvements of every kind," such a survey would furnish real estate holders in Connecticut with information "respecting . . . possessions as would guard . . . against the wiles of prowling speculators." It would prevent further "money wasted" and labor expended on the too-common search for metals and minerals "which a knowledge of those substances and the relative position they occupy would have shown to be useless."[41] The move not to fund a general natural historical survey was a decision that underscored Connecticut's emphasis on economic geology and not the generally scientific; Connecticut boasted two established colleges, Yale and Wesleyan, from where more than competent naturalists could be found. Maryland, like Connecticut, only made provisions for geology when it authorized a survey in 1833, likewise Delaware in 1837.[42] That nearly all states authorized a geological survey because it could unlock mineralogical wealth but not a natural history complement suggests that the individual legislatures did not consider botanists and zoologists to be as good an investment. Natural history might be interesting to many but it was not necessarily an interest of the state.

The state legislature and governor of New York, however, appointed a natural history team when it created its survey in 1835, employing four geologists by the time the survey finished its work: William Mather, Ebenezer Emmons, Lardner Vanuxem, and James Hall. (A fifth geologist, Timothy Conrad, left the survey in 1842 and did not contribute to the final report.) The group also included the zoologist James De Kay and a zoological draftsman, the botanist John Torrey, and the mineralogist Lewis C. Peck.[43] The completed report series, *A Natural History of New-York*, comprised five parts: the zoology, botany, and mineralogy contributions by De Kay, Torrey, and Peck as well as two parts on the geology and paleontology written by the geologists. Their multivolume work rivaled the publications of their Massachusetts colleagues and evinced similar characteristics, displaying attempts to describe the natural world using common rather than erudite language and stressing the practical and economic uses for natural resources, in particular geologic and mineralogical ones. Like the publications from Massachusetts, *A Natural History of New-York* contained maps and drawings to illustrate individual species or geologic features.[44] Notably, the commonwealths of Virginia and Pennsylvania, though equally blessed with expert naturalists like New York and Massachusetts, only made provisions for geological surveys during this period; the same is true of Kentucky, Indiana, and Ohio. Naturalists in many of these states approached the legislatures for funding unsuccessfully; apparently, natural history was not deemed as lucrative as geologic and mineralogical knowledge, its knowledge too distant from the notion of utility as defined by those in the statehouses.[45]

The state of Michigan, by contrast, authorized a geological and natural history survey less than a month after it was admitted to the union in 1837. Many state residents and boosters believed that salt would be an important commodity resource, perhaps the most lucrative, so the legislature instructed the appointed geologist, Douglas Houghton, to investigate and examine the state's salt springs and saline deposits. In his first annual report to the legislature in 1838 Houghton announced that he did not think salt harvesting in Michigan would be remunerative because the brine was too weak in concentration and too limited in quantity. By the next year, the legislature voted to include separate departments for zoological, botanical, and topographical investigations along with the geological. But resistance from opponents within the legislature about the cost and the putative rewards derived from the expanded survey required that Houghton provide "information to the direct benefits which may be anticipated to the agricultural interests of the State from the completion of the geological survey."[46] He explained in the next report to the legislature (1839) that the survey was disseminating knowledge of the soil and minerals, gathering information on destructive insects as well as plants useful and noxious; this report included more information about the viability of salt mining (too expensive) as well as a list of all the mammals, birds, reptiles, amphibians, fish, and mollusks from the survey's zoologist, Abram Sager. The botanist John Wright contributed an alphabetical list of the state's known plants. But within a year the natural history team resigned their positions after "ignorant criticisms and caricatures indulged in by members of the legislature in public debates" became too much to bear. As to why Sager and Wright had quit, Houghton was forthright: "No competent man would be willing to hazard his reputation in attempting, within the space allowed, to complete either the botany or zoology of our State."[47] The legislature canceled the zoological and botanical sections of the survey, though the geological and topographical sections of the survey continued.

The blossoming of state-supported surveys during the 1830s and 1840s signaled a new era in the relationship between government and scientific activity in the United States. Though individual critics in state legislatures remained skeptical of the value of the information and knowledge that geologists and naturalists provided them (Michigan being the most extreme case), geologists and naturalists had acquired a wider public credibility and authority through these surveys, one that the generation of naturalists before them did not possess. If some lawmakers remained hesitant about the public funding of science in all its forms, certain practices within its cluster of activities were finding allies; state legislators and state executives were willing to explore new partnerships with geologists particularly and, to a lesser degree, naturalists. That every state which conducted a geological survey made mention that it sought "economical geology" or something akin to it is not surprising; naturalists and geologists emphasized useful knowledge when petitioning the states. "Details and facts, belonging strictly to pure scientific geology," wrote William Mather to the New York state legislature, "will not be made public until the final report. The object of the annual reports is to give publicity to such facts and localities as may be of practical utility, so that the benefit may be derived from a knowledge of them during the progress of the survey."[48] Interests within and without the state legislatures were pressing for naturalists to contribute what they could toward the efficacy of various internal improvements: canals, roads, and railroads among the most prominent. Private interests were also curious about the survey findings, and because the reports were public documents, they were available for public perusal; most state legislatures also made provisions that the reports be placed in the libraries of their leading colleges, universities, and scientific societies, copies sent to the state officers and town officials, the legislatures of other states, and the Library of Congress. Among private interests who might benefit from this information were corporations and companies that wanted to know where to build a factory, excavate a mine, or plan a railroad; interest groups seeking to locate transportation routes where there would be lucrative commodities to transport; land speculators who wanted to know about the potential productivity of the soil in the unsettled areas of their states. In contributing large sums of money to public improvement efforts, individual states wanted to ensure that their money was being well spent. Legislators reasoned that geologists certainly and naturalists more obliquely could aid economic expansion though internal improvements and the speculative tendencies that accompanied those desires. Armed with better information about where (and where not) to dig canals, build roads, and lay track could only aid in better decision making and a more precise outlay of public funds.[49]

If commercial opportunity was one motivator for state legislators in funding these surveys, anxiety about falling behind other states economically was another, especially for older, eastern states that were losing population to western lands. State legislators looked covetously at the receipts New York collected from the Erie Canal and the putative multiplier effects of increased commercial activity that came from internal improvements; and they regarded enviously the gold being dug from the hills in North Carolina and Georgia, wondering if similar riches might be found within their boundaries.[50] More than one state official sounded like Connecticut governor Henry Edwards, who, when advocating for a survey, noted jealously (and ominously) that "different parts of the country" were outpacing his state and their utilization of their resources should give the Connecticut legislature reason to believe that they were not yet availing themselves of their mineralogical wealth or taking full advantage of promising topographical features for internal improvements.[51] Eastern states also regarded warily their exhausted soils, the result of decades, in some cases centuries, of intensive agriculture; decreasing agricultural yields and the shrinking size of family farms led most older states to ask naturalists for soil analyses and to look hard for marl and peat that could be used for soil rehabilitation and conditioning. Another way for older states to combat out-migration was to identify underappreciated and underutilized natural resources with which they could retain population and preserve and expand wealth. Older states had reasons to be concerned because the newly opened western states such as Indiana and Ohio were eager to have geologists and naturalists survey their economic potentialities—which they never doubted were abundant—so that they might establish a foundation of prosperity and attract settlers. If the rhetoric surrounding the need for these surveys can be believed, it appears that state legislatures thought, to some extent, that a great deal was riding on the outcome of these geological and natural history surveys: individual and state wealth, potential taxes and levies, and demographic health. After nearly forty years of arguing that their skills were essential to the success and vitality of individual states and the nation, naturalists found states listening to their pleas in the 1830s; they had finally become the aids to the health and vitality of the state they had longed to be.

But naturalists' wish fulfillment was not without consequences. As they had throughout the early years of the nineteenth century, naturalists got caught in debates about the value and utility of their skills and knowledge, but this time with the state governments and not the members of the public. The geologists could point to their educational uplift of the general populace. In Massachusetts, the state legislature provided funds for a library, an experiment station, and a college to develop better farming methods and to disseminate information about them. Geological surveys, which would provide information to all the people about their state, could be seen as a natural extension of this kind of education. Usually the geologist in charge of the survey was required to collect mineral, rock, and ore specimens and display them in some central place; he was frequently instructed to distribute suites of specimens to academies and colleges within the state. He always had to make a formal report, which, in some cases, was printed and put into the hands of state legislators and other officers and made available to educational and scientific organizations. In all states a major purpose was to locate, describe, and publicize such natural resources as coal, and ores. With this information in hand, any person, it was thought, would have a basis for judging how successfully those resources might be exploited. The educational and exploitative aspects of the surveys were thus intimately associated with each other.

But even as geologists pointed to their educational efforts and accomplishments, they were frequently confronted by general confusion and the absence of any clear conception of the task at hand. Exactly what was economically useful information in the first place was never determined, either by geologists or by state legislatures. Under such conditions, what the legislature accepted as being "useful" was necessarily the result of subjective interpretation of the geologist's report. If legislators saw that the geologist had precisely located seams of coal, and if he had determined the thickness, direction, and inclination of the vein and stated whether it was workable, and if he gave a chemical analysis and stated clearly whether the coal could be used for heating, smelting, or something else, then the work was "useful." Similarly, if he gave an analysis of the soil and clearly stated its deficiencies, suggested ways to improve it, and recommended the proper crops for each area, then his work was "useful." It was also difficult to gauge the educational value. The training received by those on the surveying teams probably did not count, nor did the information contained in the report have evident educational value unless the geologist prefaced his work with an elementary textbook of geology, as many did. But if the geologist presented an orderly display of rocks, minerals, and fossils, each specimen labeled, and the collection could be housed in some public institution it had educational value.

Those who conducted the survey's natural history components were treated with greater ambivalence. It is notable that only three states—Massachusetts, New York, and Michigan—provided extensive funding for natural history surveys during the early nineteenth century's most vigorous period of governmental funding. Whereas geology and geologists flourished, those who considered themselves naturalists—specialists in botany or zoology or both—could not convince the legislatures that they could provide the kinds of information deemed useful. Naturalists' reports on the zoological and botanical contents of the states that did provide for them are important contributions to the natural historical record of the era but appear to have made little impact in the statehouses that commissioned them. Of what utility was a natural historical account of an animal that could not be husbanded and did not pose a threat to, or an aid to, agriculture? Such information was interesting, perhaps important, but legislatures deemed natural history an unnecessary extravagance for state support, too similar to the gentlemanly generalist knowledge of the previous generation of naturalists, who also failed to secure government patronage for natural history. Out of the states' foray in the 1830s and 1840s into governmental funding for science, geology emerged considerably stronger while natural history was significantly marginalized.

Still, the lasting result of this efflorescence in funding was the establishment of enduring institutions and relationships between the state governments and the activities of naturalists. More broadly, it was the patronage by the states in the 1820s through the 1840s that ushered in a modern alignment of state-supported science, one built on self-perpetuating institutions and state-sanctioned expertise. If such an alignment was a nearly impossible goal for naturalists at the beginning of the century, it was becoming normative by the 1830s and 1840s. State-supported geological surveys continued their work and new institutions on the state and national levels came to symbolize a closer alignment between governments and scientific activity. By the end of the nineteenth century, the struggles and frustrations of the first generations of American naturalists to secure patronage were regarded in a different light.

Contrast the sentiments of W. P. C. Barton, who opened this chapter, with those of Elliot Coues, a naturalist of the late nineteenth century and the editor of an 1893 edition of the Lewis and Clark journals—the first edition published in nearly eighty years and the first to include extensively the Corps of Discovery's natural historical observations. Coues and Barton shared medical training, service as surgeons in the United States armed forces, and a deep curiosity about the natural world. Whereas Barton was part of a collection of naturalists who advocated for but rarely, if ever, received federal monies for their natural historical projects, Coues was off and on affiliated with the Smithsonian Institution and appointed expedition naturalist and secretary to F. V. Hayden's 49th Parallel boundary commission from Lake of the Woods to the Pacific coast in 1872, one of a number of the grand surveying/scientific projects during the latter half of the nineteenth century. In short, government sponsorship of science—federal, state, or local—was normative for Coues. And in the 1890s Coues, retired from military service, directed his energies toward two objectives: first, the quixotic attempt to eradicate English sparrows from North America;[52] second, rehabilitating the reputations of the nation's first federal government explorer-naturalists—Lewis and Clark as well as Zebulon Pike. If Barton is indicative of the early nineteenth century's regard of Lewis and Clark as adventurers first and naturalists a very distant second, then Coues helped shape a fin de siècle opinion of them as naturalist explorers, as scientists in government employ and in pursuit of state interests. With nostalgia for a closing frontier emerging and calls for overseas expansion growing louder, Coues regarded Lewis and Clark as the first in an august line of naturalist empire builders, a group of which he believed himself a part.[53]

The opening lines Coues's edition of the Lewis and Clark journals offered a more heroic gloss on Lewis and Clark than Barton did. In them he exhorted the "People of the Great West" to recognize the contributions of Jefferson, the individual "who gave you the country"; but it was "Lewis and Clark [who] showed you the way." All that unfolded afterward—the exploring, the cataloging, the settling—was "your own course of empire."[54] All the while valorizing the politicians and pioneers who made settling the west possible, Coues's edition of the journals credited Lewis and Clark with the discovery of numerous plants and animals, minerals, anthropological information, and natural phenomena. Coues, as much as any naturalist of the nineteenth century, helped to establish Lewis and Clark as worthy of the title of scientist, a credit not afforded them earlier in the century.[55] He also helped to shape an opinion of early American natural history that appears more certain than the experience of those who lived it.

From the years immediately following the Revolution through the 1830s, naturalists couched their pitch to aid the state in nationalist rhetoric and patriotic imagery. Coues's depiction of Lewis and Clark is the embodiment of what they longed to be. Naturalists stressed the strong links between their practices and their love of country, instructing the public in ways they could observe nature, appreciate the landscape, and celebrate the divine. Naturalists always imagined themselves as nationalist state builders, instructors in patriotic love of nature as well as creators of collective wealth and knowledge. For their efforts in fostering nationalist sentiments, naturalists were well rewarded, receiving public support in the form of audiences attending their lectures, students taking their classes, consumers reading their popular publications, and citizens sending them specimens and samples. What they did not receive, however, was the sponsorship of the state, the financial support for which they advocated and agitated. Patriotism and nationalist sentiments might bind the citizens together but it did not build the nation. That Lewis and Clark, mere collectors, came to represent the image naturalists had wished for themselves is an ironic comment on how far short of their goal naturalists ultimately fell, the amateur and the untrained occupying the role of the expert.

Scientific Practice in the Nineteenth Century

The 1840s through the end of the nineteenth century witnessed the disaggregating of early republic natural history into the recognizable modern biological disciplines. It also saw the distancing from frequent engagement with the general public of those individuals moderns would recognize as scientists. In short, the second half of the nineteenth century saw the dismantling of the democracy of facts. This process was defined in part by the winnowing of its participants. Waning slowly but steadily over this period was the ability for much of American society to contribute to the scientific conversation as competent if unequal partners; even those gentlemanly amateurs—men of wealth, some amount of leisure, and social respect and standing—who had been the backbone of scientific practice since the seventeenth century faded from view. In the second half of the nineteenth century science became a full-time occupation of paid specialists. The empire of reason emerged the victor.

The process of professionalization also institutionalized and codified the individual disciplines, and a professionalized science followed the patterns established in the practices of medicine, law, and engineering: though each had slightly different characteristics, the disciplines were defined by an abstract and systematic body of knowledge that commanded explanatory authority and fealty; formal and increasingly standardized educational requirements for its members; procedures for certifying or licensing practitioners; and associations to enforce standards, honor achievement, and exert control within the field.[1] These institutional changes and efforts at standardization were accompanied by ongoing and dogged campaigns of members to maintain status, privilege, and monopolistic domination in their field by establishing and policing institutionally sanctioned boundaries between experts and their potential rivals. Though some disciplines permit-

ted more amateur participation than others—ornithology, for example—by
the end of the nineteenth century science was a profession: specific in its
knowledge, exclusive in its participation, closed to all but the credentialed
and prepared.[2]

Natural history was not yet a profession in the early republic. Neither
was it the pursuit of amateurs. Instead, it was an open practice that sought
facts from all corners of society, evidence that was generally easy to obtain
and record. Its geographic interest was so vast that a single naturalist could
not expect to see it all. Cooperation was, to some degree, a necessity. While
specialized education and training became more important, even essential,
to some natural historical pursuits in the decades after the Revolution, the
observations of credible and capable individuals could not be dismissed out
of hand and natural history was very much a collaborative effort between
naturalists and some of the literate but not learned members of the general
public. Such relationships were far from equal and oftentimes tense as naturalists treated skeptically, if not dismissed outright, the observations of
some of their correspondents. All the while ordinary Americans questioned
or challenged naturalists' findings or conclusions that contradicted their
own experiences with nature and the natural world. Many Americans, it
appears, felt entitled to their own opinions *and* their own facts.

It is not surprising that they felt that way. The natural world of the early
republic was regarded as an exciting place, filled with novelty, wonders, and
the undiscovered. It was also uniquely American, owned by a new political
entity undergoing a grand political experiment. Naturalists helped Americans to learn about nature, taught them a new language through which to
describe it, and instructed them how to feel about it too: awe, reverence,
ownership, and patriotic pride. Naturalists consistently pitched their techniques to the public with nationalist gloss; nature study, they suggested,
should make individuals feel small with respect to the magnitude of God's
creation all the while feeling proud to know that the nature around them
was theirs. The unrestrained enthusiasm with which naturalists and ordinary Americans engaged nature—intellectually, emotionally, patrioti-
cally—is a testament to naturalists' many successes. As Americans explored,
witnessed, talked about, and wrote about nature, they generated enthusiastic observations and some less than sober conclusions. But just as many
naturalists of the period did not or would not dismiss such observations as
impossible, if improbable, so this period need not be considered a pre- or
protoscientific era. It was not, even if the democracy of facts kept alive

fantastical ideas that should have been put to rest, or if systematic thinking was regarded with suspicion in many quarters. Nor should those who used natural history primarily for entertainment or individual profit be classified as unscientific, mere entrepreneurs, cranks, or hucksters. Rather, the early republic represents a period in which natural history—a practice of fact collection first and foremost and the reporting of those facts—could be used for many ends, all of them, to one degree or another, scientific. For some, the adoption of natural historical methods and the deployment of its rhetoric was a means to turn a profit. Those same profit motives also shaped the behavior of individuals readers would regard as scientists. For as much as the early republic was characterized by a swirling debate about nature, so its most attentive students were forming clusters of likeminded individuals and settling on the proper means to observe the natural world and report their findings, coalescing around particular issues and at the same time searching for and crafting—sometimes successfully, sometimes not—the human niches where they could benefit from their knowledge and expertise. That these niches were largely in the employ and for the benefit of government bureaucracies and not with the public was part accident of history and part of the processes that marks the rise of the modern nation-state and a professionalized scientific practice.[3]

It was the fusion of nation and natural history, patriotic sentiments and observation of nature that helped to make possible the democracy of facts and allowed it to endure. By no means were Americans' every experience in the natural world informed by their thoughts about the future of their new country; every walk in the forest was not an exercise in nature study and national prognostication. But because naturalists and natural history as a practice were so closely aligned with aiding the nation by describing and uncovering its resources, because natural history sought public support and grounded its authority through appeals to Americans' pride of country, dismissing the participation of everyday Americans and ignoring their contribution smacked of not only elitism but a loss of affection for the country. Only by transposing their enthusiasms for the United States from the people to the state did naturalists and natural history evolve to become science.

Notes

Introduction

1. William Read to Thomas Jefferson, 11 February 1806, archives, MSS correspondence, American Philosophical Society, Philadelphia (hereafter cited as APS). For information on William Read, see John Michael Vlach, *The Planter's Prospect: Privilege and Slavery in Plantation Paintings* (Chapel Hill: University of North Carolina Press, 2002), 79–81.

2. On Anglophone natural history correspondence networks, see Susan Scott Parrish, *American Curiosity: Cultures of Natural History in the Colonial British Atlantic World* (Chapel Hill: University of North Carolina Press, 2006), 103–73; Anne Secord, "Corresponding Interests: Artisans and Gentlemen in Nineteenth Century Natural History," *British Journal for the History of Science* 27 (1994): 383–408; Anne Larsen, "Not since Noah: The English Scientific Zoologists and the Craft of Collecting" (Ph.D. diss., Princeton University, 1993), chap. 7.

3. On the role of slaves' expertise and assistance in New World and North American natural history, see Londa Schiebinger, *Plants and Empire: Colonial Bioprospecting in the Atlantic World* (Cambridge, Mass.: Harvard University Press, 2004); Parrish, *American Curiosity,* chap.7; James Delbourgo, *A Most Amazing Scene of Wonders: Electricity and Enlightenment in Early America* (Cambridge, Mass.: Harvard University Press, 2006), 183–89; Richard Drayton, *Nature's Government: Science, Imperial Britain, and the "Improvement" of the World* (New Haven, Conn.: Yale University Press, 2000) 93.

4. Susan Scott Parrish has argued for the instability of curiosity in the American colonies, a term that could encompass a description of an object or an individual's capacity for reliable and exhaustive observation. Used in a pejorative sense, curiosity might also signal a naturalist's obsessive fixation on useless information or a non-naturalist's propensity to fabricate the truth or tell tall tales. Read's use of "curious" appears to admit more than one of these definitions. See Parrish, *American Curiosity,* 57–64. For a discussion of early modern attitudes toward curiosity, see Lorraine Daston and Katherine Park, *Wonders and the Order of Nature, 1150–1750* (New York: Zone Books, 1998); Barbara M. Benedict, *Curiosity: A Cultural History of Early Modern Inquiry* (Chicago: University of Chicago Press, 2001).

5. Women's participation in colonial North American natural history and science

has recently been the subject of important studies. See Schiebinger, *Plants and Empire*; Parrish, *American Curiosity*; Sarah S. Gronim, *Everyday Nature: Knowledge of the Natural World in Colonial New York* (New Brunswick, N.J.: Rutgers University Press, 2007), esp. chap. 6; Gronim, "What Jane Knew: A Woman Botanist in the Eighteenth Century," *Journal of Women's History* 19 (2007): 33–59. For studies in the nineteenth century, see Nina Baym, *American Women of Letters and the Nineteenth-Century Sciences: Styles of Affiliation* (New Brunswick, N.J.: Rutgers University Press, 2002). Elizabeth B. Kenney explores women's participation in *The Botanizers: Amateur Scientists in Nineteenth Century America* (Chapel Hill: University of North Carolina Press, 1992). A still-relevant survey is Sally Gregory Kohlstet, "In from the Periphery: American Women in Science, 1830–1880," *Signs* 4 (1978): 81–96. Though focused on England, Ann Shteir's many findings about women and botany appear to hold true for the United States. See Ann B. Shteir, *Cultivating Women, Cultivating Science: Flora's Daughters and Botany in England* (Baltimore: Johns Hopkins University Press, 1996).

6. On the origins of natural history as a practice aimed at description, see Brian W. Ogilvie, *The Science of Describing: Natural History in Renaissance Europe* (Chicago: University of Chicago Press, 2006). On the early modern origins of naturalists' description of local environs, see Alix Cooper, *Inventing the Indigenous: Local Knowledge and Natural History in Early Modern Europe* (New York: Cambridge University Press, 2007); on how early republic natural history texts emulated early modern geography texts, see Martin Brückner, *The Geographic Revolution in Early America: Maps, Literacy, and National Identity* (Chapel Hill: University of North Carolina Press, 2006), 144–45. For activities of local flora and fauna inventory, see the essays in Nicholas Jardine, James Secord, and Emma Spary, eds., *Cultures of Natural History* (Cambridge: Cambridge University Press, 1996).

7. On the categories and discourse of the fact, see Mary Poovey, *A History of the Modern Fact: Problems of Knowledge in the Sciences of Wealth and Society* (Chicago: University of Chicago Press, 1998); Barbara J. Shapiro, *A Culture of Fact: England, 1550–1720* (Ithaca, N.Y.: Cornell University Press, 2000); the essays in Anthony Grafton and Nancy Sirisi, eds., *Natural Particulars: Nature and the Disciplines in Renaissance Europe* (Cambridge: MIT Press, 1999); Mary-Rose Sargent, *The Diffident Naturalist: Robert Boyle and the Philosophy of Experiment* (Chicago: University of Chicago Press, 1995); Steven Shapin, *A Social History of Truth: Civility and Science in Seventeenth-Century England* (Chicago: University of Chicago Press, 1995); Steven Shapin and Simon Schaffer, *Leviathan and the Air-Pump: Boyle, Hobbes, and the Experimental Life* (Princeton, N.J.: Princeton University Press, 1989).

8. "Centers of calculation" is a concept made famous by Bruno Latour, *Science in Action: How to Follow Scientists and Engineers through Society* (Cambridge, Mass.: Harvard University Press, 1987). On the European models for United States scientific organizations, see James E. McCellan III, *Science Reorganized: Scientific Societies in the Eighteenth* (New York: Columbia University Press, 1985); on the contemporaneous

situation in France, see E. C. Spary, *Utopia's Garden: French Natural History from Old Regime to Revolution* (Chicago: University of Chicago Press, 2000).

9. Of particular importance to this study are Shapin and Schaffer, *Leviathan and the Air-Pump*; Shapin, *A Social History of Truth*; Daston and Park, *Wonders and the Order of Nature*; Paula Findlen, *Possessing Nature: Museums, Collecting, and Scientific Culture in Early Modern Italy* (Berkeley: University of California Press, 1994); Jan Golinki, *Science as Public Culture: Chemistry and Enlightenment in Britain, 1760–1820* (New York: Cambridge University Press, 1992); William Clark, Jan Golinski, and Simon Schaffer, eds., *The Sciences in Enlightened Europe* (Chicago: University of Chicago Press, 1999); Jardine et al., *Cultures of Natural History*; Jessica Riskin, *Science in the Age of Sensibility: The Sentimental Empiricists of the French Enlightenment* (Chicago: University of Chicago Press, 2002); David N. Livingstone, *Putting Science in its Place: Geographies of Scientific Knowledge* (Chicago: University of Chicago Press, 2003); Pamela H. Smith, *The Body of the Artisan: Art and Experience in the Scientific Revolution* (New Haven, Conn.: Yale University Press, 2007); Tara Nummedal, *Alchemy and Authority in the Holy Roman Empire* (Chicago: University of Chicago Press, 2007).

10. Much of the work on colonial and early national American science predates the methodological revolution in the history of science that began in the 1980s and on which this study relies. These earlier studies stress the processes of American professional scientific development, sometimes verging into apologia for its slow progress and limited contributions in comparison to peers in Europe. See Brooke Hindle, *The Pursuit of Science in Revolutionary America, 1735–1789* (Chapel Hill: University of North Carolina Press, 1956); Raymond Phineas Stearns, *Science in the British Colonies of America* (Urbana: University of Illinois Press, 1970); Dirk Struik, *Yankee Science in the Making* (Boston: Little, Brown, 1948); Silvio A. Bedini *Thinkers and Tinkers: Early American Men of Science* (New York: Scribner's, 1975); Brooke Hindle, *Emulation and Invention* (New York: New York University Press, 1981); Whitfield J. Bell Jr., *Early American Science: Needs and Opportunities for Study* (Williamsburg, Va.: Institute for Early American History and Culture, 1955). For early republic histories of science in this vein, see John C. Greene, *American Science in the Age of Jefferson* (Ames: Iowa State University Press, 1984); George H. Daniels, *American Science in the Age of Jackson* (New York: Columbia University Press, 1968) and *Science in American Society, a Social History* (New York: Alfred A. Knopf, 1971); Charlotte M. Potter, *The Eagle's Nest: Natural History and American Ideas, 1812–1842* (Birmingham: University of Alabama Press, 1986)

11. See Richard H. Grove, *Green Imperialism: Colonial Expansion, Tropical Island Edens and the Origins of Environmentalism, 1600–1860* (New York: Cambridge University Press, 1995); Drayton, *Nature's Government*; Schiebinger, *Plants and Empire*; Schiebinger and Claudia Swan, eds., *Colonial Botany: Science, Commerce, and Politics in the Early Modern World* (Philadelphia: University of Pennsylvania Press, 2005); Jorge Cañizares-Esguerra, *Nature, Empire, and Nation: Explorations of the History of Science in the Iberian World* (Stanford, Calif.: Stanford University Press, 2006); Joyce E.

Chaplin, *The First Scientific American: Benjamin Franklin and the Pursuit of Genius* (New York: Basic Books, 2006); Chaplin, *Subject Matter: Technology, the Body, and Science on the Anglo-American Frontier, 1500–1676* (Cambridge, Mass.: Harvard University Press, 2006); Delbourgo, *A Most Amazing Scene of Wonders*; Delbourgo and Nicholas Dew, eds., *Science and Empire in the Atlantic World* (New York: Routledge, 2007); Gronim, *Everyday Nature*; Parrish, *American Curiosity*; Antonio Barrera-Osorio, *Experiencing Nature: The Spanish American Empire and the Early Scientific Revolution* (Austin: University of Texas Press, 2006). On the relationship between science and the European voyages of discovery more generally, see John Cascoigne, Science in the Service of Empire: Joseph Banks, the British State and the Uses of Science in the Age of Revolution (Cambridge: Cambridge University Press, 1998); the essays in David Philip Miller and Peter Hanns Reill, eds., *Visions of Empire: Voyages, Botany, and Representations of Nature* (Cambridge: Cambridge University Press, 1996).

12. For recent American scientific biography from the colonial era through the antebellum period, see Amy R. W. Meyers and Margaret Beck Pritchard, eds., *Empire's Nature: Mark Catesby's New World Vision* (Chapel Hill: University of North Carolina Press, 1998); Joyce Chaplin, *The First Scientific American: Benjamin Franklin and the Pursuit of Genius* (New York: Basic Books, 2007); Thomas P. Slaughter, *The Natures of John and William Bartram* (New York: Alfred A. Knopf, 1996); Joseph Ewan and Nesta Ewan, *Benjamin Smith Barton: Naturalist and Physician in Jeffersonian America* (St. Louis: Missouri Botanical Garden Press, 2007); Patricia Tyson Stroud, *Thomas Say: New World Naturalist* (Philadelphia: University of Pennsylvania Press, 1992); Donald Worster, *A River Runs West: The Life of John Wesley Powell* (New York: Oxford University Press, 2002). For history of early republic scientific institutions, see Alexandra Oleson and Sanborn C. Brown, eds., *The Pursuit of Knowledge in the Early American Republic: American Scientific and Learned Societies from Colonial Times to the Civil War* (Baltimore: Johns Hopkins University Press, 1976); Simon Baatz, *Knowledge, Culture, and Science in the Metropolis: The New York Academy of Sciences, 1817–1970* (New York: Annals of the New York Academy of Sciences, 1990); Baatz, "Philadelphia Patronage: The Institutional Structure of Natural History in the Early Republic, 1800–1833," *Journal of the Early American Republic* 8, no. 2 (1988): 111–38; Sally Gregory Kohlstedt, *The Formation of the American Scientific Community: The American Academy for the Advancement of Science* (Urbana: University of Illinois Press, 1976); Robert V. Bruce, *The Launching of Modern American Science* (New York: Alfred A. Knopf, 1987).

Chapter 1

1. Samuel Dexter, "A Letter on the Retreat of House-Swallows in Winter, from the Honourable Samuel Dexter, Esq.; to the Honourable James Bowdoin, Esq.; Pres. A. A.," *Memoirs of the American Academy of Arts and Sciences* 1 (Boston, 1785): 494–96. Dexter's letter was reprinted at least twice; see *American Museum, or Repository of Ancient and Modern Fugitive Pieces, &c., Prose and Poetical* 2 (1787): 357–59; also *Massachusetts Magazine, or, Monthly Museum of Knowledge and Rational Entertainment* 3

(1791): 621. For biographical information on Samuel Dexter, see John Arthur Garraty and Mark C. Carnes, eds., *American National Biography* 24 vols. (New York: Oxford University Press, 1999), 6:535–36.

2. Dexter, "A Letter on the Retreat of House-Swallows in Winter," 495.

3. Ibid., 495–96.

4. On the importance of probability in natural historical matters, see Ian Hacking, *The Emergence of Probability: A Philosophical Study of Early Ideas about Probability, Induction and Statistical Inference* (New York: Cambridge University Press, 1975), 146; Barbara J. Shapiro, *Probability and Certainty in Seventeenth-Century England: A Study of the Relationships between Natural Science, Religion, History, Law, and Literature* (Princeton, N.J.: Princeton University Press, 1983); Lorraine Daston, *Classical Probability in the Enlightenment* (Princeton, N.J.: Princeton University Press, 1988), 56–57. On the eighteenth-century European embrace of philosophical modesty, see Peter Gay, *The Enlightenment: An Interpretation*, 2 vols. (New York: W. W. Norton, 1996), 2:138–39; Keith Michael Baker, *Condorcet: From Natural Philosophy to Social Mathematics* (Chicago: University of Chicago Press, 1975), 87–95. For a perspective on modesty in early modern science, see Steven Shapin, *A Social History of Truth: Civility and Science in Seventeenth-Century England* (Chicago: University of Chicago Press, 1994), chap. 4; Jessica Riskin, *Science in the Age of Sensibility: The Sentimental Empiricists of the French Enlightenment* (Chicago: University of Chicago Press, 2002), chap. 3. The literature on the shock of discovery and its lasting effects is voluminous. Helpful examples include Anthony Grafton et al., *New Worlds, Ancient Texts: The Power of Tradition and the Shock of Discovery* (Cambridge, Mass.: Harvard University Press, 1992); Anthony Grafton and Nancy Siraisi, eds., *Natural Particulars: Nature and the Disciplines in Renaissance Europe* (Cambridge, Mass.: Harvard University Press, 1999); Karen Ordahl Kupperman, "Natural Curiosity: Curious Nature in Early America," *Common-Place* 4, no. 2 (January 2004), http://www.common-place.org/vol-04/no-02/kupperman/.

5. "Democracy of facts" is from Benjamin Smith Barton, *A Memoir Concerning the Fascinating Faculty Which Has Been Ascribed to the Rattle-Snake, and Other American Serpents* (Philadelphia, 1796), 50.

6. For an exploration of the politics of commonsense observation in Atlantic world science, see James Delbourgo, "Common Sense, Useful Knowledge, and Matters of Fact in the Late Enlightenment: The Transatlantic Career of Perkins's Tractors," *William and Mary Quarterly* 61 (October 2004): 643–84. On the tensions within the American naturalist community over the parameters of their practice, see Joyce E. Chaplin, "Nature and Nation: Natural History in Context," in *Stuffing Birds, Pressing Plants, Shaping Knowledge: Nature History in North America, 1730–1860*, ed. Sue Ann Prince (Philadelphia: American Philosophical Society, 2003), 76–96.

7. For a consideration of the legal foundations for natural history fact discourse, see Sargent, *The Diffident Naturalist*, chaps. 2 and 3; also, Barbara J. Shapiro, *A Culture of Fact: England, 1550–1720* (Ithaca, N.Y.: Cornell University Press, 2000), chaps. 5 and

6. Recent scholarship in the history of science and epistemological development has interrogated the means and processes by which natural knowledge was created, particularly the "fact." A host of scholars have focused attention on the social categories of "courtier" and "gentleman," highlighting local and historical differences. Other scholars trace the development of fact from its roots in English legal theory and mercantile practices and suggest a lower threshold for the admission and acceptance of truth claims. This chapter draws on this emerging and exciting historiography and finds that while genteel social standing assisted the acceptance of truth claims, by no means were claims from individuals of lesser standing precluded. See Shapin and Schaffer, *Leviathan and the Air-Pump*; Shapin, *A Social History of Truth*; and Poovey, *A History of the Modern Fact*.

8. Historians of the colonial period are uncovering the many ways in which colonists thought about and participated in natural history. While a complete listing of relevant books and articles is impossible, recent notable work include Pamela Regis, *Describing Early America: Bartram, Jefferson, Crèvecoeur, and the Rhetoric of Natural History* (DeKalb: Northern Illinois University Press, 1992); Thomas P. Slaughter, *The Natures of John and William Bartram* (New York: Alfred A. Knopf, 1996); Susan Scott Parrish, "The Female Opossum and the Nature of the New World," *William and Mary Quarterly* 54, no. 3 (1997): 475–514; Amy R. W. Meyers and Margaret Beck Pritchard, eds., *Empire's Nature: Mark Catesby's New World Vision* (Chapel Hill: University of North Carolina Press, 1998); Susan Scott Parrish, "Performances of Curiosity: British and British-American Natural Histories of the New World in the Colonial Period" (Ph.D. diss., Stanford University, 1998); Sara Stidstone Gronim, "Ambiguous Empire: The Knowledge of the Natural World in Colonial New York" (Ph.D. diss., Rutgers University, 1999); Kay Dian Kirz, "Curiosities, Commodities, and Transplanted Bodies in Hans Sloane's 'Natural History of Jamaica,'" *William and Mary Quarterly* 57, no. 1 (2000): 35–78; Joyce E. Chaplin, *Subject Matter: Technology, the Body, and Science on the Anglo-American Frontier, 1500–1676* (Cambridge, Mass.: Harvard University Press, 2003); and Prince, ed., *Stuffing Birds, Pressing Plants, Shaping Knowledge*. Older but still relevant are Brooke Hindle, *The Pursuit of Science in Revolutionary America, 1735–1789* (Chapel Hill: University of North Carolina Press, 1956), and Stearns, *Science in the British Colonies of America*.

9. David Ramsay, *An Oration on the Advantages of American Independence: Spoken before a Publick Assembly of the Inhabitants of Charleston in South-Carolina, on the Second Anniversary of the Glorious Era* (Charleston, 1778), 2. This speech was also printed in the first issue of *The United States Magazine: A Repository of History, Politics, and Literature* (Philadelphia, 1779).

10. Joel Barlow, *An Oration, Delivered at the North Church in Hartford*, 19.

11. Writing about science and the United States often positioned the nation as the location in which the long process of enlightenment from ancient Greece and Egypt to the present would culminate. See [Samuel Dexter], *The Progress of Science. A Poem Delivered at Harvard College before a Committee of Overseers, April 21, 1780.*

By a Junior Sophister ([Boston], 1780); Samuel Cooper, *A Sermon Preached before his Excellency John Hancock, Esq; Governour, The Honourable the Senate, and House of Representatives of the Commonwealth of Massachusetts, October 25, 1780. Being the Day of the Commencement of the Constitution, and Inauguration of the New Government* (Boston, 1780); Owen Biddle, *An Oration, Delivered the Second of March, 1781, at the Request of the American Philosophical Society for Promoting Useful Knowledge, Before the Society and a Large and Respectable Assembly of Citizens and Foreigners* (Philadelphia, 1781); John Gardiner, *An Oration delivered July 4, 1785, at the Request of the Inhabitants of the Town of Boston, in Celebration of the Anniversary of American Independence* (Boston, 1785).

12. Ramsay, *An Oration on the Advantages of American Independence*, 5–6. A discussion of the relationship between science and agriculture can be found in Timothy Matlack, *An Oration, Delivered March 16th, 1780, Before the Patron, Vice-Presidents and Members of the American Philosophical Society, Held at Philadelphia, for Promoting Useful Knowledge* (Philadelphia, 1780). For a more thorough treatment of the patriotic rhetoric surrounding science in the early republic, see Hindle, *The Pursuit of Science in Revolutionary America, 1735–1789*, chap. 7; Greene, *American Science in the Age of Jefferson*, chap. 1; Christopher Looby, "The Constitution of Nature: Taxonomy as Politics in Jefferson, Peale, and Bartram," *Early American Literature* 22, no. 3 (1987): 252–73; I. Bernard Cohen, *Science and the Founding Fathers: Science in the Political Thought of Jefferson, Franklin, Adams, and Madison* (New York: Norton, 1995).

13. Charles Willson Peale, *Introduction to a Course of Lectures on Natural History, Delivered in the University of Pennsylvania, Nov. 16, 1799* (Philadelphia, 1800), 10–12.

14. Jeremy Belknap, *The History of New-Hampshire. Comprehending the Events of one Complete Century from the Discovery of the River Pascataqua* (Boston, 1792), 228–29.

15. For the effects of personal and cultural corruption on science, see Ramsay, *An Oration on the Advantages of Independence*, 2–5; also Biddle, *An Oration, Delivered the Second of March, 1781*, 6; Cooper, *A Sermon Preached before his Excellency John Hancock*, 4; John Gardiner, *An Oration delivered July 4, 1785, at the Request of the Inhabitants of the Town of Boston, in Celebration of the Anniversary of American Independence* (Boston, 1785).

16. For an exhaustive treatment of the origins and repercussions of the Buffonian controversy in European intellectual history, see Antonello Gerbi, *The Dispute of the New World: The History of a Polemic, 1750–1900*, trans. Jeremy Moyle (Pittsburgh: University of Pittsburgh Press, 1973), and more recently, Jorge Cañizares-Esguerra, *How to Write a History of the New World: Histories, Epistemologies, and Identities in the Eighteenth-Century Atlantic World* (Stanford, Calif.: Stanford University Press, 2001). See also Gilbert Chinard, "Eighteenth Century Theories on America as Human Habitat," *Proceedings of the American Philosophical Society* 91, no. 1 (1947): 27–57; Greene, *Science in the Age of Jefferson*, chap. 1; Charlotte M. Porter, *The Eagle's Nest: Natural History and American Ideas, 1812–1842* (University: University of Alabama Press, 1986),

chap. 1; Richard White, "Discovering Nature in North America," *Journal of American History* 79, no. 3 (1992): 874–91; and Laura Rigal, *The American Manufactory: Art, Labor, and the World of Things in the Early Republic* (Princeton, N.J.: Princeton University Press, 1998).

17. Thomas Jefferson, *Notes on the State of Virginia*, ed. William Peden (Chapel Hill: University of North Carolina Press, 1955), 47. See Jacques Roger and L. Pearce Williams, *Buffon: A Life in Natural History* (Ithaca, N.Y.: Cornell University Press, 1997); Georges Louis Leclerc de Buffon, *Histoire naturelle, générale et particulière*, 44 vols. (Paris: Imprimeries royale, 1749–88); the English translation most often cited during the early republican period is Georges Louis Leclerc Buffon, *Buffon's Natural History: Containing a Theory of the Earth, a General History of Man, of the Brute Creation, and of Vegetables, Minerals, &c. &c. &c.*, trans. Samuel Johnson (London, 1797).

18. Samuel Williams, *Natural and Civil History of Vermont* (Walpole, N.H., 1794), v.

19. Jefferson, *Notes on the State of Virginia*, 177.

20. James Mease, *A Geological Account of the United States; Comprehending a Short Description of their Animal, Vegetable, and Mineral Productions, Antiquities and Curiosities* (Philadelphia, 1807), 86.

21. Belknap, *The History of New-Hampshire*, 229; Jefferson, *Notes on the State of Virginia*, 63–64; Benjamin Smith Barton, "Lecture on Natural Knowledge," Barton Papers, Miscellaneous Papers, APS.

22. For a discussion of implications of the Baconian reforms, see Daston and Park, *Wonders and the Order of Nature*, chap. 6. See also Paula Findlen, "Courting Nature," in *Cultures of Natural History*, ed. N. Jardine, J. A. Secord, and E. C. Spary (New York: Cambridge University Press, 1996), 57–74; on Bacon's antipathy toward popular natural history, see Paula Findlen, "Disciplining the Disciple: Francis Bacon and the Reform of Natural History in the Seventeenth Century," in *History and the Disciplines in Early Modern Europe*, ed. Donald Kelley (Rochester, N.Y.: University of Rochester Press, 1997), 239–60.

23. Francis Hopkinson, "An Address to the American Philosophical Society, held at Philadelphia, for promoting useful knowledge. Delivered January 16, 1784," in *The Miscellaneous Essays and Occasional Writings of Francis Hopkinson, Esq.* (Philadelphia, 1792), 364–66 (emphasis in original).

24. Ibid., 366.

25. See "On the Submersion of Swallows: In a letter to the Editor of the (New York) Monthly Magazine," *Medical Repository* 4, no. 2 (1800): 211–13.

26. Olaus Magnus, *Histoire des pays septentrionavs* (Paris, 1561).

27. Pierre Belon, *L'Histoire de la natvre des oyseaux, avec levrs descriptions, & naifs portraicts retirez dv natvrel* (Paris, 1555); Francis Willughby and John Ray, *The Ornithology of Francis Willughby* (London, 1678); Mark Catesby, "Of Birds of Passage," *Philosophical Transactions of the Royal Society of London* 44 (1747): 435–44. For a brief history of the controversy over swallow migration, see Jean Dorst, *The Migration of*

Birds, trans. Constance D. Sherman (Boston: Houghton Mifflin, 1962), chap. 1. For a discussion of Mark Catesby's understandings of avian migration, see Joyce E. Chaplin, "Mark Catesby, A Skeptical Newtonian in America," in *Empire's Nature: Mark Catesby's New World Vision*, ed. Amy R. W. Meyers and Margaret Beck Pritchard (Chapel Hill: University of North Carolina Press, 1998), 60–64.

28. Peter Collinson, "A Letter to the Honourable J. Th. Klein, Secretary to the City of Dantzick, from Mr. Peter Collinson, F.R.S. concerning the Migration of Swallows," *Philosophical Transactions of the Royal Society of London* 51 (1760): 459–64; Collinson, "Remarks on Swallows on the Rhine: In a Letter from Mr. Archard, in Privy-Garden, to Mr. Peter Collinson, F.R.S," *Philosophical Transactions of the Royal Society of London* 53 (1763): 101–2; Daines Barrington, "An Essay on the periodical Appearing and Disappearing of certain Birds, at different Times of the Year. In a Letter from the Honourable Daines Barrington, Vice-Pres. R.S. to William Watson, M.D. F.R.S.," *Philosophical Transactions of the Royal Society of London* 62 (1772): 265–326.

29. Thomas Pennant, *British Zoology*, vol. 2 (London, 1768), 248–53.

30. A number of the swallow writings are surprisingly scholastic, detailing the known references to swallow submersion from ancient texts to the present day. See editorial footnote to Peter Cole, "On the Disappearance of Swallows in Autumn; in a Letter from Mr. Peter Cole, to Dr. Mitchill, Dated New-York, September 25, 1798," *Medical Repository* 2 (1798); Anonymous, "On the Submersion of Swallows," *Medical Repository* 3 (1800): 241–46; and Charles Caldwell, *Medical & Physical Memoirs, Containing, among Other Subjects, a Particular Enquiry into the Origin and Nature of the Late Pestilential Epidemics of the United States* (Philadelphia, 1801).

31. Most swallow testimonies of this period reported the birds either submerging or emerging from the mud of lakes and ponds or migrating. A third alternative was that the birds hibernated in hollow trees or caves. Hibernation testimonies, though less frequent than those concerning submersion or migration, are included here because, though they vary slightly from submersion stories, they share common traits of reportage, argument, and conclusions. The controversy over swallow migration and submersion has largely escaped the notice of historians. Those who have studied the debate either consider it a vestigial remnant of early modern folk knowledge or the by-product of nature observation by the "unscientific and credulous." As a result these studies push swallow submersion to the margins of natural history practice, deeming it the fantastic result of a prescientific era. See Elsa Guerdrum Allen, "The History of American Ornithology before Audubon," *Transactions of the American Philosophical Society* 41, no. 3 (1951): 387–591. William Clarke argues that "nothing more remarkable can be found in the romance of natural history" than the belief in swallow submersion; its adherents "led mankind astray for many generations." William Eagle Clarke, *Studies in Bird Migration* (London: Gurney and Jackson, 1912), 13. See also Frederick C Lincoln, *The Migration of American Birds* (New York: Doubleday, 1939); Dorst, *The Migrations of Birds*; and Kevin R. McNamara "The Feathered Scribe: The Discourses

of American Ornithology before 1800," *William and Mary Quarterly* 47, no. 2 (1990): 210–34.

32. See Semonin, *American Monster*; Delbourgo, *A Most Amazing Scene of Wonders.*

33. This chapter is situated at the intersection of literatures on scientific epistemology and the cultural history of scientific ideas and practice. On natural historical and scientific epistemology, see Shapin and Schaffer, *Leviathan and the Air-Pump*; Paula Findlen, *Possessing Nature: Museums, Collecting, and Scientific Culture in Early Modern Italy* (Berkeley: University of California Press, 1994); and Lorraine Daston and Katherine Park, *Wonders and the Order of Nature, 1150–1750* (New York: Zone Books, 1998). For examples of the how natural historical literature can shape culture and cultural expectation, see Stephen Greenblatt, *Marvelous Possessions: The Wonder of the New World* (Chicago: University of Chicago Press, 1992); and Mary Louise Pratt, *Imperial Eyes: Travel Writing and Transculturation* (New York: Routledge, 1992).

34. On Humboldt, see Pratt, *Imperial Eyes*; Aaron Sachs, *The Humboldt Current: Nineteenth-Century Exploration and the Roots of American Environmentalism* (New York: Penguin, 2007); and Jorge Cañizares-Esguerra, "How Derivative Was Humboldt? Microcosmic Nature Narratives in Early Modern Spanish America and the (Other) Origins of Humboldt's Ecological Sensibilities," in Schiebinger and Swan, eds., *Colonial Botany.*

35. Hopkinson, Peale, Barton, Ramsey, and Barlow will be discussed further below. On the prophets of glory, see Brooke Hindle, *Pursuit of Science in Early America* (Chapel Hill: University of North Carolina Press, 1953), chap. 7.

36. The literature on revolutionary-era print culture is vast and expanding. This chapter draws on Richard D. Brown, *Knowledge Is Power: The Diffusion of Information in Early America, 1700–1865* (New York: Oxford University Press, 1989); Michael Warner, *The Letters of the Republic: Publication and the Public Sphere in Eighteenth Century America* (Cambridge, Mass.: Harvard University Press, 1990); Dena Goodman, *The Republic of Letters: A Cultural History of the French Enlightenment* (Ithaca, N.Y.: Cornell University Press, 1994); and Christopher Grasso, *A Speaking Aristocracy: Transforming Public Discourse in Eighteenth-Century Connecticut* (Chapel Hill: University of North Carolina Press, 1999).

37. Shapiro, *A Culture of Fact*, chaps. 3–4; for an extended examination of early modern understanding of marvels, see Daston and Park, *Wonders and the Order of Nature*; also Findlen, *Possessing Nature*; and Krzysztof Pomian, *Collectors and Curiosities: Paris and Venice 1500–1800* (Cambridge: Polity Press, 1990). For an examination of wonders and curiosities in the eighteenth and nineteenth centuries, see Jan Bondeson, *The Feejee Mermaid and Other Essays in Natural and Unnatural History* (Ithaca, N.Y.: Cornell University Press, 1999).

38. The conversion narrative moving from unbelief to surprised but firm belief in its reality must have resonated with a reading public already familiar with the religious

conversion narratives. Unfortunately, space constraints preclude a thorough examination of the relationship between conversion narratives and natural history practice.

39. Josiah Blakeley, "On the Retreat of Swallows," *American Museum* 3 (1789): 451–52. For accounts similar to Blakeley's, see Severyn J. Bruyn, Esq. "A Letter on the Retreat of Swallows, and the Torpid State of certain Animals, in Winter," *Memoirs of the American Academy of Arts and Sciences* 2, no. 1 (1793): 96–99; Rev. Asa Packard, "A Letter on the Retreat of Swallows in Winter. From the Rev. Mr. Packard," *Memoirs of the American Academy of Arts and Sciences* 2, no. 1 (1793): 93–95. See also Belknap, *The History of New-Hampshire*, 3:128; Williams, *Natural and Civil History of Vermont*, 115–18.

40. Blakeley, "On the Retreat of Swallows," 451.

41. Ibid., 451–52.

42. Peter Cole, "On the Disappearance of Swallows in Autumn; in a Letter from Mr. Peter Cole, to Dr. Mitchell, dated New-York, September 25, 1798," *Medical Repository* 2 (1798): 178–80 (emphasis in original).

43. H. Pollack, "On the Submersion of Swallows," *Monthly Magazine, and American Review* 3 (1800): 36–37. This letter was reprinted in *Medical Repository* 4, no. 2 (1800): 215–16; and in *Literary Tablet* 1, no. 5 (1803): 19.

44. Anonymous, "On the Submersion of Swallows," *Medical Repository* 3 (1800): 241–46 (emphasis in original).

45. For a consideration of swallow submersion in Great Britain, see I. F. Lyle, "John Hunter, Gilbert White, and the Migration of Swallows," *Annals of the Royal College of Surgeons of England* 60, no. 6 (1978): 485–91; and Paul F. S. Cornelius, "Benjamin White (1725–1794), His Older Brother Gilbert, and Notes on the Hibernation of Swallows," *Archives of Natural History* 21, no. 2 (1994): 231–36.

46. Anonymous, "On the Submersion of Swallows," 241–46.

47. Charles Caldwell, "On the Winter Retreat of Swallows," in *Medical & Physical Memoirs, containing, Among Other Subjects, A Particular Enquiry into the Origin and Nature of the Late Pestilential Epidemics of the United States* (Philadelphia, 1801), 261–63. For Caldwell's interpretation of Barton and the swallow submersion controversy, see his *Autobiography of Charles Caldwell, M.D.* (1855; reprint, New York: Da Capo Press, 1968), 168–69.

48. Caldwell, *Medical & Physical Memoirs*, 273–74.

49. Ibid.

50. "Review of Caldwell's Medical and Physical Memoirs," *American Review, and Literary Journal* 1 (1801): 178–79.

51. Ibid.

52. Stories of toads and frogs found inside rocks and boulders appear frequently in early republic letters and publications. See Samuel Harrison to Thomas Jefferson, 28 May 1808, Archives, APS; Report of Committee on H. Darlington's paper on the Migration of Swallows/ Report of Committee on a frog found in a Rock, 4 November 1808, Archives, APS; Henry Rowe Schoolcraft, "Remarks on the Prints of Human Feet,

observed in the secondary limestone of the Mississippi Valley," *American Journal of Science and Arts* 5 (1822): 223–31; John Haywood, *The Natural and Aboriginal History of Tennessee, Up to the First Settlements Therein by the White People in the Year 1768* (Nashville, 1823), 55; and William A. Thompson, "On the Vitality of Toads, &c. enclosed in firm materials," *American Journal of Science and Arts* 25, no. 1 (1834): 41–47. For a history of enclosed toads, see Bondeson, *The Feejee Mermaid*, 280–308.

53. "Review of Caldwell's Medical and Physical Memoirs," 178–79.

54. "Review of Medical and Physical Memoirs," *Medical Repository* 5 (1802): 327–28.

55. For a similar case where facts are pitted against theory, see Riskin, *Science in the Age of Sensibility*, chap. 5, esp. 180–84.

56. Robert Dunbar to Benjamin Smith Barton, 7 January 1803, Archives, MSS Correspondence, APS.

57. Dunbar to Barton, 7 January 1803.

58. "Report of Committee (Natural History) on Dunbar paper on the Submersion of Swallows, 4 February, 1803," Archives, APS. A twenty-page fragment from an unidentified but printed manuscript detailing and critiquing reports of swallow submersion exists in the Barton Papers at the American Philosophical Society. See Benjamin Smith Barton, "Facts and Conjectures on Swallows," On Swallows, Barton Misc. Papers, Box 2, APS.

59. "Report of Committee (Natural History) on Dunbar paper on the Submersion of Swallows, 4 February, 1803."

60. Colonel Frederick Antes, "On the Hibernation of Swallows, by the Late Colonel Antes. Communicated by Dr. Barton," *Transactions of the American Philosophical Society* 6, no. 1 (1804): 59–60.

61. Benjamin Smith Barton, *A Memoir Concerning the Fascinating Faculty*, 7–9, 49. This memoir was read before the American Philosophical Society (1794), later appearing in the fourth volume of its *Transactions* (1799). For a treatment of the historical roots of "the fascinating faculty," see Herbert Leventhal, *In the Shadow of the Enlightenment: Occultism and Renaissance Science in Eighteenth Century America* (New York: New York University Press, 1976), chap. 5; also Stearns, *Science in the British colonies of America*, 354–55, 580–81.

62. Barton, *A Memoir Concerning the Fascinating Faculty*, 49–53, 61–65.

63. Ibid., 63.

64. Leventhal, *In the Shadow of the Enlightenment*, 138. Also Lloyd N. Jeffry, "Snake Yarns of the West and Southwest," *Western Folklore* 14 (October 1955): 251

65. Benjamin Smith Barton, *Supplement to a Memoir Concerning the Fascinating Faculty which has been Ascribed to the Rattle-snake, and other American Serpents. In a letter to Professor Zimmermann, of Brunswick, in Germany* (Philadelphia, 1800). Barton's *Memoir* was translated into German, where it was challenged in 1798 by Johann Friedrich Blumenbach, whose *Handbuch der Naturgeschischte* Barton attacked. Blumenbach's reply, "The fascinating Power of the Rattle-Snake, with some Remarks on

Dr. Barton's Memoir on that Subject," appeared in the London publication *Philosophical Magazine* (1798), 251–55, prompting the *Supplement*.

66. Charles R. Brown and Mary B. Brown, "Cliff Swallow (*Petrochelidon pyrrhonota*)," in *The Birds of North America Online*, ed. A. Poole (Ithaca, N.Y.: Cornell Lab of Ornithology, 1995), http://bna.birds.cornell.edu/bna/species/149 (accessed 30 November 2008).

67. John James Audubon, *Ornithological Biography* (Edinburgh, 1838), 4; Michael De Jong, "Northern Rough-Winged Swallow (*Stelgidopteryx serripennis*)," in *The Birds of North America Online*, ed. A. Poole (Ithaca, N.Y.: Cornell Lab of Ornithology, 1996), http://bna.birds.cornell.edu/bna/species/234 (accessed 30 November 2008).

68. Chris Elphick, John B. Dunning Jr., and David Allen Sibley, eds., *The Sibley Guide to Bird Life and Behavior* (New York: Alfred A. Knopf, 2001), 419–24

69. Anthony J. Erskine, "Swallows Foraging on the Ground," *Wilson Bulletin* 96, no. 1 (March 1984): 136–37; Robert R. Cohen and Mark L. Dymerski, "Swallows Taking Insects from Pond Surfaces," *Wilson Bulletin* 98, no. 3 (September 1986): 483–84; Spencer G. Sealy, "Rough-Winged Swallows Scavenging Adult Midges," *Wilson Bulletin* 94, no. 3 (September 1982): 368–69.

70. Robert O. Beatty, "Behavior of Nestling Tree Swallows in Water," *Auk* 64, no. 4 (August 1947): 617–18; R. J. Robertson, B. J. Stutchbury, and R. R. Cohen, "Tree Swallow (*Tachycineta bicolor*)," in *The Birds of North America Online*, ed. A. Poole (Ithaca, N.Y.: Cornell Lab of Ornithology, 1992), http://bna.birds.cornell.edu/bna/species/011 (accessed 30 November 2008); Barnett A. Garrison, "Bank Swallow (*Riparia riparia*)," in *The Birds of North America Online*, ed. A. Poole (Ithaca, N.Y.: Cornell Lab of Ornithology, 1999), http://bna.birds.cornell.edu/bna/species/414 (accessed 30 November 2008); Charles R. Brown and Mary B. Brown, "Barn Swallow (Hirundo rustica)," *The Birds of North America Online*, ed. A. Poole (Ithaca, N.Y.: Cornell Lab of Ornithology; 1995), http://bna.birds.cornell.edu/bna/species/452 (accessed 30 November 2008); Steven L. Lima, "Ecological and Evolutionary Perspectives on Escape from Predatory Attack: A Survey of North American Birds," *Wilson Bulletin* 105 (March 1993): 1–47

71. Robertson et al., "Tree Swallow."

72. Andrew E. McKechnie and Barry G. Lovegrove, "Avian Faculative Hypothermic Responses: A Review," *Condor* 104, no. 4 (November 2002): 705–24; Robert T. Lariewski and Henry J. Thompson, "Field Observation of Torpidity in the Violet-Green Swallow," *Condor* 68 (January–February 1966): 102–3. W. L. McAtee details numerous anecdotal reports of torpidity in swallows through the modern era. See W. L. McAtee, "Torpidity in Birds," *American Midland Naturalist* 38 (1947): 191–206.

73. Brown, "Barn Swallow"; Robertson et al., "Tree Swallow."

74. Robertson et al., "Tree Swallow."

75. Benjamin Smith Barton, *Fragments of the Natural History of Pennsylvania*; Hugh Williamson, *Observations on the Climate in Different Parts of America* (New York, 1811).

76. Brown, "Barn Swallow."

77. Harold B. Wood, "The History of Bird Banding," *Auk* 62 (1945): 256–65; Sibley et al., *The Sibley Guide to Birdlife and Behavior*, 60–61.

Chapter 2

1. In 1802 United States colleges and universities housed twenty-one full time academic positions in all fields of science according to Theodore Hornberger, *Scientific Thought in American Colleges, 1638–1800* (Austin: University of Texas Press, 1945). Hornberger based this figure on Samuel Miller's *A Brief Retrospect of the Eighteenth Century* (New York, 1803). George H. Daniels confirmed this number in *American Science in the Age of Jackson* (New York: Columbia University Press, 1968), 240.

2. On the Academy of Natural Science and the Lyceum of Natural History, see Simon Baatz, "Philadelphia Patronage: The Institutional Structure of Nature History in the New Republic, 1800–33," *Journal of the Early Republic* 8, no. 2 (1988): 111–38, and "Knowledge, Culture, and Science in the Metropolis: The New York Academy of Sciences, 1817–1970," *Annals of the New York Academy of Sciences* 584 (1990): 1–269. George H. Daniels traces a steady, if uneven, rise in the number of journals that published scientific material from a low of twelve in 1805 to around sixty-five by the early 1840s. Daniels, *American Science*, 231–32.

3. For a fascinating treatment of the collision between natural history, commerce, and natural historical expertise, see D. Graham Burnett, *Trying Leviathan: The Nineteenth-Century New York Court Case That Put the Whale on Trial and Challenged the Order of Nature* (Princeton, N.J.: Princeton University Press, 2007).

4. Parrish, *American Curiosity*. See also Thomas Hallock, "Male Pleasure and the Genders of Eighteenth-Century Botanic Exchange: A Garden Tour," *William and Mary Quarterly* 62 (October 2005): 697–718; Fredrika J. Teute, "The Loves of the Plants; or, The Cross-Fertilization of Science and Desire at the End of the Eighteenth Century," *Huntington Library Quarterly* 63, no. 3 (2000): 319–45.

5. See Andrew J. Lewis, "Gathering for the Republic: Botany in Early Republic America," in Schiebinger and Swan, eds., *Colonial Botany*, 66–80.

6. John Greene describes a vibrant community of plant, seed, and botanical information exchange among botanists living in or researching North America. See Greene, *American Science in the Age of Jefferson*, chap. 10.

7. For a window into this continuity of correspondence, see William Darlington, *Memorials of John Bartram and Humphry Marshall*, ed. Joseph Ewan (New York: Hafner, 1967). Darlington records the correspondence between Bartram, Marshall, and the English naturalist Peter Collinson before and after the Revolution.

8. Manasseh Cutler, "An Account of some of the vegetable productions, naturally growing in this Part of America," *Memoirs of the American Academy of Arts and Sciences* 1 (1785): 398–99.

9. Ibid., 396–97.

10. Charles E. Ford, "Botany Texts: A Survey of Their Development in American

Higher Education, 1643–1906," *History of Education Quarterly* 4, no. 1 (March 1964): 59–71

11. Philadelphia and its environs boasted the botanical gardens of John and William Bartram, Alexander Hamilton at Woodlands, and the nurseries of William Young Jr., George Logan of Stenton, George Gray of Gray's Garden at Philadelphia's Lower Ferry, and Dr. Thomas Parke, founder of the Philadelphia College of Physicians. New York had the Linnaean Botanic Garden founded by William Prince around 1770, the Elgin Botanic Garden started by David Hossack in 1801, and another garden created by an unknown plantsman. Harvard College also had a botanic garden. See Joseph and Nesta Ewan, "John Lyon, Nurseryman and Plant Hunter, and His Journal 1799–1814," *Transactions of the American Philosophical Society* 52, no. 2 (1953): 1–69. See also David Hossack, *A catalogue of plants contained in the botanic garden at Elgin, in the vicinity of New-York, established in 1801* (New York, 1806).

12. André Michaux, *Histoire des chênes de l'Amérique . . .* (Paris, 1801); Michaux, *Flora Boreali-Americana, sisten caracteres plantarum quas in America Septentrionali collegit et detexit. . . ,* 2 vols. (Paris, 1803); François André Michaux, *Histoire des arbres forestiers de l'Amerique Septentrionale. . . ,* 3 vols. (Paris, 1810–13; the American edition was published in Paris in 1818–19). See also Gilbert Chinard, "André and François-André Michaux and Their Predecessors: An Essay on Early Botanical Exchange between America and France," *Proceedings of the American Philosophical Society* 101 (1957): 344–61.

13. Frederick Pursh, *Flora Americae Septentrionalis: Or, A Systematic Arrangement and Description of the Plants of North America* (London: White, Cochrane, 1814).

14. Thomas Nuttall, *The Genera of North American Plants, and a catalogue of the species, to the year 1817* (Philadelphia: D. Heartt, 1818); Nuttall, *A Journal of Travels into the Arkansas Territory, during the year 1819: with occasional observations on the manners of the aborigines* (Philadelphia: T. H. Palmer, 1821); William P. C. Barton, *Compendium Floræ Philadelphicæ: containing a description of the indigenous and naturalized plants found within a circuit of ten miles around Philadelphia* (Philadelphia: M. Carey, 1818); Barton, *A Flora of North America* (Philadelphia: M. Carey, 1820–23); Stephen Elliott, *A Sketch of the Botany of South-Carolina and Georgia,* ed. and intro. Joseph Ewan, 2 vols. (New York: Hafner, 1971); Jacob Bigelow, *Florula Bostoniensis. A Collection of Plants of Boston and its Environs, with their generic and specific characters, synonyms, descriptions, places of growth, and time of flowering, and occasional remarks* (Boston: Cummings and Hilliard, 1814). See Greene, *American Science,* 270–74.

15. Amos Eaton to John Torrey, 12 January 1822, as quoted in Ethel McAllister, *Amos Eaton: Scientist and Educator, 1776–1842* (Philadelphia: University of Pennsylvania Press, 1941), 218.

16. Humphry Marshall, *Aubustrum Americanum: The American Grove, or, an Alphabetical Catalogue of Forest Trees and Shrubs, Native of the American United States, Arranged According to the Linnaean System* (Philadelphia, 1785), v–ix.

17. Bernard M'Mahon, *The American Gardener's Calendar, adapted to the climates*

and seasons of the United States (Philadelphia: B. Graves, 1806). See also Robert S. Cox, " 'I Never Yet Parted': Bernard McMahon and the Seeds of the Corps of Discovery," in *The Shortest and Most Practical Route: Lewis and Clark in Context,* ed. Robert S. Cox (Philadelphia: American Philosophical Society, 2004), 102–35; Greene, *American Science in the Age of Jefferson,* 50–51.

18. Samuel Deane, *The New England farmer, or, Georgical dictionary* (Worcester, Mass.: Isaiah Thomas, 1790).

19. Charles Willson Peale, *Introduction to a Course of Lectures on Natural History. Delivered in the University of Pennsylvania, Nov. 16, 1799* (Philadelphia, 1800), 10–12, 14.

20. Jefferson, *Notes on the State of Virginia,* Queries 1–7. For commentary on *Notes* as "literature of place," see Regis, *Describing Early America,* 84–97; Myra Jehlen, "The Literature of Colonization," in *The Cambridge History of American Literature,* ed. Sacvan Berkovitz (New York: Cambridge University Press, 1995), 121–23; Robert A. Ferguson, *Law and Letters in American Culture* (Cambridge, Mass.: Harvard University Press, 1984), 40–53. See also Myra Jehlen, *American Incarnation: The Individual, the Nation, and the Continent* (Cambridge, Mass.: Harvard University Press, 1986).

21. Belknap, *The History of New-Hampshire,* 96.

22. Samuel Williams, *The Natural and Civil History of Vermont* (Walpole, 1794), chaps. 1–6.

23. Emanuel D. Rudolph, "Almira Hart Lincoln Phelps (1793–1884) and the Spread of Botany in Nineteenth Century America," *American Journal of Botany* 71, no. 8 (1984): 1161–67.

24. Samuel L. Mitchill, "Extract from a public introductory discourse to the Botanical Lectures, delivered in the Hall of Columbia College, June 12, 1793," *New York Magazine, or Literary Repository* (1793): 403–4.

25. "The Study of Botany Recommended," *Philadelphia Repository and Weekly Register* (1803), 108.

26. Parrish, *American Curiosity.*

27. Thomas Hallock, "Male Pleasure and the Genders of Eighteenth-Century Botanic Exchange: A Garden Tour," *William and Mary Quarterly* 62 (October 2005): 697–718.

28. Parrish, *American Curiosity,* 133. See also Joyce Chaplin, *The First Scientific American: Benjamin Franklin and the Pursuit of Genius* (New York: Basic Books, 2006)

29. Nicholas Collin, "An Essay on those inquiries in Natural Philosophy, which at present are most beneficial to the United States of North America," *Transactions of the American Philosophical Society* 3 (1793): v.

30. Charles Creswell to American Philosophical Society, 1809, MSS Correspondence, Archives, APS; C. Brown to Benjamin Smith Barton, 30 November 1792, Barton Papers, Correspondence, APS; D. R. Patterson to Benjamin Smith Barton, 15 March 1808, Barton Papers, Correspondence, APS.

31. William Thorton to John Vaughan, 13 December 1805, MSS Correspondence,

Archives, APS. Joseph Richardson to John Vaughan, 6 June 1805, MSS Correspondence, Archives, APS. North Carolina Gold-Mine Company, Broadside, n.d., Archives, APS. Thorton's discovery is advertised and discussed in the Barton's *Medical Repository* at least two times from 1804 to 1806, see "Domestic Intelligence," *Medical Repository* 3 (1806): 429–30; see also "Medical and Philosophic News," *Medical Repository* 1 (1803–4): 307. Samuel Latham Mitchill also appears to have assisted in the identification of this gold. For information on the North Carolina gold economy, see Richard F. Knapp, "Golden Promise in the Piedmont: The Story of John Reed's Mine," *North Carolina Historical Review* 52 (1975): 1–19; Richard D. Knapp and Brent D. Glass, *Gold Mining in North Carolina: A Bicentennial History* (Raleigh: North Carolina Division of Archaeology and History, 1999); and Jeff Forret, "Slave Labor in North Carolina's Antebellum Gold Mines," *North Carolina Historical Review* 76 (1999): 135–62.

32. Susan Scott Parrish describes the colonial period as more welcoming of Indian botanical knowledge, even if Indian participation in that knowledge making was highly attenuated. By the early national period, it appears, Indian participation was becoming less welcome. It is quite surprising how little regarded indigenous botanical knowledge is in the writings of early republic botanists. See Parrish, *American Curiosity*, 257. See also Shiebinger, *Plants and Empire*.

33. William Paul Crillon Barton, *Vegetable Materia Medica of the United States; of Medical Botany: Containing a Botanical, General, and Medical History, of Medicinal Plants Indigenous to the United States*, 2 vols. (Philadelphia, 1817).

34. Benjamin Smith Barton, *Fragments of the Natural History of Pennsylvania* (Philadelphia, 1799), viii.

35. This notice is reprinted in James Mease, *The Picture of Philadelphia, Giving an Account of its Origin, Increase, and Improvements in Arts, Sciences, Manufactures, Commerce and Revenue* (Philadelphia, 1811), 305.

36. H. B. Trout to Benjamin Smith Barton, 20 January 1814, Barton Papers, Correspondence, APS. Trout referred to Benjamin Smith Barton, *Elements of Botany: Or, Outlines of the Natural History of Vegetables* (Philadelphia, 1803). The modern classification for the opium poppy is *Papaver somniferum*.

37. It is difficult to establish a relationship between H. B. Trout and George Washington Trout, though one is likely. They lived in contiguous western Pennsylvania counties, H. B. in Somerset, George Washington in Westmoreland.

38. George Washington Trout to Benjamin Smith Barton, 16 March 1814, Barton Papers, Correspondence, APS.

39. Gabriel Crane to Secretary of the American Philosophical Society, 27 May 1817, Archives, APS.

40. Peter Curtis to Benjamin Smith Barton, 15 June 1804, Verbal Communications, APS; John D. Gillespie to John Vaughan, 23 November 1807, MSS Communications, APS; David Thomas to David Rittenhouse and the APS, 24 January 1792, Archives, APS; and William Currie, "A Sketch of the Errors which have been Discov-

ered in some of the Philosophical Opinions of the Illustrious Sir Isaac Newton, and other Philosophers of Acknowledged Genious and Talents," Archives, APS.

41. Lorraine Daston and Katherine Park, *Wonders and the Order of Nature, 1150–1750* (New York: Zone Books, 1998), esp. chap. 9.

42. Edward Johnson to Benjamin Smith Barton, 4 November 1807, Barton Papers, Correspondence, APS.

43. Unfortunately, the archives of the American Philosophical Society contain only a few outbound letters and a few reports on these matters.

44. Benjamin Smith Barton, *Collections for an essay towards a Materia Medica of the United-States* (Philadelphia, 1798), 43–45.

45. Dr. S. P. Hildreth, "Information Concerning the Frasera Carolinensis, Otherwise Called the American Colombo Plant: In a Letter from Dr. S. P. Hildreth, of Marietta, in Ohio, Dated Marietta, July 30, 1810 (with a Figure.)," *Medical Repository* 15, no. 2 (1811); James Woodhouse, "An Account of a New, Pleasant, and Strong Bitter, and Yellow Dye, Prepared from the Stem and Root of the Xanthorhiza Tinctoria, or Shrub Yellow Root; with a Chemical Analysis of This Vegetable: Communicated by James Woodhouse, M.D. Professor of Chemistry in the University of Pennsylvania, & C.," *Medical Repository* 5, no. 2 (1802): 159–64.

46. Barton, *Collections for an Essay towards a Materia Medica*, 13.

47. John Beatty to Benjamin Smith Barton, 19 April 1809, Barton Papers, Correspondence, APS.

48. Thomas T. Hewson to Benjamin Smith Barton, 11 April [1809], Barton Papers, Correspondence, APS.

49. Richard Brown to Benjamin Smith Barton, 30 October 1807, Barton Papers, Correspondence, APS.

Chapter 3

1. Elijah Backus, "Copper Coin," misc. newspaper clipping, 18 June 1801, Thaddeus Mason Harris Papers, American Antiquarian Society, Worcester, Mass. (hereafter cited as AAS).

2. Caleb Atwater to Rejoice Newton, 21 August 1818, Atwater Papers, AAS.

3. Leven Powell to Henry Snow, 12 April 1824, Archives, Correspondence, AAS.

4. Timothy Alden, *A Collection of American Epitaphs and Inscriptions with Occasional Notes* (New York, 1814), 5:256–58; see also Timothy Alden, "Antiquities and Curiosities of Western Pennsylvania," *Archaeologia Americana* 1 (1820): 308–13.

5. [Daniel Drake], "An Address to the People of the Western Country," *American Journal of Science and Arts* 1, no. 2 (1818): 203–6; Daniel Drake, *An Anniversary Discourse, on the State and Prospects of the Western Museum Society: Delivered by Appointment, in the Chapel of the Cincinnati College, June 10th, 1820, on the Opening of the Museum* (Cincinnati, 1820). For a history of one western museum, see Louis Leonard Tucker, "Ohio Show-Shop: The Western Museum of Cincinnati, 1820–1867," in *A*

Cabinet of Curiosities: Five Episodes in the Evolution of American Museums, ed. Whitfield J. Bell (Charlottesville: University of Virginia Press, 1967), 73–105.

6. Caleb Atwater to Isaiah Thomas, 14 October 1820, Atwater Papers, Miscellaneous Correspondence, AAS.

7. The most frequently referenced early republican examples of the Lost Tribe thesis are Elias Boudinot, *A Star in the West; or, A Humble Attempt to Discover the Long Lost Tribes of Israel, preparatory to their return to their beloved city, Jerusalem* (Trenton, N.J., 1816); and Mordecai Manuel Noah, *Discourse on the Evidences of The American Indians being the descendants of the Lost Tribes of Israel* (New York, 1837). See also James Adair, *The History of the American Indians* (London, 1775); Charles Crawford, *An Essay on the Propagation of the Gospel; in which there are Numerous Facts and Arguments Adduced to prove that many of the Indians in North America are descended from the Ten Tribes* (Philadelphia, 1801); Robert Ingram, *Accounts of the Ten Tribes of Israel being in America; originally published by R. Manasseh Ben Israel* (London, 1792); and Ethan Smith, *View of the Hebrews; exhibiting the Destruction of Jerusalem; the Certain Restoration of Judah and Israel; the Present State of Judah and Israel; and An Address of the Prophet Isaiah Relative to their Restoration* (Poultney, Vt., 1823). The Lost Tribes thesis gained legitimacy when a phylactery was discovered in 1815 near Pittsfield, Massachusetts; see William Goetzmann, "The Case of the Missing Phylactery," *Proceedings of the American Antiquarian Society* 95, no. 1 (1985): 69–79.

8. Clifford's article was published in the *Western Review and Miscellaneous Magazine* in 1819–20. These quotations come from "Letter V," *Western Review* 1, no. 5 (1819): 283–92. After excavation, the vessel became a part of the natural history and antiquities collection at the Lexington Athenaeum, of which Clifford was president. See George W. Ranck, *History of Lexington, Kentucky* (Cincinnati, 1872), 295. The Athenaeum closed following Clifford's death in 1820 and the vessel was dispersed with the rest of the antiquities collection. Though it is difficult to determine with absolute certainty, a flagon fitting the description of the Triune Vessel is housed in the National Museum of the American Indian Cultural Resources Center in Suitland, Maryland, catalog # 236724.000. Clifford's letters have been edited and reprinted by Charles Boewe, ed., *John D. Clifford's Indian Antiquities: Related Material by C. S. Rafinesque* (Knoxville: University of Tennessee Press, 2000).

9. Clifford, "Indian Antiquities, Letter V," 292.

10. The mounds of the Ohio River Valley belong to two cultural groups. The earlier of the two, the Adena culture, lived in the area between 1000 and 200 B.C.E. and occupied an area comprising southern Ohio, eastern Indiana, northern Kentucky, West Virginia, and southwestern Pennsylvania. The other, the Hopewell culture, occupied the Ohio River Valley from approximately 200 to 700 C.E. and describes not a group of people but shared cultural traits among different peoples. The Triune Vessel was an effigy pot manufactured by people who inhabited the Ohio and Mississippi river valleys from 1000 to 1600 C.E., referred to as the Mississippian culture because of shared cultural traits.

11. Robert Silverberg, *Mound Builders of Ancient America: The Archaeology of a Myth* (Athens: Ohio University Press, 1968), 15.

12. Angela Miller, " 'The Soil of an Unknown America': New World Lost Empires and the Debate over Cultural Origins, *American Art* 8 (1994): 26.

13. Silverberg, *Mound Builders*, 15. Other works that argue this interpretation are Roger G. Kennedy, *Hidden Cities: The Discovery and Loss of Ancient North American Civilization* (New York: Free Press, 1994); Thomas Gilbert Tax, "The Development of American Archaeology, 1800–1879" (Ph.D. diss., University of Chicago, 1973); and Stephen Williams, *Fantastic Archaeology: The Wild Side of North American Prehistory* (Philadelphia: University of Pennsylvania Press, 1991). This ridicule began as early as the nineteenth century; see Adolph Francis Bandelier, *The Romantic School in American Archaeology* (New York, 1885). For a descriptive account of archaeology during this period, see Greene, *American Science in the Age of Jefferson*, chap. 13.

14. The literature on early American magic and the occult is vast and expanding. Works that have proven invaluable for this chapter include John L. Brooke, *The Refiner's Fire: The Making of Mormon Cosmology, 1644–1844* (New York: Cambridge University Press, 1994); Jon Butler, "Magic, Astrology, and the Early American Religious Heritage, 1600–1760," *American Historical Review* 84, no. 2 (1979): 317–46; Jon Butler, *Awash in a Sea of Faith: Christianizing the American People* (Cambridge, Mass.: Harvard University Press, 1990); Herbert Leventhal, *In the Shadow of the Enlightenment: Occultism and Renaissance Science in Eighteenth Century America* (New York: New York University Press, 1976); D. Michael Quinn, *Early Mormonism and the Magic World View*, rev. ed. (Salt Lake City: Signature Books, 1998); and Alan Taylor, "The Early Republic's Supernatural Economy: Treasure Seeking in the American Northeast, 1780–1830," *American Quarterly* 38, no. 1 (1986): 6–34.

15. For surveys of some of these theories, see Lee Eldridge Huddleston, *Origins of the American Indians: European Concepts, 1492–1729* (Austin: University of Texas Press, 1967); Robert Wauchope, *Lost Tribes and Sunken Continents; Myth and Method in the Study of American Indians* (Chicago: University of Chicago Press, 1962); Paul Shao, *The Origin of Ancient American Cultures* (Ames: Iowa State University Press, 1983); and E. James Dixon, *Quest for the Origins of the First Americans* (Albuquerque: University of New Mexico Press, 1993).

16. See Drew McCoy, *The Elusive Republic: Political Economy in Jeffersonian America* (Chapel Hill: University of North Carolina Press, 1980), 17–32. See also Gladys Bryson, *Man and Society: The Scottish Inquiry of the Eighteenth Century* (New York: A. M. Kelley, 1968); Ronald L. Meek, *Social Science and the Ignoble Savage* (New York: Cambridge University Press, 1976); Robert A. Nisbet, *Social Change and History: Aspects of the Western Theory of Development* (New York: Oxford University Press, 1969).

17. James Bowdoin, *A Philosophical Discourse Addressed to the American Academy of Arts and Sciences* (Boston, 1780), 6–7.

18. Jefferson, *Notes on the State of Virginia*, 97–100.

19. Members of the Ohio Company were not the first to describe the mounds of the Ohio Valley. Travelers and missionaries in colonial America reported individual mounds, among them Peter Kalm, *Travels into North America: Containing its natural history, and a circumstantial account of its plantations and agriculture in general, with the civil, ecclesiastical and commercial state of the country, the manners of the inhabitants, and several curious and important remarks on various subjects*, ed. Johann Reinhold Forster (London, 1770); Jonathan Carver, *Travels Through the Interior Parts of North America, in the Years 1766, 1767, 1768* (London, 1781). Neither described mound groupings, however, which probably led readers to suppose that their examples were Indian burial mounds.

20. Jonathan Heart, "A Letter from Major Jonathan Heart, to Benjamin Smith Barton," *Transactions of the American Philosophical Society* 3 (1793): 214–22. A version of this letter first appeared in the *Columbian Magazine*; see "Account of some Remains of ancient Works, on the Muskingum, with a Plan of these Works. By J. Heart, Capt. in the first American regiment.; Explanation of the Plate, *Columbian Magazine* (1787): 425–27. See also Samuel H. Parsons, "Discoveries Made in the Western Country, by General Parsons," *Memoirs of the American Academy of Arts and Sciences* 2 (1793): 119–26. Winthrop Sargent, secretary of the Ohio Company, sent a similar account of antiquities to the American Academy of Arts and Sciences but his letter was not published until the Academy's 1855 volume of *Memoirs*. Winthrop Sargent, "Plan of an Ancient Fortification at Marietta, Ohio. Commonwealth of Massachusetts; Boston, March the 27th 1787. References and Explanations," *Memoirs of the American Academy of Arts and Science* 6 (1855): 25–30.

21. This theory was popularized by Noah Webster in the late 1780s and 1790s and discussed in a series of articles in his *American Magazine*. See Noah Webster, "Antiquity," *American Magazine* (1787): 15–20; Webster, "To the Revd. Ezra Stiles, D.D.L.L.D.," *American Magazine* (1788): 537–45; Webster, "Note," *American Magazine* (1789): 27–31; Webster, "Note," *American Magazine* (1790): 323–29.

22. Heart, "A Letter from Major Jonathan Heart," 217.

23. Heart relates that the location of this site is "on the east side of a small branch of the Big-Black, a river which empties itself into the Mississippi, nearly in latitude 33. north." Without more information it is difficult to determine precisely which archaeological site he is describing, but it seems likely that it is the Nanih Waiya site near Philadelphia, Miss. Heart, "A Letter from Major Jonathan Heart," 216–17.

24. Ibid., 217–18.

25. Ibid., 218.

26. James Madison, "A Letter on the supposed Fortifications of the Western Country, from Bishop Madison of Virginia to Dr. Barton," *Transactions of the American Philosophical Society* (1804): 132–33.

27. Ibid., 140.

28. Henry Marie Brackenridge, "On the Population and Tumuli of the Aborigines of North America. In a Letter from H. H. Brackenridge, Esq. to Thomas Jefferson,"

Transactions of the American Philosophical Society n.s. 1 (1818): 153. This letter was read before the APS in 1813 and printed in *Niles' Register* of that year. The *Transactions* title misattributes the article to Henry Marie's father, the Pennsylvania author and jurist Hugh Henry Brackenridge. However, it is signed H. M. and *Transactions* similarly references H. M. Brackenridge's other book, *Views of Louisiana* (1814).

29. The Delaware missionary John Heckewelder was frequently invoked as the primary authority on the Delaware history. See John Heckewelder, "An Account of the History, Manners, and Customs of the Indian Natives who once inhabited Pennsylvania and the Neighboring States," *Transactions of the Historical and Literary Committee of the American Philosophical Society* 1 (1819). James Adair was also an authority frequently cited on Indian ignorance of the mounds; see his *The History of the American Indians* (London, 1775). See also R. Douglas Hurt, *The Ohio Frontier: Crucible of the Old Northwest, 1720–1830* (Bloomington: Indiana University Press, 1996); James H. O'Donnell III, *Ohio's First Peoples* (Athens: Ohio University Press, 2004); Donald B. Ricky, ed., *Encyclopedia of Ohio Indians* (St. Clair Shores, Mich.: Somerset Publishers, 1998).

30. Mannaseh Cutler to Benjamin Smith Barton, 31 August 1792, Archives, APS.

31. Benjamin Smith Barton, "Observations and Conjectures concerning Certain Articles Which Were Taken out of an Ancient Tumulus, or Grave, at Cincinnati, in the County of Hamilton, and Territory of the United-States, North-West of the River Ohio: In a Letter from Benjamin Smith Barton, M. D. to the Reverend Joseph Priestley, L L. D. F. R. S. &c.," *Transactions of the American Philosophical Society* (1799): 181.

32. Thaddeus Mason Harris, *The Journal of a Tour into the Territory Northwest of the Allegheny Mountains; Made in the Spring of the Year 1803, with a Geographical and Historical Account of the State of Ohio. Illustrated with Original Maps and Views* (Boston, 1805), 58–59.

33. John Adams to Thomas Jefferson, 21 May 1812, *The Adams-Jefferson Letters: The Complete Correspondence between Thomas Jefferson and Abigail and John Adams*, ed. Lester J. Cappon (Chapel Hill: University of North Carolina Press, 1959), 305.

34. Thomas Jefferson to John Adams, 11 June 1812, *The Adams-Jefferson Letters*, 306–7.

35. John Adams to Thomas Jefferson, 28 June 1812, *The Adams-Jefferson Letters*, 308–10.

36. Zadok Cramer, *The navigator: containing directions for navigating the Monongahela, Alleghany, Ohio, and Mississippi Rivers* (Pittsburgh, 1808), 120–21.

37. Benjamin Smith Barton, *New Views of the Origin of the Tribes and Nations of America* (Philadelphia, 1798), v–vi.

38. Angela Miller, *Empire of the Eye: Landscape Representation and American Cultural Politics, 1825–1875* (Ithaca, N.Y.: Cornell University Press, 1993), 23–37.

39. Constantin François de Chassebœuf, Comte de Volney, *A View of the Soil and Climate of the United States of America*, trans. Charles Brockden Brown (Philadelphia, 1804), 6–7. On concerns about climate in early national life, see Conevery Valencious,

The Health of the Country: How American Settlers Understood Themselves and Their Land (New York: Basic Books, 2004).

40. Volney, *A View of the Soil and Climate of the United States of America*, 6–7, 261–62. See also Volney, *The Ruins; or a Survey of the Revolutions of Empire*, trans. Charles Brockden Brown (Philadelphia, 1799).

41. Climatic melioration through cultivation is a standard theme in early republic natural historical and antiquarian writings. These observations are taken from Hugh Williamson, *Observations on the Climate in Different Parts of America* (New York, 1811), 87. See also Benjamin Smith Barton, *Fragments of the Natural History of Pennsylvania* (Philadelphia, 1799); David Thomas, *Travels through the Western Country in the Summer of 1816. Including Notices of the Natural History, Topography, Commerce, Antiquities, Agriculture* (Auburn, N.Y., 1819); Samuel Williams, *The Natural and Civil History of Vermont* (Walpole, N.H., 1794).

42. James Foster, "Letter on the Indian Antiquities of the Western Country," *American Medical and Philosophical Register, or Annals of Medicine, Natural History, Agriculture, and the Arts* 2 (1814): 397.

43. John Heckewelder, "An Account of the History, Manners, and Customs of the Indian Natives who once inhabited Pennsylvania and the Neighboring States," *Transactions of the Historical and Literary Committee of the American Philosophical Society* 1 (1819). The legend of the Alliwegi is recounted in chapter 1, "Historical Traditions of the Indians."

44. Abbe D. Franceso Clavigero, *The History of Mexico. Collected from Spanish and Mexican Historians, from Manuscripts, and Ancient Paintings of the Indians*, trans. Charles Cullen (London, 1787).

45. Clifford, "Indian Antiquities, Letter II," *Western Review* 1, no. 2 (1819): 174–75.

46. Pierre François Xavier de Charlevoix, *Journal of a Voyage to North America*, vol. 1, ed. Louise Phelps Kellog (1761; reprint, Chicago: Caxton Club, 1923), 55.

47. Edward G. Gray, *New World Babel: Languages and Nations in Early America* (Princeton, N.J.: Princeton University Press, 1999), 125.

48. Barton, *New Views*, lxxiv–lxxv.

49. Gray, *New World Babel*, 128–31.

50. Brackenridge, "On the Population and Tumuli," 151–54.

51. Alexander von Humboldt, *Researches concerning the Institutions and Monuments of the Ancient Inhabitants of America, with descriptions and views of some of the most striking scenes in the Cordilleras. Written in French by Alexander de Humboldt, & Translated into English by Helen Maria Williams*, 2 vols. (London, 1814).

52. Brackenridge, "On the Population and Tumuli," 156–57.

53. See "Review of the Transactions of the American Philosophical Society, vol. vi. Part I. 4 to. pp. 190. Philadelphia. Atkin. 1806," *Medical Repository of Original Essays and Intelligence, Relative to Physic, Surgery, Chemistry, and Natural History* 2 (1804–5): 291–309.

54. Boewe, *John D. Clifford's Indian Antiquities*, xii.

55. Caleb Atwater, "Description of the Antiquities Discovered in the State of Ohio and other Western States," *Archaeologia Americana: Transactions and Collections of the American Antiquarian Society* 1 (1820): 109.

56. Atwater is referring to DeWitt Clinton, "A Memoir on the Antiquities of the Western parts of the State of New-York," *Transactions of the Literary and Philosophical Society of New York* 2 (1815–25): 71–85; Daniel Drake, *Natural and statistical view; or picture of Cincinnati and the Miami country* (Cincinnati, 1815); and Brackenridge, *Views of Louisiana.*

57. Atwater, "Description of the Antiquities," 110–11. The ignis fatuus, or the will o' the wisp, refers to the ghostly lights sometimes seen over bogs. Atwater quotes the Scots scholar and poet James Beattie, from *The Minstrel* (1771–72), "By the glare of false science betray'd, That leads to bewilder, and dazzles to blind."

58. The American Antiquarian Society was founded by the Worcester publisher Isaiah Thomas and titled its first issue of transactions *Archaeologia Americana.*

59. Caleb Atwater to Rejoice Newton, 30 May 1818, Atwater Papers, Miscellaneous Correspondence, AAS.

60. Caleb Atwater to Rejoice Newton, 21 August 1818, Atwater Papers, Miscellaneous Correspondence, AAS.

61. Caleb Atwater to Isaiah Thomas, 24 February 1819, Atwater Papers, Miscellaneous Correspondence, AAS. Atwater's writings did appear in this publication. The magazine published a letter from Atwater to President James Monroe, who asked him for more information about the mounds after Monroe visited Ohio in 1818. See Caleb Atwater, "Aboriginal Antiquities in the West.—Addressed to his Excellency JAMES MONROE, President of the United States," *American Monthly Magazine and Critical Review* 2 (March 1818): 333–37; Atwater, "Atwater's Notes on Ohio. Circleville, Feb. 13th, 1819. To the Editor of the American Monthly Magazine," *American Monthly Magazine and Critical Review* 4 (April 1819): 439–51.

62. See "Literary and Scientific Intelligence," *American Monthly Magazine and Critical Review* 4 (March 1819): 389.

63. Atwater was referring to a letter that appeared in Benjamin Silliman's new *American Journal of Science* that advertised the formation of a natural history museum in Cincinnati, Ohio, one that promised collectors that it would, "if required, pay a reasonable price for every article which may be deemed worthy of introduction into the museum." See "Address to the People of the Western Country," *American Journal of Science* 1 (January 1819): 203–8. Readers at the AAS could not have failed to miss the appendix to this article, which promoted Atwater's work on Ohio. This announcement signaled the formation of Cincinnati's famed Western Museum, overseen by the physician Daniel Drake. See M. H. Dunlop, "Curiosities Too Numerous to Mention: Early Regionalism and Cincinnati's Western Museum," *American Quarterly* 36 (Autumn 1984): 524–48.

64. Caleb Atwater to Isaiah Thomas, 24 February 1819, Atwater Papers, Miscellaneous Correspondence, AAS.

65. No doubt Atwater's franking privilege as Circleville postmaster made this correspondence possible.

66. Caleb Atwater to Isaiah Thomas, 2 October 1819, Atwater Papers, AAS.

67. Caleb Atwater to Isaiah Thomas, 4 October 1819, Atwater Papers, AAS.

68. Contemporary critics have ridiculed Atwater's plate for depicting the mound groupings as more regular than they actually are.

69. Atwater, "Description of the Antiquities," 111.

70. The Scots naturalist William Pennant, the English theologian Adam Clarke, Alexander von Humboldt, and the German naturalist Peter Simon Pallas.

71. Caleb Atwater, "Description of the Antiquities," 194–95.

72. Samuel L. Mitchill, "The Original Inhabitants of America consisted of the same Races with the Malays of Australia, and the Tartars of the North," *Archaeologia Americana* 1 (1820): 323–25.

73. [C. S. Rafinesque], "Archaeologia America: Transactions and Collections of the American Antiquarian Society, published by direction of the Society; Vol. 1," *Western Review and Miscellaneous Magazine* 3 (September 1820): 89–113. See Charles Boewe, "The Fall from Grace of the 'Base Wretch' Rafinesque," in *Profiles of Rafinesque*, ed. Charles Boewe (Knoxville: University of Tennessee Press, 2003), 210–13

74. Caleb Atwater to Isaiah Thomas, 29 September 1820, Atwater Papers, AAS. See also Caleb Atwater to Isaiah Thomas, 2 September 1820; Atwater to Thomas, 12 October 1820; Atwater to Thomas, 18 October 1820, Atwater Papers, AAS.

75. See Boewe, "The Fall from Grace of the 'Base Wretch' Rafinesque." See also Leonard Warren, *Constantine Samuel Rafinesque: A Voice in the American Wilderness* (Lexington: University Press of Kentucky), 138–47.

76. Charles Bottin to T. M. Harris, 6 February 1823, Archives, Correspondence, AAS; Alexander von Humboldt to George Bancroft, 5 September 1821, Bancroft Papers, Correspondence, box 1, folder 1, AAS; Henry Kretchman to T. M. Harris, 15 August 1829, Thaddeus Mason Harris Papers, AAS; Thomas Carew Hunt to Thaddeus Mason Harris, 20 March 1843, Harris Papers, AAS.

77. William Ellis wrote, "If the opinion of some American antiquaries be correct, that the skeletons found in the caverns of Kentucky and Tennessee are those of a Malay tribe, and some of the bodies were wrapped in feather cloaks similar to those used 'in the Sandwich and Figi islands,' and 'the best defined specimens of art among the antiquities of Ohio and Kentucky are clearly of an Polynesian character;' it would appear that the North Americans, Polynesians, and Malays were formerly the same people, or had one common origin." See William Ellis, *Polynesian Researches, during a Residence of Nearly Eight Years in the Society and Sandwich Islands* (New York, 1833), 1:104–5.

78. For a discussion of homologies, see David J. Meltzer, introduction to E. G. Squier and E. H. Davis, *Ancient Monuments of the Mississippi Valley*, ed. David J. Meltzer (1848; reprint, Washington, D.C.: Smithsonian Institution Press, 1998), 35–51.

79. S. Morton, "Notice of an ancient Mound, near Wheeling, Virginia," *American Journal of Science and Arts* 6 (1823): 167–68.

80. John Haywood, *The Natural and Aboriginal History of Tennessee, Up to the First Settlements Therein by the White People in the Year 1768* (Nashville, 1823). Chapters 3–5 are devoted to the ancient history of Tennessee.

81. William Pidgeon, *Traditions of De-coo-dah: and antiquarian researches, comprising extensive explorations, surveys, and excavations of the wonderful and mysterious earthen remains of the mound-builders in America, the traditions of the last prophet of the Elk Nation relative to their origin and use; and the evidences of an ancient population more numerous than the present aborigines* (New York, 1853).

82. Josiah Priest, *American Antiquities and Discoveries in the West: Being an Exhibition of the Evidence that an Ancient Population of Partially Civilized Nations Differing Entirely from those of the Present Indians Peopled America Many Centuries Before its Discovery by Columbus, and Inquiries into their Origin, with a Copious Description of Many of their Stupendous Works, Now in Ruins, with Conjectures Concerning What May Have Become of Them*, 3rd ed. (Albany, 1833).

83. C. S. Rafinesque, *Ancient History, or Annals of Kentucky; with a Survey of the Ancient Monuments of North America, and a Tabular View of the Principal Languages and Primitive Nations of the Whole Earth* (Frankfort, Ky., 1824).

84. Cornelius Matthews, *Behemoth: A Legend of the Mound-Builders* (New York, 1839).

85. Tax, "The Development of American Archaeology," 167–68, 170; Miller, "Soil of an Unknown America," 10–11.

86. William H. Prescott to T. M. Harris, 16 February 1835, Thaddeus Mason Harris Papers, AAS.

Chapter 4

1. Edward Hitchcock, *Utility of Natural History. A Discourse Delivered before the Berkshire Medical Institution, at the Organization of the Lyceum of Natural History, in Pittsfield, Sept. 10, 1823* (Pittsfield, 1823), 3.

2. Ibid., 3, 29–30.

3. Ibid., 30–32.

4. For a helpful discussion of the differences between natural theology and a theology of nature, see Jonathan R. Topham, "Science, Natural Theology, and Evangelicalism in Nineteenth-Century Scotland: Thomas Chalmers and the *Evidence* Controversy," in *Evangelicals and Science in Historical Perspective*, ed. David N. Livingstone et al. (New York: Oxford University Press, 1999), 142–76. While understandings of natural theology and theology of nature in America remain largely unexamined, British historiography is rich and extensive. John H. Brooke first suggested the concept of a theology of nature; see John H. Brooke, "Natural Theology in Britain from Boyle to Paley," in *New Interactions between Theology and Natural Science*, ed. John H. Brooke and R. Hooykaas (Milton Keyes: Open University, 1974), 5–54; John H. Brooke,

Science and Religion: Some Historical Perspectives (New York: Cambridge University Press, 1991), chap. 6; Jonathan R. Topham, "'An Infinite Variety of Arguments': The *Bridgewater Treatises* and British Natural Theology in the 1830s" (Ph.D. diss., University of Lancaster, 1993).

5. The two best treatments of science and religion in this period are Dwight Theodore Bozeman, *Protestants in an Age of Science: The Baconian Ideal and Antebellum American Religious Thought* (Chapel Hill: University of North Carolina Press, 1977), and Herbert Hovenkamp, *Science and Religion in America, 1800–1860* (Philadelphia: University of Pennsylvania Press, 1978). For shorter discussions of natural theology and natural science, see Daniels, *American Science in the Age of Jackson*, chap. 9; Greene, *American Science in the Age of Jefferson*; John C. Greene, *The Death of Adam: Evolution and Its Impact on Western Thought* (Ames: Iowa State University Press, 1959); Charlotte M. Porter, *The Eagle's Nest: Natural History and American Ideas, 1812–1842* (Tuscaloosa: University of Alabama Press, 1986); and Henry F. May, *The Enlightenment in America* (New York: Oxford University Press, 1976). Perry Miller continues to exert his influence over historiographical understandings of science and religion in this period; see Perry Miller, *Nature's Nation* (Cambridge, Mass.: Belknap Press of Harvard University Press, 1967); and Perry Miller, *The Life of the Mind: From the Revolution to the Civil War* (New York: Harcourt, Brace and World, 1965).

6. Linda Kerber, *Federalists in Dissent: Imagery and Ideology in Jeffersonian America* (Ithaca, N.Y.: Cornell University Press, 1970), chap. 3; Dirk J. Struik, *Yankee Science in the Making* (Boston: Little, Brown, 1948).

7. For a discussion of the religious attitudes within British scientific organizations, see Jack Morrell and Arnold Thackray, *Gentlemen of Science: Early Years of the British Association for the Advancement of Science* (Oxford: Clarendon Press, 1981). Evidence suggests that American scientific institutions, while not overtly secular, avoided religious controversies by taking ambiguous positions on the subject. See Simon Baatz, "Philadelphia Patronage: The Institutional Structure of Natural History in the Early Republic, 1800–1833," *Journal of the Early Republic* 8 (Summer 1988): 119. See also Edward J. Nolan, *A Short History of the Academy of Natural Sciences in Philadelphia* (Philadelphia, 1909), 6.

8. For a discussion of popular natural history works, see Margaret Welch, *The Book of Nature: Natural History in the United States, 1825–1875* (Boston: Northeastern University Press, 1998), 133–71. Examples of the various forms include *Garden Amusements, for Improving the Minds of Little Children* (New York, 1814); *Natural History of Birds, containing a Familiar Survey of the Feathered Creation. To which is Added, a Short History of Beasts* (Albany, 1808); *A Walk and Conversation, between a Fond Father and His Little Son, as they took a walk through the fields and meadows, &c. For the use of Children* (Norwich, Conn., 1804); *The Youth's Cabinet of Nature, for the Year; Containing Curious Particulars Characteristic of Each Month. Intended to Direct Young People to the Innocent and Agreeable Employment of Observing Nature* (New York, 1814); Uncle

Philip, *Natural History; or, Uncle Philip's Conversations with the Children about Tools and Trades among inferior Animals* (New York, 1833).

9. Henri Bernardin de Saint-Pierre, *Studies of Nature*, 3 vols., trans. Henry Hunter, ed. Benjamin Smith Barton, vol. 1 (Philadelphia, 1808).

10. Saint-Pierre, *Studies of Nature*, 3:17, 22–23.

11. Ibid., 24–25.

12. The caption below the engraving is the text of Genesis 2:19–20: "And out of the ground the Lord God formed every beast of the field, and every fowl of the air; and brought them unto Adam to see what he would call them: and whatsoever Adam called every living creature, that was the name thereof. And Adam gave names to all cattle, and to the fowl of the air, and to every beast of the field; but for Adam there was not found a help-meet for him."

13. Thaddeus Mason Harris, *The Natural History of the Bible: or a Description of All the Beasts, Birds, Fishes, Insects, Reptiles, Trees, Plants, Metals, Precious Stones, &c. Mentioned in the Sacred Scriptures. Collected by the best Authorities, and Alphabetically Arranged* (Boston, 1793), i. A nearly identical frontispiece can be found in George Riley, *Beauties of the Creation: or, a New Moral System of Natural History; Displayed in the Most Singular, Curious and Beatiful Quadrupeds, Birds, Insects, Trees, Shrubs & Flowers. Designed to Inspire Youth with Humanity Towards the Brute Creation; and Bring Them Early Acquainted with the Wonderful Works of the Divine Creator*, 3d American ed. (Worcester, Mass., 1798).

14. Charles Christopher Reiche, *Fifteen discourses on the marvellous works in nature, delivered by a father to his children: calculated to make mankind feel, in every thing, the very presence of a Supreme Being, and to influence their minds with a permanent delight in, and firm reliance upon, the directions of an almighty, all-good, and all-wise Creator, and Governor* (Philadelphia, 1791), iv.

15. Riley, *Beauties of the Creation*, v–vi

16. Illustrative examples of this didactic juvenile literature include T. H. Gallaudet, *The Youth's Book on Natural Theology; Illustrated in Familiar Dialogues, with Familiar Engravings* (New York, 1832); Dr. Blatchly, *The Pleasures of Contemplation, being a desultory investigation of the Harmonies, Beauties, and Benefits of Nature: Including a Justification of the Ways of God to Man, and a Glimpse of his Sovereign Beauty* (Philadelphia, 1817); James Fisher, *A Spring Day: or, Contemplations on Several Occurrences which Naturally Strike the Eye in that Delightful Season. To which is added reflections on the Nature, Qualifications, and Employment of a Retired Life* (New York, 1813); Reverend Dr. Jones, *Sermons on Botany and Natural History* (Boston, 1813); John Toogood, *The Book of Nature; A Discourse on some of those Instances of the Power, Wisdom, and Goodness of God, which are Within the Reach of Common Observation* (Boston, 1802).

17. For a mixture of the sublime and scientific, see Francis William Gilmer, "On the Geological Formation of the Natural Bridge of Virginia," *Transactions of the American Philosophical Society* n.s. 1 (1818): 187–92; for a history of these descriptions, see

Edmund Pendleton Tompkins and J. Lee Davis, *The Natural Bridge and Its Historical Surroundings* (Natural Bridge: Natural Bridge of Virginia, Inc., 1939).

18. David Nye argues that as "Americans became tourists in their own country, interest in sublime landscapes became not an idle definition but an act of self-definition." Americans, he argued, turned to the landscape as "the source of national character." See David Nye, *American Technological Sublime* (Cambridge: MIT Press, 1994), 25, chaps. 1–2; Elizabeth McKinsey, *Niagara Falls: Icon of the American Sublime* (New York: Cambridge University Press, 1985); Barbara Novack, *Nature and Culture* (New York: Oxford University Press, 1980); Leo Marx, *The Machine in the Garden: Technology and the Pastoral Ideal in America* (New York: Oxford University Press, 1965); John F. Sears, *Sacred Places: American Tourist Attractions in the Nineteenth Century* (New York: Oxford University Press, 1989).

19. Christoph Christian Sturm, *The Beauties of Nature Delineated; or, Philosophical and Pious Contemplations on the Works of Nature, and the Seasons of the Year. Selected from Sturm's Reflections by the Rev. Thaddeus M. Harris* (Charlestown, Mass., 1800), 11. Attention to seasonal changes in nature is a prevalent theme in theology of nature literature; see Fisher, *A Spring Day*.

20. Strum, *Beauties of Nature Delineated*, 23–24

21. Ibid., 28. For similar arguments, see [Thomas Branagan], *The Pleasures of Contemplation, being a desultory investigation of the Harmonies, Beauties, and Benefits of Nature: Including a Justification of the Ways of God to Man, and a Glimpse of his Sovereign Beauty* (Philadelphia, 1817).

22. Hitchcock, *Utility of Natural History*, 19.

23. Ibid., 30–32.

24. For histories of the conflict between geology and religion, see Charles Coulston Gillespie, *Genesis and Geology: A Study in the Relations of Scientific Thought, Natural Theology, and Social Opinion in Great Britain, 1790–1850* (Cambridge, Mass.: Harvard University Press, 1951); Roy Porter, *The Making of Geology: Earth Science in Britain, 1660–1815* (New York: Cambridge University Press, 1977); J. M. I. Klaver, *Geology and Religious Sentiment: The Effect of Geological Discoveries on English Society and Literature between 1829 and 1859* (New York: Brill, 1997); Rodney L. Stiling, "Scriptural Geology in America," in *Evangelicals and Science in Historical Perspective*, ed. David N. Livingstone et al. (New York: Oxford University Press, 1999), 177–92; Conrad Wright, "The Religion of Geology," *New England Quarterly* 14, no. 2 (1941): 335–58.

25. James Hutton is credited with developing the concept of uniformitarianism, his understanding of the earth as having "no vestige of a beginning, no concept of an end." His most important work, *Theory of the Earth,* was published in Edinburgh in 1785.

26. Hitchcock, *Utility of Natural History*, 27.

27. Ibid., 28.

28. Benjamin Silliman, *Outline of the Course of Geological Lectures Given in Yale College* (New Haven, Conn., 1829), 12, 30. In later writings Silliman fleshed out his

ideas on revelation and geology, though they remained remarkably consistent with his *Outline*. See Benjamin Silliman, *Consistency of the Discoveries of Modern Geology with the Sacred History of the Creation and the Deluge; Being a Supplement to the Second American form the Fourth Edition of Bakewell's Geology* (New Haven, Conn., 1833); Benjamin Silliman, *Remarks introductory to the first American edition of Dr. Mantell's Wonders of Geology* (London, 1839); Benjamin Silliman, *Suggestions Relative to the Philosophy of Geology, as Deduced from the Facts and to the Consistency of Both the Facts and Theory of Science with Sacred History* (New Haven, Conn., 1839); Benjamin Silliman, *Wonders of the earth and truths of the Bible: showing the consistency of modern geology with the Scripture account of the creation and the deluge* (London, 1843).

29. For a survey of Silliman's religious worldview, see John C. Green, "Protestantism, Science, and American Enterprise: Benjamin Silliman's Moral Universe," in *Benjamin Silliman and His Circle*, ed. Leonard Wilson (New York: Science History Publications, 1979). See also George P. Fisher, *Life of Benjamin Silliman, M.D., LL.D. Late Professor of Chemistry, Mineralogy, and Geology in Yale College. Chiefly from his Manuscripts Reminiscences, Diaries, and Correspondence*, 2 vols. (New York, 1866); John F. Fulton and Elizabeth H. Thomson, *Benjamin Silliman: Pathfinder in American Science* (New York: Henry Schuman, 1947); Leonard G. Wilson "Benjamin Silliman: A Biographical Sketch," in *Benjamin Silliman and His Circle*; and Chandon Michael Brown, *Benjamin Silliman: A Life in the Young Republic* (Princeton, N.J.: Princeton University Press, 1989).

30. Stuart insisted that the Genesis account could only be understood in six twenty-four-hour days and a short age for the earth. See Moses Stuart, "Critical Examination of Some Passages in Gen. I.; with Remarks on Difficulties that Attend Some of the Present Modes of Geological Reasoning," *Biblical Repository and Quarterly Review* 7, no. 21 (1836): 49–52. For a rebuttal, see J. L. Kingsley, "Remarks on a 'Critical Examination of Some Passages in Gen. 1.; with Remarks on Difficulties that Attend Some of the Present Modes of Geological Reasoning.' By M. Stuart, Prof. Sacred Lit. Theol. Sem. Andover," *American Journal of Science and Arts* 30 (1836): 114–30.

31. For Cooper's freethinking views on geology, see [Thomas Cooper], *Fabrication of the Pentateuch Proved, by the Anachronisms contained in those Books* (Granville, N.J., 1829); Thomas Cooper, *On the Connection Between Geology and the Pentateuch, in a Letter to Professor Silliman, from Thomas Cooper, M.D. To which is added an Appendix* (Boston, 1833). For an analysis of Cooper's views on geology and his removal trial for heresy, see Dumas Malone, *The Public Life of Thomas Cooper* (New Haven, Conn.: Yale University Press, 1926), 353–57.

32. A broadside for a "Scientific Lecture" by "Professor Edgerton of Michigan" announced the topics to be covered. They included "The Revelations of Geology" and "The Relation of Geology to Christianity." See Edgerton Broadside, Broadside Collection, #519, APS. See also the broadside syllabus for Thomas Cooper's geology lecture, Archives, III, 1, APS.

33. In later writings, Hitchcock developed his ideas about the consistency between

the biblical Flood and geology in much greater detail. His dense serial articles in the *Biblical Repository* address this subject and issues related closely to the consistency between geology and revealed religion. See Edward Hitchcock, "On the Connection Between Geology and Natural Religion," *Biblical Repository and Quarterly Observer* 5, no. 17 (1835): 113–38; Edward Hitchcock, "On the Connection Between Geology and Revelation," *Biblical Repository and Quarterly Observer* 5, no. 18 (1835): 439–51; Edward Hitchcock, "The Connection Between Geology and the Mosaic History of the Creation," *Biblical Repository and Quarterly Observer* 6, no. 20 (1835): 261–332; Edward Hitchcock, "Remarks on Professor Stuart's Examination of Gen. I. in Reference to Geology," *Biblical Repository and Quarterly Observer* 7, no. 21 (1836): 448–87; and Edward Hitchcock, *The Religion of Geology and its Connected Sciences* (Boston, 1852). For more thorough analysis of these debates, see Stiling, "Scriptural Geology in America," 177–92.

Chapter 5

1. William Paul Crillon Barton, *Vegetable Materia Medica of the United States; or Medical Botany: Containing a Botanical, General, and Medical History, of Medicinal Plants Indigenous to the United States*, 2 vols. (Philadelphia, 1817), 2: x–xiii

2. Ibid., 1:xi–xii.

3. W. P. C. Barton's thoughts on Lewis and Clark were honest but his motives were mixed. Most of the natural historical specimens and herbaria as well as the expedition journals of Lewis and Clark arrived in Philadelphia after considerable delay. Benjamin Smith Barton was enlisted to prepare the natural history material for publication but he died in 1815 and the scientific information was not published. His nephew may have cast the expedition negatively to defend his uncle from critics, downplaying its natural historical accomplishments as of little importance. See James Rhonda, "'The Writingest Explorers': The Lewis and Clark Expedition in American Historical Literature," *Pennsylvania Magazine of History and Biography* 112 (1988): 607–30; see also the introduction to Robert S. Cox, ed., *The Shortest and Most Convenient Route: Lewis and Clark in Context* (Philadelphia: American Philosophical Society, 2004), 3–11.

4. See William H. Goetzmann, *Army Exploration in the American West, 1803–1863* (New Haven, Conn.: Yale University Press, 1959); Goetzmann, *Exploration and Empire: The Explorer and the Scientist in the Winning of the America West* (Austin: University of Texas Press, 1994); Hugh Richard Slotten, *Patronage, Practice, and the Culture of American Science: Alexander Dallas Bache and the U.S. Coast Survey* (New York: Cambridge University Press, 1994); Dupree, *Science in the Federal Government*. For a more recent variation on expeditionary science, see Aaron Sachs, *The Humboldt Current: Nineteenth-Century Exploration and the Roots of American Environmentalism* (New York: Viking, 2006).

5. John Lauritz Larson, *Internal Improvement: National Public Works and the*

Promise of Popular Government in the Early United States (Chapel Hill: University of North Carolina Press, 2001), 9–37.

6. Petition to the General Assembly of Pennsylvania, 2 November 1787, APS.

7. Greene, *American Science in the Age of Jefferson*, 195–96.

8. David R. Bigham, *Public Culture in the Early Republic: Peale's Museum and Its Audience* (Washington, D.C.: Smithsonian Institution Press, 1995), 35–36, 83.

9. David Hosack, *A Statement of Facts relative to the Establishment and Progress of the Elgin Botanical Garden, and the Subsequent disposal of the same to the State of New York* (New York, 1811), 15.

10. Ibid., 3.

11. Ibid., 55–56.

12. Greene, *American Science in the Age of Jefferson*, 101–2.

13. Slotten, *Patronage, Practice, and the Culture of American Science*, 43–45; Greene, *American Science in the Age of Jefferson*, 27–36; Harold R. Burstyn, "Seafaring and the Emergence of American Science," in *The Atlantic World of Robert G. Albion*, ed. Benjamin W. Labaree (Middletown, Conn.: Wesleyan University Press, 1975), 76–109.

14. Slotten, *Patronage, Practice, and the Culture of American Science*, 42–43.

15. Ibid., 42–60.

16. Dupree, *Science in the Federal Government*, 1–43. On the Long expedition, see Goetzman, *Army Explorers*, 40–45; Todd Shallat, *Structures in the Stream: Water, Science, and the Rise of the U.S. Army Corps of Engineers* (Austin: University of Texas Press, 1994), 64–77; Howard Ensign Evans, *The Natural History of the Long Expedition to the Rocky Mountains* (Oxford: Oxford University Press, 1997); Kenneth Haltman, *Looking Close and Seeing Far: Samuel Seymour, Titian Ramsay Peale, and the Art of the Long Expedition, 1818–1823* (University Park: Penn State University Press, 2008).

17. Larson, *Internal Improvements*, 73–80; Carol Sheriff, *The Artificial River: The Erie Canal and the Paradox of Progress, 1817–1862* (New York: Hill and Wang, 1996); Ronald E. Shaw, *Erie Water West: A History of the Erie Canal* (Lexington: University Press of Kentucky, 1966).

18. Larson, *Internal Improvements*, 63–69, 180–93.

19. David Williams, *The Georgia Gold Rush: Twenty-Niners, Cherokees, and Gold Fever* (Columbia: University of South Carolina Press, 1993), 7–20.

20. Jack Repcheck: *The Man Who Found Time: James Hutton and the Discovery of the Earth's Antiquity* (New York: Basic Books, 2003); Stephen Baxter, *Ages in Chaos: James Hutton and the Discovery of Deep Time* (New York: Forge, 2006); Simon Winchester, *The Map That Changed the World: William Smith and the Birth of Modern Geology* (New York: Harper Collins, 2001).

21. See George P. Merrill, ed., *Contributions to a History of State Geological and Natural History Surveys* (Washington, D.C.: Government Printing Office, 1920; reprint, New York: Arno, 1978); and Daniels, *Science in American Society*, 192–205.

22. Amos Eaton, *A geological survey of the county of Albany, taken under the direction of the Agricultural society of the county* (Albany, 1820).

23. Amos Eaton, *A geological and agricultural survey of the district adjoining the Erie canal in the state of New York. Taken under the direction of the Hon. Stephen Van Rensselaer. Part I. Containing a description of the rock formations; together with a geological profile, extending from the Atlantic to Lake Erie* (Albany, 1824).

24. The full text of Olmsted's letter to the North Carolina Board of Internal Improvements is published in Merrill, *Contributions to a History of State Geological and Natural History Surveys*, 363–65.

25. Ibid., 365.

26. Charles E. Rothe, "Remarks on the Mines of North Carolina," *American Journal of Science* 13 (1828): 201–17

27. Richard F. Knapp and Brent D. Glass, *Gold Mining in North Carolina: A Bicentennial History* (Raleigh: North Carolina Division of Archives and History, 1999).

28. A portion of the Act of the General Assembly, quoted in Merrill, *Contributions to a History of State Geological and Natural History*, 459.

29. Ibid., 275.

30. Ibid., 149–53. The details on the legislative origin of the survey can also be found in the preface to Hitchcock's final report to the state: Edward Hitchcock, *Report on the Geology, Mineralogy, Botany, and Zoology of Massachusetts* (Amherst, 1835).

31. Edward Hitchcock, *Final Report on the Geology of Massachusetts*, iv.

32. Edward Hitchcock, *Report of a Geological Survey of Massachusetts* (Amherst, Mass., 1832).

33. Hitchcock, *Report on the Geology*, 13.

34. Ibid., 1–72.

35. Ibid., 83.

36. Merrill, *Contributions to a History of State Geological and Natural History Surveys*, 153.

37. Ibid., 154–55.

38. [Agustus Addison Gould], *Report on the Invertabrata of Massachusetts, comprising the Mollusca, Crustacea, Annelida, and Radiata* (Cambridge, Mass., 1841); [Thaddeus William Harris], *Report on the Insects of Massachusetts, Injurious to Vegetation* (Cambridge, Mass., 1841); [Chester Dewey and Ebenezer Emmons], *Report on the Herbaceous Plants and on the Quadrupeds of Massachusetts* (Cambridge, Mass., 1840); [George B. Emerson, David Humphreys Storer, and William Bourn Oliver Peabody], *Reports on the Fishes, Reptiles, and Birds of Massachusetts* (Boston, 1839).

39. [Dewey], *Report on the Herbaceous Plants*, 3.

40. [Hitchcock], *Final Report on the Geology of Massachusetts*.

41. Merrill, *Contributions to a History of State Geological and Natural History Surveys*, 45–48.

42. Ibid., 137–45, 51–53.

43. Ibid., 327–36.

44. John Torrey, *A Flora of the State of New York, comprising full descriptions of all the indigenous and naturalized plants,* 2 vols. (Albany, 1843); James E. De Kay, *Zoology of New York, or the New-York Fauna; comprising detailed descriptions of all the animals hitherto observed within the state of New York,* 5 vols. (Albany, 1842); Lewis C. Beck, *Mineralogy of New-York Comprising Detailed Descriptions of the Minerals Hitherto Found in the State of New-York, and Notices of Their Uses in the Arts and Agriculture* (Albany, 1842).

45. Merrill, *Contributions to a History of State Geological and Natural History Surveys,* 507–12, 428–34, 100–104, 72–73, 387–98.

46. Ibid., 158–68, 162–63.

47. Ibid., 175.

48. Walter B. Hendrickson, "Nineteenth Century State Geological Surveys: Early Government Support of Science," *Isis* 52 (September 1961): 367.

49. Larson, *Internal Improvements,* chap. 6.

50. Ibid., 195–96.

51. Merrill, *Contributions to a History of State Geological and Natural History Surveys,* 45–46.

52. Michael J. Brodhead, "Elliott Coues and the Sparrow War," *New England Quarterly* 44, no. 3 (September 1971): 420–32; Paul Russell Cutright and Michael J. Brodhead, *Elliott Coues: Naturalist and Frontier Historian* (Urbana: University of Illinois Press, 1981).

53. Frederick Jackson Turner, *Rereading Frederick Jackson Turner: "The Significance of the Frontier" and Other Essays,* ed. John Mack Faragher (New Haven, Conn.: Yale University Press, 1999).

54. Elliot Coues, ed., *History of the Expedition under the command of Lewis and Clark,* 4 vols. (New York: Francis P. Harper, 1893): 1, iii.

55. Reuben Gold Thwaites, superintendent of the State Historical Society of Wisconsin, edited a volume of the journals and, like Coues, emphasized their natural historical contributions. See Reuben G. Thwaites, ed., *Original Journals of the Lewis and Clark Expedition,* 8 vols. (New York, 1904–5).

Epilogue

1. The literature on the professionalization of nineteenth-century American science is vast and contentious. Pioneering but still relevant work on this question includes Nathan Reingold, "Definitions and Speculations: The Professionalization of Science in the Nineteenth Century," in Oleson and Brown, eds., *The Pursuit of Knowledge in the Early American Republic,* 33–69; George H. Daniels, "The Process of Professionalization in American Science: The Emergent Period, 1820–1860," *Isis* 58 (1967): 151–66; and Howard S. Miller, *Dollars for Research: Science and Its Patrons in Nineteenth-Century America* (Seattle: University of Washington Press, 1970). More recent and theoretically informed works include Andrew Abbott, *The Systems of Professions: An Essay on the Division of Expert Labor* (Chicago: University of Chicago Press, 1988),

and Samuel Haber, *The Quest for Authority and Honor in the American Professions, 1750–1900* (Chicago: University of Chicago Press, 1991). An efficient summary of the professionalizing literature can be found in Mark V. Barrow, *A Passion for Birds: American Ornithology after Audubon* (Princeton, N.J.: Princeton University Press, 1998), 4–6.

2. On ornithology, see Paul Lawrence Farber, *Discovering Birds: The Emergence of Ornithology as a Scientific Discipline, 1760–1850* (Baltimore: Johns Hopkins University Press, 1997); Barrow, *A Passion for Birds.*

3. The role of cartographers and scientific experts in creating both domestic and imperial spaces are explored in Patrick Carroll, *Science, Culture, and Modern State Formation* (Berkeley: University of California Press, 2006); Matthew Edney, *Mapping an Empire: The Geographical Construction of British India, 1765–1843* (Chicago: University of Chicago Press, 1997); D. Graham Burnett, *Masters of All They Surveyed: Exploration, Geography, and the British El Dorado* (Chicago: University of Chicago Press, 2000).

Index

Page references in italics refer to illustrations

Acknowledgments

I am forever indebted to the many individuals and institutions that have contributed to the production of this book. Those many debts begin with Chris Grasso, who showed me that a career in academics was worthwhile and exciting. These debts continue with Jon Butler and John Mack Faragher, who pushed, cajoled, read, and reread its pages and encouraged me in this project. I also offer thanks to my colleagues in American studies, particularly Kathleen Donegan and Kirk Swinehart, who made early America come alive.

Along the way I was able to research and study at the American Philosophical Society, where Rob Cox and Roy Goodman were so helpful. I spent a very productive fellowship at the American Antiquarian Society, with its unparalleled staff. They seemed to know more about this book than I did. An extended stay at the Huntington Library was not only productive but exceptionally pleasant.

In Washington, D.C., I owe tremendous thanks to Karin Wulf, who provided me counsel and friendship that I will always treasure. I found a tremendous colleague and dear friend in Philip Stern, who bolstered my confidence to see this project to completion. Finally, Kate Haulman helped me find value in my work after I had become disillusioned and discouraged.

The McNeil Center for Early American Studies was an incredible environment in which this project grew, was nurtured, and matured. The year spent there as a fellow was intellectually rewarding and wonderful, as were my colleagues, particularly Denver Brunsman, Ben Irvin, and Jennifer Janofsky.

I owe tremendous thanks to my editors at the University of Pennsylvania Press, Bob Lockhart and Dan Richter. To Bob I am indebted for his enthusiasm and tremendous patience as he far surpassed my expectations for what editors are supposed to do. To Dan I owe thanks for his vision and his commitment to clear thinking and precise prose. This book is far better for his contributions to it. Thanks too to the anonymous readers, editor Erica Ginsburg, and my copyeditor, Lynn Walterick.

I owe thanks to my sister, Wendy Sue Swanson, and my parents, Karen Lewis and John Lewis. They have accomplished so much in their own lives and they serve as reminders for what can happen with sustained and committed effort.

Finally, this book would not be what it is without the assistance of my wife and children. Nancy Kadowitz has seen me though many ups and downs and remained a source of encouragement, love, and resolve. My children, Asher Jacob and Phoebe Olivia, came along at the right time. They are my great distractions, fonts of joy, and my reason to finish writing this book.